THE HIGHEST
GLASS CEILING

THE HIGHEST GLASS CEILING

Women's Quest for the
American Presidency

ELLEN FITZPATRICK

HARVARD UNIVERSITY PRESS

Cambridge, Massachusetts
London, England
2016

First printing

Library of Congress Cataloging-in-Publication Data
Names: Fitzpatrick, Ellen F. (Ellen Frances), author.
Title: The highest glass ceiling : women's quest for the American
presidency / Ellen Fitzpatrick.
Description: Cambridge, Massachusetts : Harvard University Press, 2016. |
Includes bibliographical references and index.
Identifiers: LCCN 2015045620 | ISBN 9780674088931 (alk. paper)
Subjects: LCSH: Woodhull, Victoria C. (Victoria Claflin), 1838–1927. |
Smith,
Margaret Chase, 1897–1995. | Chisholm, Shirley, 1924–2005. |
Women—Political activity—United States—History. | Presidential
candidates—United States—Biography. | Women presidential
candidates—United States—Biography.
Classification: LCC HQ1236 .F49 2016 | DDC 320.0820973—dc23 LC rec-
ord available at http://lccn.loc.gov/2015045620

In memory of
Lindy Hess

CONTENTS

THE HIGHEST
GLASS CEILING

PROLOGUE

New Hampshire, 2008

On a winter's evening in early 2008, presidential candidate Hillary Clinton stood on the stage of a crowded, dimly lit high school auditorium in Salem, New Hampshire. By all appearances, it was the kind of campaign event that was routine for—even required of—hopefuls stumping in the nation's first presidential primary. Surrounded by her supporters, Clinton started to deliver a line that was born of her Iowa caucus defeat to Barack Obama just days earlier. "Everybody in this race is talking about change," Clinton began. "But what does that mean? Some people think you bring about change by demanding it . . ." In the next moment, before she could finish her sentence, a heckler stood up in the audience, holding a sign and shouting its message. "Iron my shirt! Iron my shirt!" he yelled insistently. Another sign was hoisted; another heckler joined the chorus. Together their shouted demands succeeded in drowning out the candidate.

Pacing back and forth, microphone in hand, Clinton paused and asked, above the din, that the lights be raised. "Oh! The remnants of sexism—alive and well," Clinton said with laughter as officials quelled the disturbance and escorted the young men from the audience. The candidate would later be praised for her adroit pivot back to her campaign message. "As I think has just been abundantly demonstrated," she offered, "I am also running to break through the highest and hardest glass ceiling for our daughters, for our sons, for our children and for our country and really for women around the world." The demonstrators, it would later turn out, had been deployed as a stunt by a Boston radio station.[1]

The "Iron my shirt!" outburst was a memorable moment in the 2008 Democratic presidential primary. The ridicule visited upon Hillary Clinton that day as a woman who was running for the nation's highest office seemed both outlandish and entirely plausible given the tenor of contemporary American politics. By 2008, the vast majority of citizens expressed no reservations in principle about electing a woman president. Many, indeed, voiced enthusiasm about casting their vote for the nation's first female chief executive. But it remained a fact that no individual woman aspirant had yet prevailed in American politics' longest and most arduous race.

In 2008, Hillary Clinton mounted the most successful campaign of any woman presidential candidate in American history. She still lost a very close race for the

Democratic nomination to a young, charismatic African American senator who would go on to win the general election and serve two terms as president. The battle between the front-runners unfolded over many months against a remarkable backdrop that received relatively little attention amid the thrust and parry of the immediate race. Either candidate, if victorious in their bid for the nomination, would make history as the first African American or the first woman to become the standard-bearer for a major political party. The November triumph of Barack Obama represented an extraordinary milestone in the history of the nation. Clinton's loss deferred to another time, and perhaps another candidate, the election of the country's first woman president.[2]

In the postmortems that followed Clinton's campaign, many touched on its pathbreaking nature. Amid those assessments, however, the larger history that preceded and, in some ways, framed her bid for the White House received very little attention. Clinton may have been the most successful female presidential candidate, but she had emerged from a longer race. Indeed, it was still possible to hear during her 2008 campaign echoes of the skepticism that greeted Victoria Woodhull, the first woman to run for president nearly a century and a half ago. In 1872, Harriet Beecher Stowe posed a memorable question, in her thinly veiled satire of Woodhull's candidacy. "What sort of brazen tramp of a woman," she asked, would seek the presidency? A man running for the office could anticipate having "his character torn off from his back in shreds" only to be "mauled, pummeled, and covered with dirt by every filthy paper all over the country." A woman, Stowe predicted, would be "dragged through every kennel, and slopped into every dirty pail of water like an old mop." Would a woman who survived "an ordeal that kills a man" be the "kind of a woman that we would want to see at the head of our government?" Stowe queried. Then, as now, not a few people wondered the same thing.[3]

Women's quest for the American presidency has a rich history—one marked by ambition and failure, doubt and possibility. The texture of this history is revealed in the stories of three of its central protagonists, who, over the course of a century, reached for the nation's highest office in a political world mostly inhospitable to their aims. Each, to be sure, achieved important firsts for women—Victoria Woodhull as the first woman to seek the office in 1872, Margaret Chase Smith as the first woman to have her name placed in nomination by a major political party in 1964, and Shirley Chisholm as the first African American woman to be similarly placed in nomination for the presidency in 1972. Yet the crossing of those thresholds from 1872 to 1972 reveals little of the warp and woof of their experience and of their legacy.

From each of their stories, we can learn something

about "the kind of woman" who sought the presidency—the question raised so pointedly by Harriet Beecher Stowe. We can also see in stark relief the obstacles women have faced and the prospects they uncovered in their drive for the nation's most exalted office. Perhaps most important, we can recapture an enduring theme in the history of American democracy. As citizens who defied constraints on their political participation, rights, and liberties, they seized historical moments they believed were rife with possibility. In defeat, each imagined a successor who would eventually reach the presidency. Each was supported and challenged by political forces, historical conditions, particular constituencies, and, of course, character traits that remain visible elements in the landscape of presidential politics today.

More than two hundred women have sought, been nominated, or received votes for the office of president since Woodhull's bid in the 1870s. As is true of most male presidential aspirants, the overwhelming majority gained very little traction. Until the late twentieth century, women candidates surfaced most often as independents, on third-party tickets, or as quixotic candidates whose stars briefly rose during political conventions. They have been and are easily forgotten. Few failed candidates for president—male or female—leave their mark upon the pages of history, and perhaps few should. This book tells the story of three exceptional women who did.[4]

VICTORIA WOODHULL

"A Very Conspicuous Position"

Nearly a century and a half ago, in July 1871, an unlikely candidate for the American presidency penned a "letter of acceptance" agreeing to run as the standard-bearer for a fledgling political party. She was responding to a "letter of nomination" she had recently received. The exchange of letters reflected the custom of the day. For it was a time, very unlike our own, when political parties reigned supreme and their presidential nominees were expected to stand waiting in the wings at a dignified remove. The candidate's supporters had urged their nominee to respond favorably and to outline in response her political beliefs. Victoria Woodhull took pains in her reply to explain why she was "the proper person" to lead "a great political party, and actually to guide the state."

She began by dismissing the ruling Democratic and Republican political parties as "of the past." Riven by partisanship and incapable of unifying the nation behind its exalted ideals, they could produce no leader akin to the country's founding president. "General

Washington's popularity extinguished for the moment all partizan opposition, and made of the whole nation one grand fraternalizing party," Woodhull recalled. The "advent of the first woman" president might well produce, she predicted, the "next great . . . jubilee." "Little as the public think it," Woodhull observed, "a woman who is now nominated may be elected next year. Less change of opinion than has occurred already . . . will place her in the White House."[1]

For someone who claimed to have powers as a clairvoyant and who kept company with spirits who foretold what the future would bring, the thirty-two-year-old Woodhull proved a poor prognosticator to say the very least. She would be more than eighty years old before the Nineteenth Amendment to the U.S. Constitution conferred voting rights on American women in 1920. The twenty-first century would dawn without a woman ever reaching the presidency. Nonetheless, the confidence Woodhull expressed in 1871 is telling. Her bid for the presidency certainly reflected her unique qualities, including bravado, grandiosity, and, as some would have it, her relentless appetite for celebrity. But it also emerged as old institutions and mores seemed vulnerable amid the upheaval of Reconstruction-era politics and society. As the United States attempted to come to terms with the consequences of secession, war, and the end of slavery, a swirling debate ensued about the very meaning of freedom, citizenship, and democracy. Woodhull seized that moment to mount her bid for the presidency.

Indeed, Woodhull explicitly linked her unprecedented effort to the turmoil that roiled the nation in the years after the Civil War. "I am well aware," she admitted, "that in assuming this position I shall evoke more ridicule than enthusiasm at the outset. But this is an epoch of sudden changes and startling surprises. What may appear absurd to-day will assume a serious aspect to-morrow." It was, perhaps, a forgivable assumption. Americans such as Woodhull who had lived through the Civil War witnessed in its aftermath once unthinkable transformations remaking the social and political landscape. During Reconstruction, three sweeping amendments to the United States Constitution, ending slavery and expanding citizenship, had been ratified in a five-year period. Four million emancipated slaves could now claim rights as citizens, though African American women would remain deprived of voting privileges reserved for men. A brave vanguard of African American men pursued and won electoral office. In some instances, they displaced the very leaders who had fought vigorously to prevent their freedom. "The blacks were cattle in 1860," Woodhull noted, "a negro now sits in Jeff Davis' seat in the United States Senate." Tested by secession and a brutal war, a triumphant national government appeared poised to vigorously assert its power over states and localities wedded to outmoded traditions and institutions.

Like many feminists of her era, Woodhull imagined that in this environment women's rights were on the horizon. "The spirit of this age," she insisted, "is unbounded emancipation." "While the curse of slavery covered the land," Woodhull observed, "progress was enchained." But the "torrent of war" had "swept away" slavery, allowing "the voice of justice" to be heard. "Let those, therefore, who ridiculed the negro's claim to exercise the right to 'life, liberty and the pursuit of happiness,' and who lived to see him vote and hold high public offices," she wrote, "ridicule the aspirations of the women of the country after equality with the blacks as much as they please. They cannot roll back the rising tide of reform. The world moves."[2]

The nation would not, of course, move to elect a woman president in 1872. Indeed, by the end of the nineteenth century, the new political rights for African Americans that had been enshrined by law during Reconstruction were being steadily eroded. Systematic efforts at disfranchisement and spreading segregation made a mockery of the liberties secured by hard-won constitutional amendments. The forces of localism in American society proved far more resistant to the country's nationalizing impulses than many had predicted. Reconstruction itself would soon be judged an unspeakable "tragedy" by those who rejected its daring experiments. Nor would women's suffrage be much closer to advancement.[3]

Woodhull, who had achieved a measure of renown as the first woman to seek the presidency, became little more than a historical footnote. In time, her presidential aspirations would figure rather superficially even in accounts of her own personal history. Woodhull's vivid life as a spiritualist healer, stockbroker (she and her sister opened the first brokerage house run by women on Wall Street in 1870), feminist, free-love radical, and essential player in one of the great sex scandals of her era came to vastly overshadow her failed reach for the presidency.[4]

Although Woodhull's presidential run has been largely dismissed as frivolous, her bid for the White House, in fact, figured centrally in the dramatic arc of her larger story. It also set in motion a quest that engaged the interest of many late nineteenth-century citizens. Most important, it foreshadowed what future female candidates would face when they entered the field of presidential politics. Marginalized by gender, law, age, and experience from the centers of organized politics, Woodhull succeeded in posing a challenge to women's exclusion from the arena that reverberated across the country. She paid a high price for her glittering moment and left a legacy for future female presidential aspirants that remains worthy of reflection.[5]

Of all women to reach the national political stage, few followed a more unlikely path to it than Victoria Woodhull. The seventh of Buck and Roxanna Claflin's ten children, she was born in September 1838 in the small farming town of Homer, Ohio. Her father has been variously described as a confidence man, swindler, snake oil salesman, river rafter, barkeep, real estate investor, horse thief, hotelier, and sometime lawyer. It is a list of endeavors not at all incompatible with his status as a rootless young man struggling to rise in early nineteenth-century America. He appears to have enjoyed some initial financial success, only to lose his gains not long after Victoria's birth. Whether callous or "partially crazed," he was "impartial in his cruelty to all his children," Woodhull claimed. "Worked like a slave and whipped like a convict"—such would be her lot in a childhood remembered as "an unbroken heartbreak." She received very little education—three years, at best, according to the most reliable estimation.[6]

Woodhull's mother, described as "never wholly sane," could provide little stability for her daughter. Instead she offered the comfort of a "spirit world" beyond our own with whom only a privileged few could communicate. Her mother's religious enthusiasm had been nurtured in the revivals held by Methodists who traveled through Ohio during the Second Great Awakening, seeking new followers in their stirring camp meetings. A woman who "saw visions and dreamed dreams," she nonetheless swung wildly between moods of rapture and deep melancholy. She was said to "pray till her eyes are full of tears, and in the same hour curse till her lips are white with foam." Yet Mrs. Claflin's religious passions clearly left their imprint on her daughter. Before she was ten, Woodhull reported to her mother that she had been visited by angels "who told me I was to be in their charge, and that they were to constantly guide, instruct and care for me so that I should be, when grown, fitted to do their work on earth." Her name alone, Woodhull would later remind her campaign supporters, evoked the example of Queen Victoria, after whom she was named and who might yet be "her elder sister in sovereignty." (Queen Victoria was coronated in the year of Woodhull's birth and would reign until 1901.) As a girl, Victoria Woodhull also took courage from a spirit who foretold that she would "rise to a great distinction . . . that she would become the ruler of her people." Such visions perhaps allowed Woodhull to survive her childhood and to acquire early a sense of election, as it were, to a special destiny.[7]

The narrative of her youth sketched above, which Woodhull endorsed and helped elaborate and disseminate, served a political purpose in the early 1870s. It emerged first, in fact, during Victoria Woodhull's presidential campaign as she sought the support of spiritualists, women, and laborers. Spiritualism, which held that the soul was immortal and that the living could access the spirits of the dead, was a powerful force in nineteenth-century America. It flourished partly as an antidote to the anxieties and grievous losses of the Civil War era. Among the leading political figures intrigued by its beliefs were Presidents Grant and Garfield, as well as Speaker of the House, Republican presidential nominee, and Secretary of State James Blaine. The movement, however, proved especially attractive to women, who found in Spiritualism a welcome emphasis on equality and a satisfying sphere of activity. Mediums who presided over séances and "trance speakers" were among the first women to address public audiences of both men and women. Their leadership within the movement ensured a welcome reception to those who promoted the cause of women's equality. Spiritualism thus would intersect powerfully with the women's rights movement in the mid-nineteenth century. Both were instrumental in shaping Woodhull's campaign for the presidency.[8]

The message of the mid-nineteenth-century women's rights movement surely resonated deeply with Victoria Woodhull when she learned of its existence. It laid bare, of course, the wholly undemocratic exclusion of women from the panoply of civil and political rights then enjoyed by privileged (white) male citizens. But it also emphasized the "repeated injuries" inflicted on women from the "tyranny" many endured in the private sphere. The *Declaration of Sentiments* unveiled at the 1848 Seneca Falls women's rights convention decried the inequality suffered by a woman upon marriage. She was then considered not only "civilly dead" but "compelled to promise obedience to her husband, he becoming, to all intents and purposes her master—the law giving him power to deprive her of her liberty, and to administer chastisement." That was a state of affairs only too familiar to Woodhull.[9]

With parental approval, she had been married off at the age of fifteen to a physician nearly twice her age who had been called in to treat her for a fever. The dapper, handsome Dr. Canning Woodhull soon morphed into a Mr. Hyde. The young bride discovered she had married a philandering alcoholic who could support little more than his penchant for barrooms and brothels. She "grew ten years older in a single day," Woodhull later recounted. Thirteen months after her marriage, in late December 1854, and now living in Chicago, the sixteen-year-old "child-wife" endured "in almost mortal agony" a deeply traumatic labor and delivery presided over by her drunken husband. The baby, named Byron, suffered from a severe mental disability. He became "a daily agony" to his mother—"a sad and pitiful spectacle" who "roams from room to room, muttering noises more sepulchral than human." When, as a grown woman, Victoria Woodhull met feminist Lucretia Mott and her sister, she succinctly summarized these years of horror: "All that I am I have become through sorrow."[10]

What Woodhull lacked in fortune in these early years she made up for in grit. She learned early to live by her wits. Struggling to support her young boy and her husband, she moved across the country working as a seamstress in San Francisco, then briefly as an actress, only to wind up in Indiana, where by the 1860s she drew notice as a medium and clairvoyant. She was said to use the guidance of the spirits to heal the sick. It was a peripatetic existence. But her talent as a "spiritualistic physician," enhanced no doubt by her striking physical beauty, reaped, she claimed, "a golden harvest" as "money flowed in a stream toward her." It also harvested a second husband, Colonel James Harvey Blood, a Civil War veteran from St. Louis. Blood and Woodhull met when he consulted her for healing. An extremely attractive man, with dark wavy hair, deepset penetrating eyes, and muttonchop whiskers, Blood was president of the Spiritualist Society in St. Louis. Nonetheless, he "was startled" upon meeting Woodhull when she quickly fell "into a trance, during which she announced, unconsciously to herself, that his future destiny was to be linked with hers in marriage." The attraction was mutual; they felt joined "by 'the powers of the air.'" She married Blood in 1866, having left Canning Woodhull after the birth (in another traumatic botched delivery) of their second child, Zula, a healthy daughter, five years earlier. But she retained the name of Woodhull, as her biographer Theodore Tilton explained in 1871, like "many actresses, singers, and other professional women whose names have become a business property to their owners."[11]

By 1868, Woodhull and Colonel Blood were in New York City, with Victoria's younger sister Tennessee Claflin, who was seven years her junior. An experienced medium and beautiful young woman, Tennessee had been exploited since her youth by her father. He promoted her variously as a clairvoyant, medium, fortuneteller, and child healer. Mr. Claflin conveniently manufactured an elixir with his lovely daughter's picture on it as adjuvant therapy. The counterfeit treatment was foisted for a price on a gullible public in various towns and cities, mostly in the Midwest. All this became too much even for Woodhull. She believed in her sister's powers as a medium but saw that Tennessee was being used to advance a "fraudulent business." After freeing her sister from her father's clutches, Woodhull decamped with her two children, Colonel Blood, and Tennessee to New York. There they began a career that would lead Victoria to wealth and to politics.[12]

Wealth came first. As fate and luck would have it, one of the country's richest men was a superstitious eccentric, drawn to Spiritualism and the comfort provided by mediums. He was also in the habit of welcoming strangers who showed up at the door of his Greenwich Village mansion. "Commodore" Cornelius Vanderbilt had amassed a fortune in shipping and rail-roads. By the spring of 1868, when Woodhull and her sister entered his orbit, the Commodore was seventy-four years old. Soon to be widowed, he was more than happy to make the acquaintance of attractive women with a reputation for their ready access to the spirits. Woodhull would later claim that a "spirit guide"—none other than Demosthenes, the great Athenian ora-tor, statesman, and defender of democracy—had in-structed her to "journey to New York." Whatever the inspiration, her association with Vanderbilt proved de-cisive in launching Woodhull to fortune and fame. Smitten with her sister, Vanderbilt embraced Victoria for her powers as a medium who offered remarkably prescient stock tips along with messages from the dead. While many of the details of their financial arrange-ments remain murky, Vanderbilt clearly staked Wood-hull and her sister. His investment allowed them to be-gin speculating in gold and bonds. That enterprise would soon make them extremely wealthy women.[13]

As this new chapter in her life unfolded, Woodhull also began to surface in the circles of the women's suf-frage movement. In January 1869, she attended an im-portant national women's rights convention held in Washington, D.C. A volatile debate took place at the gathering about the Fourteenth (then ratified as of July

1868) and Fifteenth (currently under debate) Amendments to the United States Constitution. Woodhull may have learned of the meeting through *The Revolution,* Susan B. Anthony and Elizabeth Cady Stanton's new publication. She later credited the journal with doing "heroic work" in 1868 as Congress debated the parameters of the Fifteenth Amendment, which prohibited restricting voting rights on the basis of "race, color, or previous condition of servitude." Petitions seeking to include women in the expanded suffrage provisions of the new amendment had flooded Washington. But the writing was on the wall by the time the 1869 national convention met. Women would not gain voting rights under the Fifteenth Amendment. Key women's rights activists, including Stanton and Anthony, felt betrayed that the Reconstruction amendments advanced citizenship and access to the vote for African American men but not for women. This matter would deeply divide the suffrage movement itself and some of its staunchest allies, including the great ex-slave, abolitionist, writer, and now elder statesman Frederick Douglass, who was also present at the January gathering.[14]

Tensions were palpable as Woodhull observed some of the great feminists of her era address the crowded meeting. Stanton gave an impassioned speech before an audience that included politicians, senators, congressmen, and suffragists. She urged a sixteenth amendment enfranchising women. In making her case, Stanton argued that the extension of "manhood suffrage" had actually produced for women "the lowest depths of political degradation." A "white man's government," she observed, had now become "a man's government." In her outrage, Stanton pandered to prevailing prejudices. "The Fifteenth Amendment," she pointed out, "takes in a larger population than the 2,000,000 black men on the Southern plantation." It would also enable "the ignorant foreign vote" of immigrants, as men of any background or lineage enjoyed privileges denied to women. Stanton did not confine her criticism to voters she saw as undesirable members of the electorate. In the setting of the nation's capital, she called attention to the political corruption she believed governed national politics. "When the highest offices in the gift of the people are bought and sold in Wall Street," she charged, "it is a mere chance who will be our rulers. Whither is a nation tending when brains count for less than bullion, and clowns make laws for queens?"[15]

If Stanton's remarks offended some attendees, and they did, the debate surely cast in stark relief for Woodhull the conflicts that would divide the women's movement. "The discussion between colored men on the one side and women on the other," *The Revolution* reported, "as to whether it was the duty of the women of the nation to hold their claims in abeyance, until all colored men are enfranchised, was spicy, able and affecting." In fact, opinion on this question crossed lines of race and sex. Some women suffragists rejected Stanton's approach. And at least one African American man, abolitionist Robert Purvis, spoke eloquently for the imperative of universal suffrage.[16]

Woodhull herself, who had attracted the interest of reporters in attendance, for reasons not entirely opaque, confessed that she "only partly" agreed with "the doings" of the convention. "She believes in woman most completely," one journalist noted with approval, "but she also believes in man just as thoroughly." The reporter waxed eloquent about Woodhull's "fine and commanding figure," "her spiritual eyes, 'flashing like sun-lit gems,'" and a "face and form" of "bewildering loveliness." He predicted a great future for his subject: "this woman is to rise to a very conspicuous position." That opinion was echoed in a Washington press story that likewise forecast that Woodhull "was destined to act no inferior part in the coming conflicts and reforms in the country."[17]

Thoroughly engaged by the drama of the meeting, Woodhull also pictured herself a future *participant* rather than a spectator in the excitement. As she watched Stanton, Susan B. Anthony, Clara Barton, and other notables assembled on the platform, Woodhull later recalled "how important I felt. It had been the dream of my life to vote and really at that time I thought the 'Millennium,' otherwise Woman's day, was soon to materialize." At thirty-one, Woodhull was considerably younger, and some would apparently have it, more physically alluring, than the suffrage lionesses who occupied the limelight. Perhaps awareness of that fact contributed to her reverie. For Woodhull fantasized about a far greater role for herself than simply voter. "Visions of the offices I would hold," she remembered, "danced before my imagination." Ironically, the very Wall Street influence that Stanton lambasted would grease Woodhull's entry into national politics.[18]

For within the year, Victoria Woodhull had amassed a very considerable fortune. And it was about to grow exponentially larger. In what measure her gains came from shrewd investments, speculating in gold, or financial rewards heaped upon her by Vanderbilt—or some combination of all three—cannot be precisely discerned. Nor is it possible to know exactly the extent of her affluence. In January 1870, she told a reporter that she had earned over $700,000—a net worth that today would exceed ten million dollars—"since she had been in the business in New York—some two or three years." The claim may well have been extravagant given that it was coupled with the announcement that Woodhull and her sister had established their own brokerage firm on Wall Street. They were now open for business and seeking clients. But if Woodhull was worth even a tenth of what she claimed, she had become an extraordinarily wealthy woman. She was initially coy about revealing Vanderbilt's financial backing of the new establishment of Woodhull, Claflin & Co. Nonetheless, Victoria and her sister readily invoked him as a valued advisor. Customers would have not missed the Commodore's portrait hanging on the wall of the firm's offices. The press, in any case, trumpeted the connection. The first headlines describing "The Queens of Finance" identified them as "Vanderbilt's Proteges."[19]

Vanderbilt did not deny his association with the "lady stock operators of Wall Street." A prospective female client of Woodhull & Claflin, who checked with the Commodore to ensure the sisters' legitimacy, was satisfied, to some degree, with his endorsement. Advised by the firm to invest "some $18,000 or $19,000 in New York Central stock," a railroad Vanderbilt incidentally controlled, the patron asked the Commodore if he endorsed the suggestion. "He said yes," she later reported, "that was the thing to do; that it would go up 22% in three months." She continued: "I asked him why. He said Mrs. Woodhull was a spiritual medium, and while in a clairvoyant state had told him so. I told him I would invest the $18,000 in the stock if he would give me a written guarantee that it would rise that much. He said he didn't do business that way." However, Vanderbilt was happy to reassure the investor of his confidence in the brokers. "I told him that Mrs. Woodhull said he owed her a good deal of money," the investor indicated. "He said yes—that they were clairvoyants, and he was helping them, and he owed them money; he was furnishing the funds to carry on the business."[20]

The novelty of Woodhull and Claflin's financial endeavor attracted immediate attention. Crowds gathered at their Wall Street offices in the first days as scores of onlookers sought to catch a glimpse of the unlikely brokers. Their celebrity was fueled by avid press coverage, which the sisters invited. A cartoon of the "lady brokers" was published a month after the firm's opening. It depicted them driving a carriage drawn by "bulls and bears" with men's faces which they lashed with whips. Elaborate descriptions of the women themselves—Victoria was depicted in one early story as "plainly dressed, having no ornament but a single rose tastefully inserted in her hair" with a diamond ring on her left hand—and the firm's lavishly appointed Broad Street offices made for irresistible copy. So did the specter of women entering a decidedly male domain—a phenomenon some characterized as familiar in a time when discussion of women's rights flourished.[21]

Initial coverage of Woodhull and Claflin expressed fascination and skepticism in equal measure. Although a few papers (notably the *New York Times*) acidly ridiculed the venture, many stories were surprisingly respectful. "How are we ever to make the masculine names of the stock brokers common to both sexes?" mused the New York *Evening Post*. "Can Mrs. Woodhull, of whom we would speak with only the highest respect, be ever properly mentioned as a bull or Miss Claflin, to whom we would always pay the homage that is due her, as a bear?" Noting the experience of women doctors, the writer concluded: "Whether woman goes out of her proper range in entering the stock-market or the dissecting room may be a moot point, perhaps; but wherever she goes, maintaining her self-respect, she is entitled to the courtesy of 'Us.'" The *New York Herald* likewise welcomed with enthusiasm Woodhull and Claflin's firm as an "experiment of great importance." "If successful," the *Herald* reported, "it opens a new and boundless field of employment to women . . . But if it should fail? Fail! These ladies of the new banking firm, they say, are backed by a capital of half a million and that they cannot fail. At all events, we like the experiment as a new thing, and we wish it success." A San Francisco paper similarly concluded that it "speaks well for the onward sentiment of the age" that the women brokers were treated seriously.[22]

Within short order, Woodhull and Claflin also attracted the attention of suffrage leaders. Susan B. Anthony visited the brokerage house and heaped praise in *The Revolution* on what she found at 44 Broad Street. She admired especially the sisters' "pluck, energy and enterprise," as well as their "personal appearance, manners and lady-like deportment." The firm would allow women, Anthony stressed, the opportunity to pursue their "financial business" in a congenial setting rather than having to conduct their transactions "through men" and face "the gauntlet of Wall Street." Indeed, she noted the steady stream of female clients filing into the firm's office. Predicting that Woodhull and Claflin would "stimulate the whole future of woman by their efforts and example," she wished "success to the new firm."[23]

Woodhull and Claflin scarcely needed Susan B. Anthony's endorsement. By the early spring of 1870, Woodhull was riding a wave of success. She was a wealthy woman, living in a stately Murray Hill mansion, a stone's throw from Fifth Avenue, enjoying growing celebrity and remarkable public recognition as an apparent player in high finance. It had been quite a journey from her homely childhood in Homer, Ohio, where her dreams of future greatness had improbably been nurtured. But all that she had achieved did not yet seem to realize that "previous prophesy." Her riches opened the door to even larger ambitions—a not uncommon story in Gilded Age America. Woodhull's desires took shape in part through the influence of the wide circle of reformers, spiritualists, and radical intellectuals she came to know in New York City. Entertaining on a grand scale, she brought together a host of unlikely guests, including leading finance capitalists, journalists, politicians, mediums, and anarchists. Two men, however, both radical, became Woodhull's most influential muses. The first was her husband, Colonel

Blood, a man of "philosophic and reflective cast of mind," who considered himself a communist even as he kept the brokerage business humming. The second was utopian philosopher and radical labor activist Stephen Pearl Andrews, whom Blood appears to have brought into the mix. An avid student of Marx, and a committed exponent of women's rights, Andrews wrote prolifically about his vision of a just society. Among the targets of his criticism was the institution of marriage, which he believed oppressed women. His support of liberalized divorce laws and individual sexual freedom earned him a reputation as a "free-love" advocate—a highly controversial stance in Victorian America. Andrews became close to Woodhull, who helped him to stay afloat financially. Together Blood and Andrews would assist Woodhull in laying claim to her next objective—the American presidency.[24]

Woodhull's run for the presidency evolved in two stages. In the spring of 1870 came her opening salvo, a letter to the *New York Herald* announcing her candidacy. From the start, Woodhull proved a highly unorthodox candidate. This was not simply because she was a woman, who could not vote, and did not meet the minimum age for president mandated by the Constitution (thirty-five). There was also her "self nomination." To be sure, eccentric independent male candidates had surfaced with some regularity in nineteenth-century presidential races. Two such men,

Daniel Pratt, an oddball itinerant lecturer, and George Francis Train, a supporter of Stanton and Anthony, wealthy founder of the Crédit Mobilier holding company, and a virulent racist, had already declared when Woodhull entered the 1872 race. (In fact, Train's involvement in women's suffrage perhaps led Woodhull to entertain the idea of running.) But serious presidential aspirants invariably emerged from political parties. As a woman, Woodhull enjoyed neither voting rights nor access to power within the mainstream political parties of her era. Thus she shrewdly bypassed the normal political apparatus and took her case directly to the people through the available media of her day—a newspaper.[25]

Woodhull's timing was also noteworthy. The announcement came on April 2, 1870, just three months after her brokerage firm opened but *two years* before the presidential election of 1872. In contemporary America, long prologues devoted to fundraising, primary battles, debates, media operations, and barnstorming have become commonplace. This was not usually the case in the nineteenth century, despite the equally premature entry of Messrs. Pratt and Train. Even bona fide nominees ran the risk of appearing unstatesmanlike, and therefore unworthy of the office they sought, if they asked for votes on their own behalf and actively promoted their own candidacies. The parties largely ran the show; quixotic presidential candidates still often stood behind the fig leaf of a formal political organization. Stumping for votes, even after winning a place on the ticket, remained a somewhat suspect activity as late as the 1870s. In 1872, the *Hartford Courant* labeled Democratic nominee Horace Greeley "the great American office beggar" when he embarked on a limited campaign swing. Greeley seemed to think, the *Courant* complained, that a "man should seek the office rather than the office the man." A lack of dignified reserve was, of course, the least of Woodhull's problems in declaring her intention to seek the presidency.[26]

Woodhull would later confess that her April 1870 announcement was "mainly for the purpose of drawing attention to the claims of woman to political equality with man." Hers would be, in other words, a symbolic presidential candidacy—a path well trod by others in the nineteenth century. Yet the terms in which she framed her bid foreshadowed how her campaign would evolve in the two years ahead. She made the candidate—in this case herself—the central offering. Though her declaration emphasized her bonds with other women, it accented her own exceptional achievements. "I happen to be the most prominent representative of the only unrepresented class in the republic, and perhaps the most practical exponent of the principles of equality," she wrote in her letter to the *Herald*. Such a stance again anticipated the pitch of modern presidential candidates. Today aspirants to the Oval Office commonly champion their individuality, rather than their allegiance to party principles, in their efforts to persuade voters of their fitness for national leadership. In an age that highly prized at least the appearance of virtue, modesty, and rectitude in its would-be presidents, Woodhull pursued an unusual tack. She used the forum of a newspaper to tout her bid for office. Diverging from a political culture wherein party and platform trumped, for the most part, candidates, Woodhull advanced herself as an embodiment of a cause rather than its selfless representative.[27]

In fact, Woodhull took pains to distinguish herself even from the most visible female voices in national politics—the suffrage leaders. "While others of my sex devoted themselves to a crusade against the laws that shackle the women of the country," she noted pointedly, "I asserted my individual independence." She continued: "While others prayed for the good time coming, I worked for it; while others argued the equality of woman with man, I proved it by successfully engaging in business; while others sought to show that there was no valid reason why woman should be treated socially and politically as a being inferior to man, I boldly entered the arena of politics and business and exercised the rights I already possessed." Her record as a self-made woman, successful in business, assertive in a world of male privilege, courageous in the pursuit of her varied interests and endeavors, in other words, had prepared her to lead her sex and her country. "I there-fore claim the right to speak for the unenfranchised women of the country," Woodhull asserted. "Believing as I do that there will be more female officeholders than female voters for some time to come, and that the prejudices that exist in the popular mind against women in public life will soon disappear, I now an-nounce myself as a candidate for the Presidency."[28]

Woodhull's announcement reflected more than brag-gadocio. It contained a central insight that diverged from the views most prevalent among suffrage leaders. In a democratic society, Woodhull maintained, equal-ity could not be realized by persuading the public of the principle in theory. It needed to be actualized and made concrete. A national candidate for whom men and (she hoped) women could cast their ballots might well demonstrate broad support for women's equality. As Woodhull put it: "All that has been said and writ-ten hitherto in support of equality for women has had its proper effect on the public mind, just as the anti-slavery speeches before secession were effective; but a candidate and a policy are required to prove it. Lincoln's election showed the strength of the feeling against the peculiar institution; my candidacy for the Presidency will, I confidently expect, develop the fact that the principles of equal rights for all have taken deep root." Woodhull praised women's rights activists for their "respectable known strength." But she suggested that a far greater "undercurrent of unexpressed power" existed in the country that was "only awaiting a fit opportunity to show itself." A woman presidential candidate would test the proposition of women's political equality. Win or lose, by embarking on such a run "we shall be able to understand the woman question aright, or at least have done much toward presenting the issue involved in proper shape." "I claim to possess the strength and courage to be the subject of that test," she insisted.[29]

In advancing herself and her cause, Woodhull dismissed the existing political parties as entities without "great principles of policy or economy." Voters would be hard-pressed to find meaningful differences in politics or "sentiment" between the parties. Instead, political life had become an arena for demagoguery. "Political preachers paw the air; there is no live issue up for discussion," she asserted. The only topic that seemed to engage and divide politicians was "the dead issue of negro equality"—dead, she believed because the war and Reconstruction had established it as fact. Nonetheless, to some "political leaders" seeking to perpetuate discord the matter remained "a harp of a thousand strings." An election that engaged "a great national question," Woodhull believed, was "wanted to prevent a descent into pure sectionalism." Political equality for women, she held, should be that issue. She insisted that no matter more important would "arise before the Presidential election." An array of other concerns should command the attention of the nation's next leader, Woodhull added. She sketched out a platform that endorsed prison reform, more effective "internal improvements," "some better means" of assisting "the helpless and indigent," attention to the needs of working people, as well as a neutral foreign policy. Only "a complete departure from the beaten track of political parties and their machinery" could advance the country.[30]

Woodhull added to her announcement an unsparing critique of the sitting Ulysses S. Grant administration. The public already widely recognized its deficiencies, she claimed. But "as I have now taken a decided stand against its continuance for another term of four years, and offered myself as a candidate for the Presidential succession," she wrote, she felt compelled to itemize its failings. Grant's administration, she charged, had been a "failure from the very beginning; weak, vacillating, and deficient in moral courage." Its policies lacked the "decision and firmness" that were the hallmarks of Grant "the victorious soldier who is now President." She faulted the administration for failing to support rebels in Cuba who sought the island's independence from Spain. Grant's tariff and taxation policies she deemed neither coherent nor fair. And she discussed at some length the matter of the public debt amassed during the Civil War—at more than $2 billion, it was massive by the standards of the time. It required no hasty liquidation, in Woodhull's view. Economic growth would enable the nation to easily erase its debt in time. In the interim, the nation needed to invest in itself. That position was consonant with the views of many labor, antimonopoly, and reform activists of the period.[31]

Reaction to Woodhull's presidential announcement was abundant and swift. The *Herald* on the day it printed her letter welcomed Woodhull's bid. "There can certainly be no objection to such a competition as this," the editors wrote. "It possesses the merits of novelty, enterprise, courage and determination." If women were enfranchised under a sixteenth amendment, the paper predicted, Woodhull could anticipate a "triumphant election." Indeed, it portrayed Woodhull's run as "a fitting opportunity for women throughout the land to show their might . . . by voting for a candidate for the Presidential succession of 1872, and by inducing the men to vote, 'just this once,' in favor of a woman for President." The *Herald* imagined that a groundswell of support would exist among women for a female candidate whatever her political posture. "Women always take the part of each other," the *Herald* claimed (inaccurately), "and if the women can be allowed to vote Mrs. Woodhull may rely on rolling up the heaviest majority ever polled in this or any other nation." Such a prospect did not seem to trouble the editors. On the contrary, the newspaper concluded enthusiastically: "Now, then, for another amendment and victory for Victoria in 1872."[32]

A day later, the *Herald* returned to the subject, sarcastically surveying what was becoming a crowded field of independent candidates two years before the election. If a woman ran for president could a person of color be far behind? "We shall probably next have Senator Revels, Downing, the oysterman, or Frederick Douglass, as the African candidate, and the famous Koopmanschap as the Chinese labor candidate . . . and in the course of the next two years a half dozen more candidates may turn up, which will make things very lively," the paper observed. But the *Herald* viewed "Victoria C. Woodhull" as the candidate who had "all the advantages that point to success." "Who can tell the extent of her financial resources among the brokers, bulls, and bears?" the paper asked. A wealthy woman, "a smart and handsome woman" at that, she was, the *Herald* declaimed, "the proper person to stand forth against the field as the woman's rights candidate for the White House." The *Herald*'s editors went so far as to publish over the course of several months ten dense theoretical and historical essays on government and politics purportedly written by Woodhull. They were likely the work of Stephen Andrews. Impenetrable, abstract, and mind-bendingly convoluted, they surely challenged the perseverance of even the most committed reader of a daily mass-circulation newspaper. An editorial in the *Chicago Tribune* rendered this dismissive verdict: "When a woman begins to talk about 'the tendencies of government,' and takes two columns of the *Herald* to make her way from Nimrod to Sardanapalus, we feel inwardly thankful that, whatever may be the point she is coming to, we are not obliged to listen to the argument."[33]

From Maine to California, Woodhull's foray into presidential politics garnered notice from the press. Nearly 100 stories reporting her candidacy appeared in just the first month after the *Herald* published her announcement. Most simply noted her entry into the race, though some wags could not resist editorializing. The *Jackson* [Michigan] *Citizen Patriot* observed that Woodhull joined a field occupied by George Francis Train and Daniel Pratt. "Of the three distinguished candidates for the White House above named," it offered, "Mrs. Victoria is the best man, by all odds." The *Mobile* [Alabama] *Register* described Woodhull's letter to the *Herald* as a "powerful women's rights document," under the headline "A Woman in the Ring for President." But a San Francisco paper was left incredulous. Noting that the "bulls and bears" of Wall Street had already been "gazing with a more or less dazed expression of countenance, upon the curious phenomenon of a female broker's office," they were now further jolted by Woodhull's presidential announcement. "It is evident," the *Weekly Alta California* concluded, "that we live in right lively times, and that not only Wall street, but the whole country, has reason to rub its eyes."[34]

As Woodhull had predicted, her intentions were, indeed, openly ridiculed by some. The *Albany Argus* attempted to tar Woodhull with a broad women's rights brush: "The announcement of this lady's candidacy . . . must have gladdened the heart of Mrs. Stanton, and made that of Miss Anthony leap for joy." Referring to the candidate variously as "the enchanting Woodhull," "this lady," "the lovely money changer," and "the lady-bird," the reporter echoed the surprise of many of his contemporaries: "Truly, the world moves. To say the least of it, this proclamation of Mrs. Woodhull's is a little bit startling." "It is possible, though perhaps not quite probable," the reporter mused, "that the American people will elect her, and hail her as Victoria, the American sovereign, at least as the 'Queen of Hearts.'" He concluded, however, that perhaps a Woodhull White House would be no worse than the Grant administration. "The old women whom she might select as her cabinet advisers," he speculated, "would hardly be found less calculated to adorn and fill worthily their posts, than those against whose incapacity and extravagance the nation is now so generally protesting." A Georgia newspaper reached a similar conclusion in the summer of 1870, when it offered that "a petticoat government" led by Woodhull "would be a vast improvement on the present gift enterprize concern by which the nation is ruled."[35]

Woodhull left nothing to chance, however, in her dealings with the press. She had relied upon newspapers to disseminate word of her presidential bid. But she had no intention of leaving to established journalists the important business of defining her as a candidate. At a time when highly partisan newspapers decisively shaped the political culture, she recognized the need to have a reliably sympathetic news outlet that would fairly report upon her. Thus Woodhull decided to devote some of her considerable resources to establishing her own journal. It was a costly proposition, and Woodhull spared no expense in finding office space on Park Row, a devoted staff, heavy paper stock, and a first-rate press. Her wealth left these expenditures easily within her grasp. Enlisting Andrews and Blood to assist her with the venture, she released the first issue of *Woodhull & Claflin's Weekly* just six weeks after announcing her campaign for president.[36]

"Upward & Onward" read the slogan under the *Weekly*'s masthead. The journal's inaugural issue touted its independence even as it affirmed its central objective: the promotion of Woodhull's presidential candidacy. "This Journal will be primarily devoted to the vital interests of the people, and will treat of all matters freely and without reservation," it promised. But in a paradox that perfectly captured the contradictions of late nineteenth-century print journalism, it likewise announced: "It will support VICTORIA C. WOODHULL for President, with its whole strength; otherwise it will be untrammeled by party or personal considerations, free from all affiliation with political or social creeds, and will advocate Suffrage without distinction of sex!" Sports news, including cricket scores, financial reports, poetry, fashion, and boating race outcomes shared space with articles on women's suffrage, essays on "labor and capital," book reviews, and literary contributions, including a translation of George Sand. Initial reviews were very favorable. The *Herald,* predictably, pronounced the first issue "interesting and agreeable" and suggested Woodhull and her sister were doing more for women's advancement in publishing the journal than the leading (and "squabbling") suffrage organizations. The *Leavenworth* [Kansas] *Bulletin* applauded Woodhull and Claflin for publishing "a handsome sheet of sixteen pages, moderate in tone, advocating all practicable social reform movements, and furnishing the reader a really spicy, well-edited hebdomidal." That assessment was echoed by the Harrisburg, Pennsylvania, *Morning Patriot,* which praised the paper's "talented editresses," wishing them "abundant success." The *Coldwater* [Michigan] *Sentinel* suggested the journal had appeal for "all tastes from the strong minded woman to the weak minded one."[37]

By all accounts, Woodhull's news outlet enjoyed

early success. But if its purpose was to advance Victoria Woodhull's presidential campaign, *Woodhull & Claflin's Weekly* proved to be a blunt instrument. For the first sixth months of its existence, the journal expounded regularly and at length on the merits of women's voting rights and equality. Many of these stories ran under section headings that read the "Sixteenth Amendment." The paper covered closely political news from Washington, where a bill for a sixteenth amendment guaranteeing women the right to vote, in fact, remained stalled in committee. But it did little to showcase explicitly Woodhull herself as a potential leader of the country. That posture was, of course, consistent with Woodhull's later claims that initially she sought the presidency to advance the cause of women's equality. Suffrage surfaced in virtually every issue of the *Weekly*. The election itself was distant. Even a determined candidate in the 1870s might well have been doing far less than Woodhull at this juncture.

The *Weekly* was, in truth, becoming somewhat of a creature of Andrews, who wrote extensively for the paper. After the first few editions, his views on politics, his advocacy of a universal world government (with himself a reigning "Pantarch"—a weird kingly figure), and his meditations on the iniquities of marriage appeared more regularly. A short piece entitled "What Is Prostitution?" ran in August 1870 that suggested the term well described unhappy women trapped by dependence in marriage. Such contributions to the *Weekly* did not go unnoticed by the press. The *Cleveland Plain Dealer* flagged the marriage stories. Another critic suggested Andrews' views could be found in *Woodhull & Claflin's Weekly* by "those who care to befuddle themselves with enlightenment." And in mid-September 1870, the *Idaho Statesman* asserted very directly that the *Weekly* had "fallen a prey to evil counsels and we fear has been seduced from original good purposes by designing men." Woodhull's brokerage business, presidential bid, and new journal startled but had been taken in stride. Suspicions grew, however, once the *Weekly* made space for Andrews' radical views about the family, sex, and marriage. In particular, Andrews' reputation as an apostle of "free love" and a critic of marriage potentially imperiled Woodhull's reputation. Mindful of the danger, Woodhull initially took pains to insulate herself from any guilt by association. In November 1870, the *Weekly* published a disclaimer of sorts in response to blowback received about a Stephen Andrews article. "We do not necessarily endorse *anything* which appears in our columns over another's signature. We frequently differ widely from much which appears thus," the editors stressed even as they defended their journal as a forum for open discussion.[38]

That apologia might well have been missed by readers whose attention would have been drawn to another article, running under bold headlines and Victoria Woodhull's byline, in the same November issue. The headline read: "STARTLING ANNUNCIATION! A New Political Platform Proclaimed! Woman's Right of Suffrage Fully Recognized in the Constitution and Completely Established By Positive Law and Recent Events—The Sixteenth Amendment a Dead Letter! Victoria C. Woodhull Triumphant as the Most Prominent Candidate for the Presidency in 1872." It was a lot of news for one lead-in. Woodhull went on to explain. She noted that when she announced her run for president on April 2, she "knew then" that the United States Constitution *as written and ratified* already provided for "woman's complete political equality with man." She held back this insight, Woodhull wrote, because "the time had not come for this announcement." The ongoing debate about women's rights had yet to run its course. But now the moment was at hand. "As I have been the first to comprehend these Constitutional and legal facts," Woodhull continued, "so am I the first to proclaim, as *I now do proclaim to the women of the United States of America that they are enfranchised.*"[39]

Woodhull based this claim on an interesting constitutional interpretation. She argued that if any state in the Union allowed women to vote, then under the U.S. Constitution's "privileges and immunities" clause (Article 4, Section 2), no woman in any state could be denied the franchise. (Wyoming, though still then a territory, had conferred voting rights on women in 1869.) In making this claim, she drew on an approach that had, in fact, been advanced over a year earlier by Francis and Virginia Minor. This husband and wife from Missouri, active in the suffrage movement, argued that the provisions of the Constitution, especially when bolstered by the new Reconstruction amendments, already conferred voting rights on women. (Woodhull knew of the Minors' position, which she heard discussed at the 1869 suffrage meeting she had attended in Washington.) The Minors' legal reasoning differed from Woodhull's, but nonetheless the implication was the same. The Minors held that if women were already enfranchised, they should show up at the polls and demand a ballot. If barred, they should use the court system to sue for their voting rights. Woodhull called for another level of political engagement—mobilization on behalf of her presidential candidacy. Noting that "the question of female suffrage being thus definitely settled," it was time for women to "unite in purifying" government. She reviewed the political platform she had unveiled in April, now adding to the list a call for the abolition of capital punishment.[40]

Woodhull concluded her "Startling Annunciation" with a broad request for support in her bid for the presidency. In the eternal language of presidential candidates, she depicted herself as a "friend of equal rights, a faithful worker in the cause of human advancement;

and more especially the friend, supporter, co-laborer with those who strive to encourage the poor and the friendless." She took pains to invite support from everyone "in the social scale." But she departed from traditional campaign rhetoric when she alluded to a future improved by the guidance of a woman president. "If I obtain this support, and by it the position of President of the United States," Woodhull offered, "I promise that woman's strength and woman's will, with God's support, if He vouchsafe it, shall open . . . a new career of greatness in the race of nations," which, she argued, had been lost "under despotic male governments."[41]

In the winter of 1870, Woodhull moved from the arenas of New York business and publishing into the den of national politics. Her constitutional argument, now improved by careful legal reasoning, provided the occasion for her sojourn in Washington. U.S. Congressman Benjamin Butler, a controversial Massachusetts Republican, supporter of women's suffrage, and new acquaintance of Woodhull, played a major role in the unfolding of this chapter. He helped ensure that a memorial—a petition, in modern parlance—to Congress that Woodhull had drawn up (likely with Butler's assistance) would be presented and heard and that Woodhull herself would be invited to speak on its behalf. The Woodhull Memorial, as it became known, asserted that women were already enfranchised under the terms of the Fourteenth and Fifteenth Amendments. It turned, in brief, around a straightforward syllogism. The Fourteenth Amendment established that "all persons born or naturalized in the United States" were citizens. It further stipulated that no state could pass a law abridging the rights of citizens. The Fifteenth Amendment affirmed, as she saw it, the voting rights of citizens. Thus any law barring women from voting was unconstitutional and no new amendment was needed to enfranchise women. Woodhull called upon the Congress to issue a declaratory act affirming that as citizens, women had a right to vote that was already established in the U.S. Constitution.[42]

The memorial was submitted by sympathetic members to the House and Senate in late December and referred to each chamber's judiciary committee. Woodhull's scheduled appearance before the House Judiciary Committee on January 11, 1871, as it turned out, coincided with a national suffrage meeting in Washington, D.C. Suffrage leaders had neither been consulted nor informed of Woodhull's impending date with members of Congress. But once they learned of it, arrangements were hastily made to attend the hearing in force and to have a constitutional lawyer appear on behalf of the thousands of women who had already petitioned Congress for their voting rights. Such expansive efforts well predated Woodhull's engagement in the issue. Nonetheless, she had scored an incredible coup in getting a hearing before the House Judiciary Committee.

Indeed, when she arrived in the hearing room that January day, she made history as the first woman to address a committee of Congress. Her political adroitness astounded seasoned suffrage leaders, including Susan B. Anthony, Elizabeth Cady Stanton, and Isabella Beecher Hooker. In fact, Anthony expressed confidence that Woodhull had brought new power to the proceedings: "We propose to obtain the ballot with telegraphic speed. Wall street has appeared in Congress to demand the ballot." Although Woodhull's voice was said to have "trembled slightly with emotion" as she began her statement, one reporter noted that it "only made the reading the more effective." The committee respectfully received Woodhull and listened closely to her argument.

The suffrage leaders in attendance pronounced themselves persuaded of the value in pressing the Congress to act directly. That very afternoon Woodhull repeated her testimony at the national suffrage convention. Efforts to advance the sixteenth amendment were dropped almost immediately in favor of a new strategy. Anthony embraced a lobbying campaign designed to pressure Congress to declare women enfranchised under the existing amendments. Spirits ran high even after the House Judiciary Committee rendered its majority report in late January decisively rejecting Woodhull's petition. Two members of the committee (Butler and William Loughridge, a Republican from Iowa) filed a minority opinion strongly supporting Woodhull's argument. Despite the memorial's rejection, many suffragists felt galvanized by the hearing and minority report. Some remained behind in Washington to continue their lobbying. The entire event was clearly a victory for an aspiring presidential candidate. Woodhull appeared to have deeply impressed both the committee members and many of those in attendance.[43]

To be sure, Woodhull's appearance in Washington elevated her standing with suffrage leaders, who lauded her accomplishment. A reporter from the *New York Times* picked up the buzz and offered: "Beecher Hooker and Miss Anthony appear on the surface as chief fugle-women . . . In fact, Woodhull's name is in constant use among them, and they are all exceedingly lavish of their praises." Certainly the suffrage leaders' private communications confirmed that assumption. "Bravo! My Dear Woodhull," wrote Susan B. Anthony. "I have never in the whole twenty years' good fight felt so full of life and hope. I know now that Mr. Train's prophesy —nay, assertion—three years ago . . . that 'the women would vote for the next President,' is to be realized." Anthony made no promise to vote for Woodhull, however. But she ended with a blessing: "Go ahead! bright, glorious, young, and strong spirit, and believe in the best love and hope and faith of S. B. Anthony."[44]

Isabella Beecher Hooker also extolled Woodhull. "This is a remarkable woman," Hooker later wrote to her friend Anthony, "and of a sweetness I have seldom seen." She admitted that Woodhull was "wild on only one point—and that was her conviction that she was to be President next time and thus *ruler of the whole world*—our country being destined to lead all others." Hooker advised the young woman "to keep this to herself and she appeared to after that." *The Revolution* concluded that the suffrage convention in Washington had been "a great success and this success has mainly been owing to Mrs. Victoria C. Woodhull." Her involvement had, the journal noted, "attracted the attention of a class of people who have never before recognized the cause."[45]

Press coverage was widespread, with many stories praising Woodhull for her composure, effectiveness, and physical attributes. The *New York Herald* ran a headline reading "A Delegation of Fair Ones Before the House Judiciary Committee—Grand Display of Ancient and Tender Loveliness—A Female Candidate for the Presidency." Mrs. Woodhull, the article reported, "will be a candidate for the Presidency in 1872, should Congress legalize female suffrage and intends to run as an independent candidate on the platform of free suffrage and equality before the law." The press noted that "even the matrons" (Susan B. Anthony was then fifty years old) displayed a "scrupulous attention to tidiness and attractive appearance." It was Woodhull, however, who most commanded attention. Her "voice was very clear," and at her conclusion she "bowed gracefully," one reporter noted. "Other speeches were made, but Woodhull had captured the committee, and the others were not needed." Woodhull's youth and beauty surely enchanted some reporters, who contrasted Woodhull with the older generation of suffrage leaders. "The Woman's Rights army this year," the *Boston Herald* reported, for example, "contains all the veterans who have been here before, besides a number of recruits, some of them young and handsome, and it is generally conceded that the personal charms of some of these recruits adds weight to the cause."[46]

So impressed was the *New York Tribune* by Woodhull's achievement that it elevated her to an exalted position in a movement she had only relatively recently discovered. "Mrs. Woodhull," it declaimed, "has at last risen to her rightful place as the legitimate leader of the Woman Suffrage movement in its formal demand made yesterday upon Congress for recognition." A less romantic scribe referred to her as "the banker of the party," perhaps because she breezily pledged $10,000 at the suffrage meeting when Susan B. Anthony called for donations. Even the *Cincinnati Daily Enquirer,* which referred to Woodhull as "the frisky Wall Street heifer," suggested that she represented a new vanguard. "Mrs. Victoria C. Woodhull," it reported, "is monopolizing all the glory of the Woman Suffrage campaign at Washington. MRS. STANTON has retired from the field and even SUSAN rasps a secondary fiddle."[47]

There were discordant notes sounded. One foreshadowed where Woodhull's bold efforts to enter American political life at the top ultimately were headed. In late February 1871, a little more than a month after Woodhull's well-regarded performance before the congressional committee, the *New York Times* published an account of a legal action that raised questions about Woodhull's character. A female client of Woodhull and Claflin had sued the brokerage firm over what she claimed were mishandled funds ($500). The client testified that Woodhull offered to invest her funds in gold and to refund the principal if no profits were forthcoming. Woodhull vehemently denied that she had ever made such a promise. She explained that she had, on the contrary, warned the client of the risks involved in gold speculation. This was by no means the first disgruntled client to land Woodhull in legal trouble. Nor was it the first press account to raise questions about Victoria Woodhull's character. The *New York Times* had, in fact, suggested that Woodhull and her sister were frauds in the story they published when the brokerage business opened. But that was before Woodhull expressed an interest in politics. Now the headline the *Times* attached to the story was telling: "Woman's Right to Speculate—A Presidential Candidate in an Unsuccessful Gold 'Pool'—A Country Governess Launches Her Bark on the Troubled Waters of Wall Street and Gets Swamped." While the jury found for the plaintiff and called for restitution of the lost funds, the media coverage potentially inflicted a different sort of damage. It certainly suggested that this presidential aspirant, who claimed to favor women's rights, had, in fact, ruthlessly exploited another woman to enrich herself. A presidential candidate who based so much of her suitability for office on her character would be particularly vulnerable, of course, to such negative coverage.[48]

The *Times*'s adverse story was largely buried, however, by an avalanche of favorable coverage of Victoria Woodhull in the late winter and early spring of 1871. She followed her triumph in Washington with a series of public lectures in New York, Philadelphia, and Boston, where she attracted large audiences. The *Chicago Republican* characterized her travels as "in preparation for her elevation to the presidency in 1872," noting they had set off "a great bustle among the newspapers." "We have constantly supported the claims of Mrs. Woodhull for that high position," the *Republican* continued but joked that it disapproved of any "bustle"—a double entendre evoking the padding underneath a Victorian woman's skirt. "Why, indeed, should she consider such an article necessary for a President? Washington never wore a great bustle made of newspapers; nor did John Adams, nor James Buchanan, nor Andrew Johnson, nor any of them." Changes in Woodhull's hairstyle, dress, and accessories remained fertile subjects for comment.[49]

A second phase of Woodhull's presidential campaign had indeed ensued after her triumph in Washington. In late January 1871, *Woodhull & Claflin's Weekly* unveiled with new vigor Woodhull's ongoing candidacy. A giant front-page graphic announced the "Cosmo-Political Party Nomination for President of the U.S. in 1872 Victoria C. Woodhull—Subject to Ratification by the National Convention." Thus was heralded Woodhull's intention of creating a "cosmopolitan" political party to back her bid for the nation's highest office. The image appeared for months afterward on the *Weekly*'s first page without elaboration.[50]

Woodhull's paper served a very useful purpose in swatting stories from other press outlets that threatened to become more than annoyances. In late March 1871, the *Weekly* ran a piece entitled "Mrs. Woodhull and the Poodles of the Press" that went aggressively after a newspaper editor who impugned Victoria's moral character. His evidence was derived from an article the *Weekly* ran criticizing marriage laws that made divorce extremely difficult. Such commentary again raised the red flag of "free love" for those who conflated liberalized divorce laws with advocacy of sexual licentiousness. In any case, the *Weekly* had reprinted the story from a London journal, as it was quick to point out in rejoinder. And it went to great lengths to disassociate Woodhull from any free-love advocacy. "There seems to us no kind of immorality and license to free love," it stressed, in the original essay's insistence that women need not be forced to love, honor, and obey a man who was no longer loveable, honorable, or "just and reasonable" in his commands. Nor was the editor just in smearing Mrs. Woodhull for printing another writer's opinion to that effect. "It by no means follows," the *Weekly* scolded, "that Mrs. Woodhull indorses the sometimes very queer and crude crotchets of her correspondents, neither does it follow that this editor has the right to try and make it appear that Mrs. Woodhull is the person who puts forth the views contained in the Marriage Law article." Such misrepresentations seemed highly suspicious to the *Weekly*, which suggested the editor sought to deliberately dethrone Woodhull, "the head of the women's movement." His effort to "blacken her character" and make of her "a very black sheep" would fail. "The little editor man strikes at high game," the *Weekly* warned, "but he won't bring it down." In this particular instance, and for the moment, that was correct.[51]

May 1871 brought a cascade of events, however, that would set Woodhull's presidential bid, her entire public career, and ultimately her personal life on a disastrous course. The month began on a high note when Woodhull gave a well-received lecture on May 8 at the Cooper Institute in New York City. Her audience was the American Labor Reform League, an eclectic gathering of leftists and reformers intent on addressing the exploitation of the working class in the burgeoning American industrial economy. Woodhull fully aligned herself with labor in its struggle against capital, and she spoke with feeling about the "insatiable avarice" of "obese corporations," the "despotism" of "bank and railroad combinations," and the "greed of capital" that sought to "swallow up the rights of labor entirely." It was rich stuff coming from a Wall Street broker. But there could be no doubt that Woodhull embraced the cause. She would publish countless antimonopoly and prolabor articles in the *Weekly* in the ensuing months. And by the summer she would be a major figure in an American section (known as 12) of the International Workingmen's Association (IWA), or First International, a diverse federation of radical labor activists. At the Cooper Institute, she urged labor reformers to seize power by engaging directly in the political process. And she certainly meant to cultivate their support for her own aspirations in politics. Labor, as Woodhull saw it, would be a vital component of the new political party she hoped to launch and lead, one that she believed could take her all the way to the White House.[52]

Those sympathetic to suffrage constituted, of course, a key constituency. As would be true of women presidential candidates who would succeed her, Woodhull expected and cultivated the support of other women. In May 1871, a national suffrage meeting would be held in New York at Apollo Hall. Woodhull was to have a major role in the proceedings. She would give a keynote speech on May 11, just three days after her appearance at the Cooper Institute. Woodhull had devoted considerable energy over the spring to her relationships with major suffrage figures. Now she could showcase her leadership abilities and, she hoped, draw support from suffragists for the new political party she planned to serve as standard-bearer. Before the day of her speech arrived, however, a family drama unfolded that raised all the old traumas. Her mother, who lived with Victoria, her children, Colonel Blood, Tennessee, and various other members of the Claflin family in the Murray Hill mansion, showed up at the Essex Market Police Court on May 4. She had come to swear out a criminal complaint against her son-in-law. Mrs. Claflin charged that Blood had alienated both her daughters from her, and used them to blackmail and defraud wealthy married men. She complained that the colonel played fast and loose in his management of the brokerage business, failing to keep records and warning that the firm could not survive scrutiny. Last, but certainly not least, she revealed that her son-in-law had threatened variously to commit her to a "lunatic asylum" or to kill her. It was a bill of particulars guaranteed to stoke the smoldering fires of scandal that seemed to constantly warm her daughters. Within a day of Mrs. Claflin's visit to the police, the story appeared in newspapers across the country.[53]

Most press accounts let the salacious details speak for themselves. Many took pains to quote Woodhull's denial of her mother's charges. But Woodhull's prominence fed the story. She had, indeed, become a national figure—one who had found a pathway to politics by emphasizing her personal character and by inviting news coverage. That strategy had made Woodhull one of the most famous women of her day. But it also meant that Woodhull could not escape infamy when her fortunes shifted. "New Scandalous Developments about the Noted Wall Street Firm," "Soiled Linen," and "Mrs. Woodhull in Trouble" were among the headlines. The *Cincinnati Commercial* published Mrs. Claflin's entire affidavit as well as sworn statements from one of Victoria's sisters and her husband, supporting the charges. A single line in Mrs. Claflin's sworn affidavit would inflict a world of pain on her daughter. Having established that she lived with Victoria until the end of April at the Murray Hill address, Mrs. Claflin made a further revelation that proved damning. She swore that "there also resides Dr. Canning Woodhull, who was formerly the husband of deponent's daughter, Victoria." Bad enough in Victorian America for a prominent woman, in an unorthodox profession, to aspire to political power. The story revealed that Woodhull lived in a chaotic household with two men, both of whom she had married.[54]

In an effort at damage control, Woodhull invited the press to her Broad Street office to deny allegations of immoral behavior. She threatened to sue any newspaper that printed the "black and infamous lies." Her mother, she claimed, "aged and weak of mind," had been induced to file the charges by, it was said, "persons who are endeavoring to blackmail herself and her sister." But Woodhull couldn't stanch the ink that flowed from the press. The *Chicago Republican* probed Woodhull's past and reported her "antecedent history" in an article that carried the headline: "THE WOODHULL CLAFLIN FAMILY. The Mother of a Future President Endeavors to Relieve Her Daughter From Entangling Alliances." Rumors had long abounded that Woodhull and her sister lived unrespectable lives in the past and had no place in polite society. But now the scandal and the prospect of unending investigations brought distant history into the present.[55]

Suffrage leaders already nervous about their association with Woodhull grew more anxious about this matter. Although Stanton and Isabella Beecher Hooker remained loyal to Woodhull, they knew turbulent waters roiled around her. As early as March 1871, before Mrs. Claflin's unfortunate complaint against Colonel Blood, Hooker sought to get to the bottom of a rumor that had reached and troubled her. The tale originated with her brother, the highly regarded Protestant clergyman Reverend Henry Ward Beecher. Beecher had heard from a parishioner that Woodhull had engaged in improper relationships with prominent men. Hooker investigated and managed to reassure herself that no proof of such assignations could be established. But she suggested to Elizabeth Cady Stanton that efforts be made to probe further into Woodhull and her sister's background.[56]

Stanton was disgusted by the notion and provided a ringing defense of Woodhull's right to personal privacy and respect for her autonomy. In a letter to Lucretia Mott on April 1, 1871, she wrote: "I have thought much . . . of *our dear Woodhull* & all the gossip about her & come to the conclusion that it is a great impertinence in any of us to pry into her affairs. How should we feel to have everybody overhauling our antecedents & turning up the whites of their eyes over each new discovery or invention. There is to me a sacredness in individual experience that seems like profanation to search into or expose." Woodhull, Stanton asserted, "stands before us to day one of the ablest speakers & writers of the century . . . Her face form manners & conversation, all indicate the triumph of the moral, intellectual, spiritual over the sensuous in her nature. The processes & localities of her education are little to us, but the grand result is everything." Indeed, Stanton suggested that individuals of humble origins who had triumphed over "every phase of social degradation, poverty, vice, crime, temptation in all its forms, & yet tower above all their kind," provided "unmistakable proof of their high origin, the moral grandeur of their true nature."[57]

Stanton and Anthony both saw the attacks on Woodhull as an example of women being set against each other in ways that did nothing but continue their oppression. "We have had women enough sacrificed to this sentimental, hypocritical, prating about purity. This is one of man's most effective engines, for our division, & subjugation. He creates the public sentiment, builds the gallows, & then makes us hangman for our sex," Stanton observed. "We are ever cruel to each other," she mourned. Anthony briskly instructed another suffrage friend and colleague: "When we women *begin* to *search individual records* and antecedents of those who bring influence, brains or cash to our work of enfranchising woman—we shall *begin* with *the men*." Stanton echoed that sentiment when she concluded: "If Victoria Woodhull must be crucified, let men drive the spikes & plaite the crown of thorns."[58]

It would not take long for the spikes to be driven. On the very day Woodhull was to deliver her speech at the May suffrage meeting, an article in the *Cincinnati Commercial* offered a prescient prediction of what would happen to Woodhull in the days ahead. It read: "The startling revelations just made in New York concern-

ing the marital, or supra marital relations of MRS.
VICTORIA WOODHULL, the female broker, female
suffrage advocate, and self-nominated female candidate for the Presidency, will, we fear, be fatal to her
Presidential aspirations, if not to her brokerage business and her influence as an advocate of women's
rights." All that was therein predicted, in fact, would
come to pass. The author questioned whether "even if
women were voters" they would vote for a woman of
dubious morals and questionable reputation. While acknowledging that "under certain circumstances, men
may vote for a candidate who is somewhat less than
immaculate," women risked their own reputation if
they followed suit. "This would assuredly involve the
application of a dreadful test to female political candidates, but still it would have to be unflinchingly applied," the writer insisted.

Whatever Woodhull had accomplished counted for
nothing, in short, if her moral virtue was in question.
As the Cincinnati newspaper put it, "It is not enough
that a female aspirant for the Presidency be the owner
of a weekly paper which supports her cause, it is not
enough that she run on a 'cosmological' platform, it is
not enough that she be a public advocate of all moral,
social, political and scientific reforms, it is not enough
that she has written a book on the art of government
and the principles of legislation, but she herself, at the
same time, must be a paragon of propriety, if she would

secure the feminine vote of the country in support of her political ambition." Certainly it was too late for Woodhull to be that candidate in 1871. Within one week of her mother's accusations and revelations, obituaries for Woodhull's public life appeared in newspaper reports across the country. "BUSTED," an *Atlanta Constitution* headline blazoned. "The Cosmo-Political Party Gone to Smash and Woodhull & Clafflin Disgraced."[59]

Yet in the face of this barrage of criticism, Woodhull stood her ground. She continued her efforts to build a new political party, unveiling her platform at the suffrage meeting on May 11. She called upon those in attendance to reject the Republican and Democratic parties. They had, after all, rejected women. In the summer of 1871, she accepted the nomination of the political party she helped invent—the Equal Rights Party—as their candidate for president. She was determined to create a new coalition of labor, spiritualists, women's rights supporters, and reformers that might yet sweep her into office. She would continue on through the fall and winter of 1871, and through much of 1872, lecturing, drawing large crowds, and advocating for a revolution that would never come.

But Woodhull also went on the offensive. It was a fateful choice that brought what she had achieved to ruin. In late May 1871, she wrote a letter to the *New York Times* explaining why she had lived with both her current and her ex-husband. She and Colonel Blood had taken in Dr. Canning Woodhull when her first husband became ill and disabled. Far from being evidence of licentiousness, she had displayed compassion. "I esteem it one of the most virtuous acts of my life," she wrote, "but various editors have stigmatized me as a living example of immorality and unchastity." Woodhull indicated that she could accept criticism of her "opinions and principles." But what she would not tolerate was the hypocrisy of her "self appointed judges and critics" who were "deeply tainted with the vices they condemn." She now readily admitted, "I advocate free love . . . as the only cure for the immorality . . . by which men corrupt and disfigured" marriage. It was a bold and transgressive stance that came to define Woodhull in ways that soon overshadowed her reach for the presidency.

Woodhull went further. Outraged by the public criticism unjustly heaped upon her, she lashed out at her "judges," who, she charged, "preach against 'free love' openly, practice it secretly." She raised as an example "a public teacher of eminence, who lives in concubinage with the wife of another" distinguished man. That teacher, whom Woodhull would eventually name in the pages of the *Weekly,* was the leading Protestant minister of the day, Henry Ward Beecher. Beecher's alleged inamorata was Elizabeth Tilton, whose husband, Theodore, was a friend both to the clergyman and to Woodhull.

Woodhull's charge against Beecher precipitated a great and prolonged sexual scandal that would lead three years later to one of the nineteenth century's most riveting trials. When Theodore Tilton sued Beecher for alienating his wife's affection in 1874, the press lavishly reported every detail of the proceedings. Woodhull's fate unfolded with far greater speed. She was prosecuted on obscenity charges within days of publishing and mailing an account of Beecher's purported indiscretions in the *Weekly*. On election day in 1872, the first woman to seek the American presidency was in prison.[60]

MARGARET CHASE SMITH

"The Elephant Has an Attractive Face"

In mid-November 1963, a week before he left for the campaign trip that would bring him to Dallas, Texas, and his death, John F. Kennedy held the last press conference of his presidency. Among the questions he fielded was one about the upcoming 1964 presidential race. "Would you comment on the possible candidacy of Margaret Chase Smith, and specifically what effect that would have on the New Hampshire primary?" a reporter asked. The question alone provoked merriment among the largely male press corps. The prospect of a female presidential contender clearly seemed preposterous to many in attendance. But Kennedy was prepared for the query. Since August, rumors had swirled that Maine's three-term Republican senator might enter the presidential race. In fact, the archconservative *Dallas Morning News,* no admirer of Kennedy's administration, had prominently featured stories in late August and September speculating favorably about a Smith run. One of those reports asked whether Senator "Margaret Chase Smith, a wide-awake Maine

Republican," might actually "be the sleeper of the 1964 campaign." Kennedy parried the question gracefully: "I would think if I were a Republican candidate, I would not look forward to campaigning against Margaret Chase Smith in New Hampshire, or as a possible candidate for President." The gathered reporters laughed heartily. "I think she is very formidable, if that is the appropriate word to use about a very fine lady," Kennedy continued. "She is a very formidable political figure."[1]

A few days later Robert Healy, the *Boston Globe*'s Washington correspondent, filed a story that served as a sharp rejoinder to his colleagues. Under the headline "Sen. Smith's Candidacy—No Laughing Matter," Healy underscored President Kennedy's assessment of Smith as "formidable." Her potential candidacy, according to Healy, unsettled leading GOP hopefuls Nelson Rockefeller and Barry Goldwater, neither of whom were laughing "about campaigning against a woman for President." Least of all did they welcome competing against Smith in her neighboring state of New Hampshire. In truth, Smith was "a real independent" who proved difficult to predict and manage. She had disappointed her own party leaders repeatedly over her long career in the House and Senate. Her voting record tacked abruptly across the political spectrum from liberal to conservative from the day she entered the House in 1940 through her twenty-four years in the U.S. Senate. "If she votes with us," one of her Republican colleagues in the Senate once said, "it is a coincidence."

The many "firsts" Smith piled up reflected both achievement and isolation—further ballast, perhaps, for her storied independence. The first woman elected on her own to the Senate, she was also the first woman to serve in both houses of Congress. Smith won these initial elections when very few women served in either chamber. Only a handful of women held seats in the House when she went to Congress in 1940. She had no female colleagues when she joined the Senate in 1949. She remained the only female senator to serve as a result of her victory in a general election (as opposed to a special election or appointment) until the 1960s. None of this seemed to trouble her Maine constituents. They sent Smith back to Washington term after term. She served in the Senate longer than any woman in the twentieth century.[2]

By 1963, Smith had held office alongside four presidents—FDR, Truman, Eisenhower, and now her fellow New Englander, John F. Kennedy. She sparred, on occasion, with most of them. Certainly she had been a thorn in the side of the Kennedy administration. In August, she had voted against the Nuclear Test Ban Treaty that JFK deemed one of his signal achievements. Smith and Kennedy had by then known each other for nearly two decades through their membership in the House and Senate. They once anchored the New England delegation. Nonetheless, "when John F. Kennedy was President," Kennedy assistant Richard Donahue later recalled, "we couldn't get Margaret Chase Smith" to vote "for adjournment."[3]

Smith considered her grit and independence a birthright—qualities as quintessentially Maine as her state's rocky coastline, pine forests, quiet villages, and resilient working men and women. But her self-reliance emerged, in part, from the way she rose in American politics. To the end of her days, Senator Smith attributed her political career to a sort of mystical "destiny." It was a claim a century removed but no more persuasive than Victoria Woodhull's assertion that the spirits had guided her to politics. "It was just to be and I had little to do about it," Smith insisted as she neared the age of ninety. In fact, she followed the most predictable, though still rare, route to the Congress trod by women of her generation. She found her way to national electoral office through her husband.[4]

Indeed, had Margaret Chase never married Clyde Smith, it seems very unlikely that she would have ever risen to the stature she attained. The oldest of six children born to George and Carrie Chase, Margaret grew up in Skowhegan, Maine, a mill town situated alongside the banks of the Kennebec River. Wool, logging, and wood pulp drove Skowhegan's industrial base. The town was prosperous during the early twentieth century, when Margaret Chase came of age. Her family was less so. Her father, a barber, made a modest living and struggled with alcohol. When inebriated, Margaret later recalled, he became mean and angry. She viewed her mother, by contrast, as a saintly figure. A portrait of her mother hung over her bed until Margaret's final day. Mrs. Chase was devoted to her children and very hardworking. She took on a variety of jobs including factory worker, waitress, store clerk, and laundress to support her family. Home wasn't a tranquil place. Before Margaret was ten, she had seen two of her younger brothers die of disease in early childhood. In the face of such sadness, she assisted her mother dutifully. By the age of thirteen, Margaret too began to work for wages when free from school. Her sense of responsibility, drive, and ambition were in early evidence, although she turned out to be an indifferent student. At Skowhegan High School athletics engaged her, and she stood out as a member of the girls' basketball team. She focused her studies on typing, shorthand, and bookkeeping, with an eye toward the growing number of secretarial positions that had become an important source of mobility for women.[5]

While still in high school, Margaret landed a part-time job at night as an operator for the Maine Telephone Company. She loved the wizardry of the switchboard, which connected her to operators around the state and allowed her to eavesdrop on her Skowhegan neighbors—which she did, freely. Her duties for the phone company led Margaret Chase to make the acquaintance of Clyde Smith before her high school graduation. Smith purportedly called the operator to inquire about the time—a nightly affair, it was said, once he found Miss Chase on the other end of the line. Divorced and nearly forty years old—her mother's age, in fact—Smith was then a successful businessman who served as Skowhegan's selectman. A man-about-town with an appetite for politics and attractive young women, he took an avid interest in Margaret Chase, who welcomed his attention.[6]

The couple did not marry for nearly a decade and a half after meeting, though it is clear they maintained a relationship throughout the 1920s. Its nature cannot be discerned from extant sources. When asked late in life about this period, Chase Smith rejected "courting" as a characterization of this interlude in their story. It is certain that she was not Clyde Smith's sole object of interest. She recorded her ongoing anxiety about the relationship in her diary in 1920. Then twenty-two years old, she could neither free herself of her preoccupation with Smith nor reassure herself that he would ever provide the steady love and companionship she craved. She expressed then longing for a nice home, for marriage, and for a baby even as she discouraged other suitors. She struggled to comprehend Smith's intentions. His duplicity especially troubled her. She noted on one occasion that Clyde "called me twice. Said he was going to Boston tomorrow. I'd like to know if he really has to go. He hates to so it seems rather funny he would go twice. Feeling rather blue. But what is the use?" In the winter of 1920, she waited night after night for his calls and often seemed upset even when Smith delivered. "Said he was going to work all the evening. Wonder how true it is?" "You can never tell when he is telling the truth," she observed on another occasion. Smith had told her he was returning home rather than paying her a visit. She thought about checking up on his story but noted that she was "too lazy to walk down and find out." "Oh, I am so lonesome for someone to like me," she lamented. "Wish I was decent. Mother says I hate myself + everyone around me. Guess she is right." Of Smith she imagined "people can hardly tell just what we are to each other. I don't wonder when it['s] as blind to me as it is." At other times she "wished he would go away," confessing that she was "tired" of the entire affair.[7]

If such torment consumed her late at night, work filled Chase's days. She seemed especially proud of her ability to earn and save. "I worked every spare moment I could get," she would later recollect. After spending a miserable fall and winter in a frigid one-room schoolhouse following her 1916 high school commencement, she turned her back on teaching. Instead, she actively pursued a series of jobs each of which improved in some way her prospects. Having abandoned the schoolhouse, she landed a higher-paying clerical position for the phone company. Two years later, she signed on with the editor and publisher of Skowhegan's weekly newspaper, the *Independent-Reporter*. As something of a girl Friday, she thrived in this environment and eventually became highly successful as circulation manager. She stayed until 1928, when she accepted a job working as an office manager for Willard Cummings, who owned the Cummings woolen mill in Skowhegan. She remembered to the end of her days distributing to the factory workers their paltry wages. For their exhausting labor in punishing conditions the textile workers earned a little more than twenty-five cents an hour.[8]

Her active involvement with women's clubs in the 1920s foreshadowed most of all Chase's future career in politics. Perhaps it also provided an antidote to her social anxiety. The two clubs she favored, Sorosis and the Maine Federation of Business and Professional Women's Clubs (BPW), belonged to national networks of clubwomen. Before suffrage, such organizations served as a primary means by which women could participate energetically in civic life and influence public policy. They remained a vital form of political participation even after women won the vote in 1920. The clubs also offered more prosaic rewards, including opportunities to socialize with like-minded women. The local BPW club in Skowhegan, for example, acquired a welcoming space downtown where members could meet for lunch and evening entertainment. Some younger members, including Chase, were much taken by the accomplished women who led these clubs. Hearing Lena Madesin Phillips, the national president of the BPW, speak at a convention in Portland, Maine, proved to be a thrilling experience for the young Margaret Chase. She remembered her as "a very prominent young attorney, a very attractive young woman. . . . I was quite intrigued with her and fascinated with her speech, and came home and decided that Skowhegan was large enough to have a club."

Chase herself quickly attracted attention within the women's clubs for her zest. Within two years of joining Skowhegan's chapter of Sorosis in 1920, Margaret became its president. By 1925, Chase was head of Maine's BPW. She traveled around the state visiting the BPW's many local chapters and left her mark as editor of the *Pine Cone,* the Maine Federation's magazine. Smith's attendance at national meetings and her leadership at the state and local level of these organizations helped her forge lasting ties to a huge network of activist women. They would prove to be valuable assets when she entered national politics.[9]

It was Clyde Smith rather than Margaret Chase, however, who first sought electoral office. In fact, before Margaret Chase was born, Smith had won a seat at twenty-one in the Maine legislature. He served two terms and left to pursue other ventures, but he never

lost sight of politics. Smith's success as Skowhegan selectman led to repeated bids for further office; he ran
successfully again for the Maine House (1919–1923)
and then the state Senate (1923–1929). By the late
1920s, Margaret had also become active in local and
county Republican politics. Her participation began
with the Skowhegan Republican Committee; she served
the group as secretary and two years later performed
similar duties for the county Republican organization.
Once she began working for the woolen mill, she became engaged in party politics at the state level. Her
boss, Willard Cummings, encouraged—she would say
demanded—her involvement. A powerhouse in Maine
Republican politics, Cummings sought to stack the
state Republican Committee with his associates and
pressed Margaret into service. She ran for a seat on
the State Committee, thus winning her first election in
1930. By then Clyde Smith had set his sights on Maine's
governorship. That ambition, unfulfilled though it
turned out to be, perhaps led him to finally marry Margaret Chase in the spring of 1930. She was then thirty-
two years old; Smith was fifty-three and already facing
health problems. He was treated for a "nervous" disor-
der the summer after they married and suffered a cardiac event two years later. Neither deterred him for
long, and in 1936, with prodigious help from his wife,
he successfully campaigned for a seat in the U.S. House
of Representatives.[10]

As he campaigned in 1936, Smith's political opponents fanned rumors about his extramarital sexual behavior. There appeared to be no shortage of material.
In addition to Smith's many dalliances, a woman factory worker in Skowhegan had a young child rumored
to be Smith's daughter. She had been born only four
months after Margaret and Clyde Smith's 1930 marriage. (Perhaps the imminent arrival of the child also
encouraged Smith to marry—someone other than the
baby's mother.) Smith never publicly acknowledged either the gossip or the daughter. It is unclear if Margaret knew about the child in the 1930s. But she knew
her husband and could not have been surprised by the
talk about him. It hurt and embarrassed her. "He gave
me many heartaches," she admitted late in life. Smith
"loved the ladies and they loved him," she confided to
historian Janann Sherman when Chase Smith was in
her nineties. "I took it after a fashion." The marriage
was less "a great love," she then reflected, than a "business arrangement." It is hard to evaluate whether such a
comment, from the distance of more than half a century, truly reflected Chase Smith's feeling going into her
marriage. What is certain is that the couple formed a
firm partnership that was soon tested. The move to
Washington proved difficult for Margaret Chase Smith.
She had never lived outside of Maine, and she felt
somewhat self-conscious in the social whirl of the nation's capital, given her modest origins and her lack of

education. Chase Smith overcame her inhibitions in part by immersing herself in her husband's office. She joined his staff and, indeed, earned a salary (which she insisted on) for her expansive duties as his secretary.[11]

Clyde Smith was a progressive who had supported restrictions on child labor, pensions for the aged, and workmen's compensation while serving in the Maine legislature. He continued that record as a Republican in the U.S. Congress. In the late 1930s, he attempted to navigate the shoals of New Deal legislative battles by attending to the often conflicting demands of Maine's unionized workers and its industry leaders. Amid these challenges, his health continued to decline, and he suffered a serious heart attack in his first term. In truth, Smith was suffering from advanced, untreated syphilis—a diagnosis his doctors conveyed to the congressman late in 1938. In an age before antibiotics, this sexually transmitted disease was difficult to treat under the best of circumstances. In its late stages, syphilis could ravage its victims. Their suffering was augmented by the shame, imposed by a judgmental society, that many also endured. However, no public knowledge of Smith's true malady appears to have surfaced in his or his wife's lifetime. Indeed, Smith initially denied that he even suffered from a cardiac condition. How did he get away with such evasion? The congressman held office in an era when prevailing notions of propriety, including among journalists, helped shield a candidate's personal life from close public scrutiny if not from gossip.[12]

Whatever the veil of secrecy hid or revealed, Margaret, by necessity, took over more of her husband's duties. She increasingly became his link to his constituents. She kept up a brutal pace commuting between Washington and Maine, appearing on his behalf especially during his campaign for re-election in 1938. Her confidence as a public figure grew so much that on some occasions she was less a surrogate articulating Congressman Smith's positions than a competing voice laying out diverging opinions. This happened most consequentially when Chase Smith appeared in October 1938 at the Kennebec Women's Republican Club. In crafting her remarks, she noticed that her visit coincided with the observation of Navy Day. The patriotic holiday thus provided a theme for her presentation.

Although Clyde Smith was an isolationist who opposed increased defense spending, his wife apparently saw things differently. She said so in no uncertain terms before the Women's Republican Club in the fall of 1938. Chase Smith emphasized the urgency of American military preparedness. A month after Chamberlain's ill-fated appeasement of Hitler at Munich, she warned that the United States could not afford to ignore the gathering storm in Europe. She made the case for enlarging expenditures for the United States Navy.

"Those who oppose naval protection," she insisted, presciently as it would turn out, "fail to perceive that the real attack, if any, probably will come by way of sea. Development of our Navy is necessary self-preservation." Her assertion that "the best insurance for peace is preparation for war," echoed that of Franklin Roosevelt even if it diametrically opposed the stated views of her husband. Chase Smith's remarks surely spoke to Maine's central economic stake in defense spending. The state was home to the Portsmouth Naval Shipyard, located in Kittery and run by the U.S. Navy, as well as the Bath Iron Works, a ship-building facility generously rewarded with defense contracts.[13]

Invited to reflect on "The Experiences of a Congressman's Wife in Washington," Chase Smith veered sharply off her hosts' expected course. But she did no political damage to her husband. The voters returned Clyde Smith to office that year. By the spring of 1940, however, he was dying. In April he released a statement urging "his friends and supporters" to "support the candidate of my choice, my wife and my partner in public life, Margaret Chase Smith," if he was unable to run in the forthcoming primary or general election. "I know of no one," Smith insisted, "who has the full knowledge of my ideas and plans or is as well qualified as she is, to carry on these ideas and my unfinished work for my district." Smith died a day later.[14]

Congressman Smith's plea to his constituents on

his wife's behalf drew upon a custom with which they would both have been familiar—the "widow's mandate." (Alice Roosevelt Longworth once referred to the practice less romantically as using "coffins as springboards.") The term describes a convention that emerged after women won the vote in 1920. It involved appointing or advancing by special election a woman to finish out the congressional term of a husband or other male relative. Uncodified by law, but favored by elected officials and their political parties, the custom blended sentimentality, practicality, and *realpolitik* in equal measure. A widow's closeness to her late husband and her familiarity with his political beliefs offered at least the veneer of continuity as well as a tasteful, if temporary, memorial to the deceased officeholder. As Mae Ella Nolan, the first widow elected to finish out her husband's term in 1923, put it: "I owe it to my husband to carry on his work. . . . No one better knows than I do his legislative agenda." The prevailing assumption was that such women, lacking entirely political ambition of their own, would act as placeholders, serving only until the political parties could settle upon an appropriate male successor.

"The widow's mandate" was always more complicated, however, than that soubriquet suggested. Many women who attained office in this way cooperated fully. But not all who slipped into the congressional chambers through this flap door wished to exit. Appointed by the governor of Arkansas to her late husband's seat in 1931, Senator Hattie Caraway stayed put for fourteen years. "Silent Hattie," as she was known, spoke from the Senate floor on average about once a year over her entire senatorial career. "I haven't the heart to take a minute away from the men," she once explained. "The poor dears love it so." Caraway remained in office until she was defeated in the 1944 Democratic primary by J. William Fulbright, who would go on to represent Arkansas for thirty years. For all its limitations, the widow's mandate allowed a few individuals to circumvent the obstacles the major political parties placed before women would-be candidates. It unquestionably created an avenue that allowed Margaret Chase Smith to enter national politics. But her own drive and ambition made a decisive opportunity of fate's accident.[15]

That became clear immediately after Clyde Smith's death. On the day of his funeral, Maine's governor set a date for a special election to fill his seat. Margaret Chase Smith's nomination papers had been secured before her husband drew his final breath. Now supporters had to be lined up and the state's Republican party leaders brought on board. The gentility of the "widow's mandate" prevailed. Smith faced only token opposition in the special primary and none in the general election. She won her husband's seat handily. "Mrs. Smith Goes to Washington" proved an irresistible headline when newspapers reported the outcome of Maine's special congressional election. Describing Chase Smith as an "unusually attractive" and "versatile" woman with a "long and popular business career," the *Christian Science Monitor* noted her extensive record of engagement in Republican politics and women's clubs. She "was well established in her own right as a candidate for public office," the paper generously reported. "Vivacious and attractive," the *Boston Globe* called the new representative in a story that ran under the following headline: "Maine Is Sending a Housekeeper Who 'Took Care' of a Thirty Room Home in Skowhegan to Congress." Chase Smith had assumed "man sized responsibilities" in her career, the *Globe* observed, but had also "retained her femininity . . . She plays an extraordinary hand of contract, but never smokes or sips a cocktail." Smith thoughtfully invoked her husband's legacy in her comment, promising to carry on his commitment to advancing "old age assistance, labor activities and adequate preparedness to fight off the danger of invasion or war." These were winning commitments given her constituency in Maine's Second Congressional District, which included unionized industrial workers in the populous cities of Waterville, Auburn, Lewiston, and Augusta.[16]

Smith had little time to savor her victory. The special election gave her only slightly more than six months in office. Indeed, she faced four male Republican opponents in a June 1940 primary fight only a week after taking over her duties in the Congress. The winner would run in the general fall election for a regular term in Congress. War in Europe and the ongoing debate about American neutrality made Smith especially vulnerable to those who doubted women's capacities to serve well in a time of international crisis. One of her Republican primary opponents argued that the stakes were too high to trust Maine to a woman representative—"a flick of the wrist and a smile won't do it," John G. Marshall warned. That line of argument gained enough traction to prompt a *Portland Sunday Telegram* columnist to note that the primary seemed to turn more on a "question of sex" than on "ability."[17]

Such concerns would especially come to dog women presidential candidates amid the wars of the twentieth century. Traditional notions about the inherent capacities of men and women that emphasized the former's strength, aggression, courage, dispassion, and hence natural ability as warriors and military strategists fueled doubts about women's ability to serve as commander in chief. The strong historical association between activist women and the peace movement appeared to lend credence to these worries. Some of the most visible women in American public life were pacifists who had linked the cause of women's suffrage to peace during the first World War. Their argument was straightforward. Enfranchising women, whom they claimed by nature abhorred war, would help advance peaceful solutions to international conflict.

That was the message of the International League of Women for Peace and Freedom, organized in opposition to World War I and led by Jane Addams. Addams would win the Nobel Peace Prize in 1931 for her activities as a pacifist. (Her successor as league president, Emily Balch, would be similarly honored.) The first woman ever elected to national office likewise was a staunch pacifist. Jeannette Rankin, a Republican from Montana, served two terms in the House from 1917 to 1919 and 1941 to1943. Rankin voted against American entry into the First *and* Second World Wars. (She tendered the only no vote in the entire Congress when she opposed issuing a declaration of war on Japan after Pearl Harbor.) When Margaret Chase Smith joined the Congress in the summer of 1940, a *New York Herald Tribune* article noted that "5 of 8 Women in Congress Are Isolationists." The five, "who never act as a bloc," nonetheless agreed in an interview conducted after the fall of France "that the United States is safely isolated from the European war" and should remain so. Yet a subheadline seemed to mischievously challenge the notion that their attitudes reflected the legislators' inherent moral superiority as women. "Majority Oppose Admitting Child Refugees," the paper also noted. Even the "only blonde" among the congresswomen rejected asylum for children from England.[18]

Although the *Tribune* counted Margaret Chase Smith among the female isolationists, she early staked out an entirely different approach to American foreign policy—one that could not be accused of being "feminine." From the moment she assumed her husband's congressional seat, she vigorously championed building up national defense and aggressively promoted Maine as a site for new military installations. She made preparedness a major focus of her first serious primary run in June 1940, reminding her constituents of her 1938 Navy Day remarks endorsing rapid naval expansion. As she campaigned each weekend in factories, small towns, and every precinct in her district, Smith promised to advance the interests of Maine's working people and protect the state's security. The state's long coastline, Smith stressed, and proximity to Canada, with that nation's ties to Britain, made Maine a potential target of Nazi invasion. "We must remember that Greenland, now under German domination, is only 1500 miles from us," she warned in a speech before the Daughters of the American Revolution. (Even as she sounded this alarm, Smith urged her audience to remain "free from hysteria and set an example of bravery.") The *Lewiston Journal* dubbed Smith the "Preparedness Prophetess" as she promoted the need for new weapons of war, naval bases, air stations, and military training. Nothing short of "immediate and complete preparation . . . for the defense of the United States," in her view, was in order. Mindful of Maine's fealty to Republican principles of fiscal conservatism, Smith contended that "money spent in this way is not extravagance. It is an insurance against involvement in war." She did not wish to see American soldiers "sent into battle on foreign soil," a position President Roosevelt himself also maintained in June 1940. But she cautioned that war might come to the United States however much it sought to avoid the conflagration.[19]

If Smith's attention to rearmament and war mobilization alienated female voters, there was little evidence of it in Maine. Women's clubs and organizations professed nonpartisanship, but many of their members campaigned actively for her. Smith also drew on the support of fellow Republicans—male and female—with whom she had become familiar through her long service in state party politics. She knew her constituents well; she had handled her husband's correspondence for years, taking pains to ensure that their concerns were personally addressed. After trouncing her four Republican opponents in the primary, Smith breezed on to victory in the fall election. She won by a larger plurality than her husband had amassed in either of his two congressional bids. Somehow amid perhaps the worst personal crisis of her life, Smith had managed to thread the needle. She mobilized women energized by her candidacy even as she sought to downplay the significance of her gender. She had buried a husband, carried on his "legislative business," kept his Washington office going, and "run campaigns for two primaries and two elections in five months."[20]

Amid all this Smith was forced to confront, perhaps for the first time, the knowledge that her now deceased husband had, in fact, fathered a child a decade before—just around the time of their marriage. In July 1940, as executor of Clyde Smith's estate, his widow signed a legal agreement that bound her to pay a Skowhegan lawyer a monthly sum to be dispersed for child support. The document stipulated that Margaret Chase Smith would continue providing these funds until Clyde Smith's daughter turned eighteen. It is unclear whether the contract simply formalized an arrangement, perhaps casual, that her husband had made with his child's mother, or whether it represented a response to a fresh demand. In either case, the understanding forbade the child's mother from ever contacting Margaret Chase Smith directly. Although rumors of such an arrangement would surface when she ran for the Senate in 1947, they gained little traction. It remains impossible to know how Smith absorbed her husband's betrayal. She did allow late in life that 1940 "was a pretty heavy year."[21]

Nonetheless, Smith found and kept her footing in the Congress. A powerful conservative Republican who objected to Clyde Smith's support for New Deal labor reform kept her from the Labor committee assignment she coveted. But she proceeded adroitly and soon found other allies, including Harold Ickes, Roosevelt's secretary of the interior, and Frances Perkins, secretary of labor, both of whom had spent time in coastal Maine. (Perkins was, in fact, Smith's constituent.) Like others of wealth and means who vacationed there, they loved Maine's craggy coast, quiet villages, and Down East character. (President Roosevelt's family had long owned a summer retreat on Campobello Island off the coast of Maine in New Brunswick, Canada.) They also understood its many problems and needs. Early in her first term, Smith approached Ickes directly in an effort to ensure that Maine remained supplied with heating oil and gas during the war. Ickes responded cordially to her, as did other prominent New Dealers who appreciated her foreign policy stance, including Undersecretary of the Navy James Forrestal and the powerful financier and Roosevelt adviser Bernard Baruch. Events in 1941 were, after all, moving in Smith's direction even if she alienated powerful GOP leaders, including "Mr. Republican"—Ohio's Senator Robert Taft—when she voted in favor of FDR's war-mobilization efforts. She was one of only twenty-four Republican members to support the Lend-Lease bill in February 1941, allowing the United States to send aid to Great Britain. Legislation expanding defense spending and instituting a peacetime draft likewise earned her approval. Alone among Maine's three Republican representatives, and one of just twenty-two Republicans in the entire House, she favored repeal of the 1939 Neutrality Act in November 1941.

By then the attack on Pearl Harbor that would bring the United States into World War II was only weeks away. Smith would benefit politically from her prescience in supporting preparedness. She was the only member of the Maine House delegation to consistently do so. Indeed, by mid-November, one Maine Republican party official warned fellow members that "Republican members of Congress are digging the grave of their party by consistent, blind, unreconstructive opposition to the Administration's policies . . . this smells of politics to me, politics played without regard to the state of their country." It was a mistake Margaret Chase Smith would not make. Whatever standing she lost in abandoning influential isolationists in the GOP, she gained in her home state. The Gannett newspaper chain, then a dominant force in the state and decidedly Republican in its sympathies, praised Smith for her patriotism and courage. It noted that she was the only representative who seemed to understand that Maine was "not the home of pacifism and isolationism."[22]

Smith's approach to political service embodied principles that would both earn admiration and ultimately doom her candidacy when she sought to compete in the realm of presidential politics. To the corridors of power in Washington that she now walked on her own, she brought independence of mind and strict work habits. She ran her congressional outpost with the skills of the office manager she had once been. She held fast to a set of values as clear and bracing as Maine's frigid waters. She accepted no campaign contributions and would return with a letter of explanation even a single dollar. She took pride in how little she spent on her campaigns. Thrift checked even necessary office expenditures. One Senate staff member confided to a journalist in 1964: "Nobody so much as charges a personal phone call to the office or takes so much as a paper clip from supplies paid for with taxpayers' money." He meant it. The voters of Maine had sent her to Congress to conduct their business, not to enrich herself or compile a campaign war chest, she would explain.

Nor did Smith ever appear to lose sight of her constituents, bringing the same attention to detail and high level of interest to their needs as to the demands of Congress. She responded to every single constituent's letter on the day she received it. She persuaded the local press to run a column entitled "Washington and You," which she authored monthly. It was designed to inform those she represented of what she was doing in Congress. She returned to Maine on the weekends, speaking at local functions and ensuring that she visited each precinct monthly. But she also strove to be at hand for the business of Congress. (She set a record when in the Senate for being present for nearly 3,000 consecutive roll calls.) No Democratic challenger could best her when she ran for re-election in 1942 and 1946, and while she served in the House no Republican even tried to wrest the party's nomination from her. She had created a bond with those she represented more valuable than the patronage bestowed by the power brokers in her political party's apparatus.[23]

Stature in the House of Representatives, with its firm hierarchies, elaborate traditions, and complex rules governing committee assignments proved more difficult to acquire. She initially won appointments to low-prestige committees focused on education, invalid pensions, and post offices and post roads. But in 1943, the assignment she most coveted on the Naval Affairs Committee (later known as the Armed Services Committee) finally came through. It was a plum given the war emergency. And it allowed Smith to burnish her credentials in the realm of military affairs and foreign policy. Ironically, given her husband's secret history, she was assigned first to a subcommittee charged with addressing the threat of venereal disease to military personnel deployed in port cities.

Smith bristled throughout her career when asked if she was a feminist, even though she repeatedly voted for the Equal Rights Amendment and, in fact, in 1945 cosponsored the measure. (Consideration of the constitutional amendment was an annual event in Congress after its initial introduction in 1920.) She rejected what she felt was the label's implication that she cared more about women, because she was a woman, than about the rest of humanity. Nor was Smith comfortable with any suggestion that her status as a woman was or should be a variable in her advancement. "I never asked for any special privileges," she once said of her experience in Congress, "and I can assure you I never got any." Despite these protestations, she spent considerable energy on the Naval Affairs Committee addressing the impact of the war on women.[24]

Her concerns were evident as Naval Affairs probed the "congested areas" adjacent to military installations and defense plants. Periodic dragnets rounding up prostitutes had led to deplorable conditions for incarcerated women, Smith emphasized in committee hearings. Some had been jailed simply because they happened to be on the street in the evening; others were indeed engaging in prostitution—many, Smith emphasized, out of economic desperation. Nothing justified their appalling treatment. She did much to ensure that her colleagues paid attention to the difficulties faced by women who worked in industry as a result of the war emergency. Criticized for high rates of absenteeism on the job, these workers were ably defended by Smith and Secretary of Labor Frances Perkins during congressional hearings. They stressed that the lack of housing, child care, decent health care services, and reasonable hours augmented the crushing burden of their double duty—as full-time workers, and as wives, mothers, and homemakers. Smith joined with other congresswomen in 1943 to prevent passage of an amendment that would have cut the already meager federal support for child care. The first congressional legislation she initiated in 1941 sought to equalize the minimum wages for men and women engaged in defense industries. The status of women in the military also became a focal point of Smith's interests during the 1940s. After much resistance, she eventually succeeded in helping to advance bills that improved the status, rank, and pay of military nurses in the Army and Navy. Years of effort eventually led to a bill that upgraded the standing of women in the armed forces to give them permanent status.[25]

Smith's service on the Naval Affairs Committee also wrought changes in her personal life—indeed, it led to the closest and most lasting relationship she would ever experience. William Lewis, Jr., served as chief counsel to the House Naval Affairs Committee. Fifteen years younger than the congresswoman and then an assistant to Undersecretary of the Navy James Forrestal, Lewis was an Oklahoman, with a bloodline partially traceable to Chickasaw Indians. The thirty-one-year-old naval lieutenant held an M.B.A. from Harvard and a law degree from the University of Oklahoma. By the time he met Smith, he knew his way around Washington. In the late 1930s, Lewis had worked as a lawyer for the Securities and Exchange Commission. But the war led the naval reservist to be summoned back to active duty working in an administrative position. Bright, confident, financially secure (in part from family money), Lewis sensed Smith's vulnerability on the entirely male committee. Seated next to the congresswoman, he began passing her encouraging notes, and over the next several months a warm friendship grew.

Working together long hours, traveling for the committee, an unattached man and woman with a shared passion for politics, on their own in Washington, D.C., amid the heightened emotions stirred by the war, Smith and Lewis became extremely close. In fact, Smith would eventually move into an apartment in the home of Lewis's parents in the Washington suburbs. Both of the Lewises had been lawyers, and like their son they admired and took a warm interest in the congresswoman. By the end of Smith's term in the House, Lewis had become Smith's executive assistant and remained so for the rest of her political career. His fierce and protective loyalty, absolute commitment, and deep involvement in her congressional work sustained her. The relationship between the lifelong bachelor and the widow set tongues wagging; the gossip never really abated. To this day, no one can say for sure what intimacies they did or did not share. They took those secrets to their graves. "We loved each other," she affirmed to a biographer late in life. But she added: "I could not marry a younger man," or anyone at all, "and keep my job."[26]

Lewis played a critical role in helping Smith advance to the United States Senate in 1948. The retirement of Maine's senior senator created the vacancy, coveted by Republican party leaders including the state's sitting governor and his predecessor. Few in the party elite considered Smith a contender. Nor could she command loyalty from the party from which she so often had strayed. "She is a party all by herself," the *New York Times* reported. The risks for Smith were considerable despite her popularity in Maine. No woman had ever been elected to the Senate running on her own anywhere in the United States, without the benefit first of a special election or previous appointment. In seeking the Senate seat, she was behaving like a male politician who had served his time in the House and felt entitled to be considered for a promotion. The norm for women was a game of waiting on the sidelines. A Senate run also meant giving up her seat in the House; she was up for re-election in 1948.

Without the backing of party leaders, Smith lacked the money, organization, support of power brokers, and endorsements that flowed to her opponents. Lewis was convinced, nonetheless, that she could prevail anyway. He proceeded to mastermind an impressively organized grassroots campaign. For the first time, Smith agreed to accept contributions to her campaign—an acknowledgment that a statewide bid against wealthy opponents could not be fought entirely in the old way. In this she benefited enormously from the assistance of shipping tycoon Clifford Carver, who agreed to serve as her campaign finance manager. Still, small donations of a dollar or two, sometimes ten, were the norm. The campaign would largely rely on other strengths.[27]

Notable among them were female voters, organizations, and members of the press. Estimates that 64 percent of Maine's voters were women offered Smith an opportunity that could be exploited when her primary opponents suggested that her sex disqualified her for such an august post. Smith characterized as "a direct challenge to every woman in Maine" any assertion that "the Senate was no place for a woman." But she also insisted that as "proud" as she was of being female, she sought no votes "because I am a woman." She ran instead on her achievements in the House of Representatives and the promise that she would bring her strengths to the Senate. Her campaign literature stressed simultaneously that she was "no feminist" *and* that she was a "champion for the women." In the culture of immediate post–World War II America, as returning veterans sought employment, defense industries demobilized women workers, and a romance with domesticity scented the air, that was no contradiction. Women's groups in Maine, including the BPW, and the

Women's Christian Temperance Union understood the distinction and again set aside their nonpartisanship to assist her campaign.

Female members of the press corps, especially Gannett's irrepressible Washington correspondent May Craig, filed story after story about the campaign, many flattering to Maine's congresswoman. Their accounts made Smith's Senate bid a national news story. "It would be difficult to think of Mrs. Smith as a 'politician' in the sense in which that word is often used," wrote the women's editor of the *Christian Science Monitor*, "but she does impress one as an able public servant who places the interests of her country and her state before personal considerations." A woman reporter from the *Washington Post* encouraged readers to make note that a "Sleeping Giantess Stirs" as candidates such as Smith gave evidence of a "new political aggressiveness" among American women. Their presence was especially vital, the journalist claimed, so that "congressional committees . . . will not continue to handle the Nation's affairs as a committee of men might run a household." Stories advancing women as serious candidates provided a counterweight to the standard fare that ran. A sketch of senatorial candidate Smith in the *Boston Globe* stressed that her friends admired the casual suppers of baked beans and brown bread she cooked herself. It ran under the headline: "Maine Candidate for U.S. Senator Baked Bean Champ."[28]

In truth, Smith won the Maine Republican Senate primary on the ground. The campaign mailed tens of thousands of postcards costing a penny each urging voters to choose Smith. The candidate made a virtue of her lack of financial resources, contrasting her modest campaign operation with the lavish spending of her opponents. "I have made no campaign promises and I shall make none," she asserted. As she had always done, Smith relied on shoe leather—in her case high heels—tirelessly visiting the small towns and big cities, grange halls, local clubs, and factories, all across the state that had produced her remarkable rise in politics. A reporter who traveled with her in the campaign's last days was especially impressed by her ease and familiarity with her fellow citizens. "I stood at her elbow while long lines of Maine people filed by to greet her—many of them addressing her as 'Margaret' with the natural privilege of old friends. . . . Hers is not a political smile, varying in degree according to the importance of the person she is greeting. With each one she is sincerely, graciously charming."[29]

An eleventh-hour smear operation, accusing her of communist sympathies because of her support for labor, New Deal legislation, the United Nations, the Truman Doctrine, and the Marshall Plan, among other positions she had taken, outraged the candidate. Engineered by her Republican competitors, and by anonymous forces, perhaps out of state, this effort aimed to tar Smith with the brush of communist sympathizing then gaining strength in postwar America. By 1948, the tentacles of the ongoing anticommunist investigations being pursued by the House Committee on Un-American Activities (HUAC) reached the pine tree state's senatorial campaign. Unsigned literature linking Smith's voting record to a prolabor representative from New York, widely perceived as a "communist spokesman," began to circulate. Smith was convinced that Maine's Republican party leadership was orchestrating the attack. Certainly Maine's senior United States senator, Ralph Owen Brewster, echoed her critics' assertions when he hurled the ultimate epithet: "She's been a New Dealer from the start!" Ironically, given the accusations, Smith's previously loyal labor constituency expressed hesitation about her senatorial bid. In 1946, the Maine Congress of Industrial Organizations (CIO) enthusiastically asserted that "Mrs. Smith is the best man we have in Washington." However, the unions felt betrayed by the congresswoman's vote for the unpopular Taft-Hartley Act (1947) that restrained organized labor.

More personal accusations that she was actually French Canadian (a maligned ethnic group among some in Maine) or a woman of loose morals also circulated. Her campaign fought the charges vigorously, but they clearly shocked the congresswoman. In the end, the effort to denigrate her and tarnish her record gained little traction. When the primary votes were counted she had crushed the opposition. "Mrs. Smith Victor over Three Men," announced the *New York Herald Tribune.* She won her Senate seat in a landslide in the general election.[30]

Smith's improbable victory in Maine made her a national figure as well as a heroine in her home state. "Say Margaret Smith Could Be President," read a headline in the *Boston Globe* the day after the primary in a story that surveyed public opinion in Maine. A Skowhegan taxi driver and lifelong Democrat admitted, "We all have to hand it to that lady who is doing a lot of good for this state." It was a judgment, the *Globe* reported, that was "just an echo of what could be heard all over this part of Maine today." One elderly man mildly protested: "At least she mighta left those fellows a few votes in their own precincts. . . . It sort of makes a fellow feel that politics have changed too much." So many Republican women were hopeful as they gathered for the GOP's national convention in Philadelphia. They greeted news of Smith's victory with a "whoop and holler" from the convention floor. When Smith officially took her place in the Senate in January 1949, women's groups organized an array of celebrations. Smith's election, they expected, would be another arrow in their quiver that could speed their legislative goals in Congress. Many were elated when a week after claiming her seat, Smith joined a group of twenty-seven male senators in introducing yet again the Equal Rights Amendment for consideration by Congress.[31]

The new Maine senator welcomed such expectations. At a BPW lunch honoring her shortly after her swearing in, Smith indicated that she held herself "in readiness to be a voice of America's women on the floor of the Senate and in committees." In reflecting on the lessons of her election, she cut to the quick: "I am not a United States Senator today simply because I am a woman. . . . To the contrary, I was elected in spite of the fact that I am a woman. And that in itself was a victory for all women, for it smashed the unwritten tradition that the Senate is no place for a woman." She went on to explain "the point that so many miss." "Women do not blindly support some candidates just because they are women: we are not headed for an Amazonian world," she insisted. The goal instead was "that no one should be barred from public office just because she is a woman." She hoped her victory reflected a broader change in the culture—a "growing realization," as she put it, "that ability and proved performance, rather than sex, are the best standards for political selection just as much as they are for any other kind of selection. I like to think that I am a symbol of this." In truth, a general sense of anticipation seemed to greet Maine's new senator. "Republican Senator Margaret Chase Smith of Maine, a one-time dime-store clerk who made

good on her own," a *Boston Globe* society column reported, "is the new sweetheart of Capitol Hill."[32]

Smith quickly cut short the honeymoon. Less than a
week after being sworn in, she delivered a provocative
speech to the Women's National Press Club blaming
the Republican party leadership for losing "five straight
Presidential elections." They had lost, she said, because
they "thought the government should not intervene in
the economic affairs of the people." Although willing to
bury the hatchet with the party elders who had worked
against her in Maine, she was apparently not about to
do so without another wide swing of the axe. "They
have refused to recognize a simple principle of politics,"
Smith asserted of the GOP's leaders. "Nor is this a mere
question of expediency, for the little fellow has a right
to economic security just as the big man wishes to protect his own interests when he requests legislation ben-
eficial to his business." Smith urged her fellow Republicans to recognize the thirst for fairness and equality
among Americans. "This winning edge is too thinly
cut," she warned, "to permit the Democratic party to
be identified as the labor party." "The people have
clearly shown," she continued, "that they don't want a
'big business' Republican party or a 'labor' Democratic
party. The people want moderation with each group
having a fair share instead of unfair privileges for special groups. They want equality and not extremes. They
want the traditional compromise of the greatest good

for the greatest number." Government, she argued, had a critical role to play in arbitrating these claims as "protector of the public interest." The speech presaged the generally liberal Republican stance on domestic issues that would characterize Smith's Senate years.[33]

She would prove to be more conservative on foreign policy issues. Smith's career in the Senate took shape amid the growing tensions of the Cold War. By 1949, the wartime alliance between the United States and the Soviet Union had been sundered. Disputes over the political and economic reconstruction of Western and Eastern Europe and conflicting security interests fueled the enmity. In the United States, growing fears of Soviet expansionism and a three-year monopoly on the atomic bomb encouraged a "get tough" approach in the Truman administration. Smith applauded this shift in tone and, indeed, urged the president to go further in neutralizing the Soviet Union. Her first public comments as a senator in January 1949 had emphasized women's special responsibility to advance peace. Looking to Indonesia's struggle to free itself from Dutch colonial rule, she had called upon Queen Juliana of the Netherlands to "exercise the power that is hers to stop the Dutch-Indonesia fighting." Holland had "defied," Smith asserted, a United Nations resolution with "police action" in Indonesia that had led to widespread killing. By ending the violence the queen could demonstrate to the world "the will and the power of women for peace."

At home, however, the nation's pioneering woman senator favored the eagle's talons more often than the olive branch. She backed an aggressive foreign policy during the Cold War, strongly supporting each element of the national security state that emerged in this period. She vocally endorsed the buildup of the nation's weapons arsenal, and during the Korean War she advocated using nuclear weapons against North Korea and China. Smith had always stood for a robust military to be sure. Mobilization for World War II was one thing, however. Saber rattling in the nuclear age—the Soviet Union had acquired the bomb in 1949—constituted another.

Nothing in the events of the 1950s and 1960s dissuaded Smith from the view that the menace of Soviet communism, exported worldwide, might require the use of nuclear weapons. Atomic bombs were, indeed, immoral weapons, she asserted, but they remained a vital instrument in the U.S. effort to contain the immorality of communism. To a greater or lesser degree, every American president harbored similar views about the potential necessity of deploying nuclear weapons in the Cold War era. Eisenhower, Kennedy, Johnson, and Nixon all entertained scenarios that involved using the bomb in Korea, Cuba, and Vietnam variously.

(Truman, of course, had deployed atomic weapons in Hiroshima and Nagasaki.) And all considered nuclear stockpiles, as did Smith, a deterrent to a catastrophic war once the Soviet Union had acquired such weapons. Nonetheless, Smith's position discomfited some of her supporters. In the long run, her unswerving support of American intervention in Vietnam would end her political career in 1972. But in the 1950s and early 1960s, she conveyed the hard-eyed toughness prevalent among her male colleagues.[34]

There were, however, boundaries to Smith's support of anticommunism, and they were traversed early in her Senate career. Perhaps because she herself had been smeared as a communist sympathizer in her 1948 campaign, she recoiled at the anticommunist crusade led by her Republican colleague Joseph McCarthy. A first-term senator from Wisconsin, McCarthy was largely unknown when he burst onto the national scene in February 1950. But that soon changed when he delivered an infamous speech to a Republican Women's Club in Wheeling, West Virginia. In it, he accused the state department—a place "thoroughly infested with communists"—of knowingly employing security risks. These traitors, he charged, were working actively to ensure that the United States lost the Cold War. Their treachery was all the more dangerous for the high status they occupied by virtue of wealth, education, and breeding.

McCarthy elaborated on and enlarged these claims in the Senate over the next months as he sought to uncover the "enemies from within" so that they could be "swept from the national scene." He was supported in his efforts by many of his colleagues, some because they sat by silently. Others would endorse and participate in his reckless, damaging, and ever-expanding investigative hearings. The Wisconsin senator perfected a "politics of fear" that cowed politicians and government officials in both parties. To challenge McCarthy was to run the risk of being dragged into the inquiry with all the accompanying publicity and potential ruin. For within a matter of a few short months, McCarthy had cast off obscurity to become "a towering national figure," widely covered in the press, and increasingly powerful.[35]

Smith had had the ill luck of being assigned as a freshman senator to serve on two committees with Joseph McCarthy. She already knew the Wisconsin senator slightly. As the Senate began investigating his charges against the state department, she increasingly disliked what she saw of him. Loud, boorish, demeaning of others, prone to exaggeration, drawn to drink, and sadistic in his treatment of those he considered weak, effete, and "phony," McCarthy operated in a manner that was anathema to Smith. She certainly shared his concerns about the dangers of the communist threat. She listened carefully as McCarthy elaborated on his assertions, waiting for the evidence. But she also felt uncomfortable with the Senate's using its investigative powers and the immunity its members enjoyed to stalk individuals. (Smith had opposed legislation making HUAC a permanent committee in 1945, and voted against appropriations for its work a year later.) McCarthy seemed to be taking these senatorial privileges to an extreme while earning plaudits from the public for his "straight talking." Republican party strategists in Wisconsin saw in McCarthy's approach a winning tactic. "Our party is finally on the attack and should stay there . . . we may get rid of many Communist sympathizers and queers who now control policy." Democrats did little to curb McCarthy either. Some approved of his actions; others simply lacked the stomach to challenge him. Moderate and liberal Republicans were left similarly flatfooted. "Mental paralysis and muteness," Smith later recalled, "set in for fear of offending McCarthy."[36]

By spring, Smith began to express her doubts directly to the Wisconsin senator. "Margaret, you seem to be worried about what I am doing," she recalled him saying. "Yes, Joe," she responded. "I want to see the proof. I have been waiting a long time now for you to produce proof." She concluded in May that none was forthcoming. Urged by liberal journalists and friends to take on the senator, Smith at first demurred. She was a junior member of the Senate, finding her way, and however much celebrated for the achievement, she was the only woman among ninety-five men. But she changed her mind when no other senator came forth; she decided to challenge McCarthy from the Senate floor with a speech of her own. She asked five carefully selected Republican Senate colleagues to join her statement; they agreed to do so but in the end "only Wayne Morse was to hold his ground and not show any subsequent misgivings . . . signs of retreat and partial repudiation." When she boarded the "little Senate subway train" on June 1 to make her way to the floor, Smith caught sight of McCarthy himself. She long remembered their encounter: "'Margaret, he said, 'you look very serious. Are you going to make a speech?' I said, 'Yes, and you will not like it.'" As she sat at her desk in the Senate Chamber, waiting to be recognized, McCarthy sat two rows behind her. When recognized, she rose and gave the speech of her lifetime.[37]

"Mr. President, I would like to speak briefly and simply about a serious national condition. It is a national feeling of fear and frustration that could result in national suicide and the end of everything that we Americans hold dear," she began. Far from dismissing the threat that communist infiltration posed in the United States, she affirmed its dangers. She criticized at length the "lack of effective leadership" in the Truman administration in confronting its evils. No one in attendance, however, missed the real object of her criticism—the

United States Senate and its most reckless member. "I speak as a Republican. I speak as a woman. I speak as a United States Senator. I speak as an American," Smith explained. "The greatest deliberative body in the world," she continued, had "been debased to the level of a forum of hate and character assassination." Smith never mentioned McCarthy by name. But to those who listened, her jeremiad was all the more effective for that omission. "Those of us who shout the loudest about Americanism in making character assassinations are all too frequently those who, by our own words and acts, ignore some of the basic principles of American-ism: The right to criticize; The right to hold unpopu-lar beliefs; The right to protest; The right to independ-dent thought," she asserted. "The exercise of these rights should not cost one single American citizen his reputation or his right to a livelihood." Although pub-lic opinion polls charted McCarthy's growing popular-ity, Smith took pains to speak for what she believed was the essential fairness of the American people. "The American people are sick and tired of being afraid to speak their minds lest they be politically smeared as 'Communists' or 'Fascists' by their opponents," she in-sisted. "Freedom of speech is not what it used to be in America. It has been so abused by some that it is not exercised by others."[38]

Smith's speech included a highly partisan attack on

the "present ineffective Democratic Administration." But it was perhaps even more pointedly addressed to the weaknesses Smith located in her own party. The nation needed a change of administration and a change of party. But to "displace it with a Republican regime embracing a philosophy that lacks political integrity or intellectual honesty would prove equally disastrous to this nation." Indeed, she warned her fellow party members of a pyrrhic victory: "I don't want to see the Republican Party ride to political victory on the Four Horsemen of Calumny—Fear, Ignorance, Bigotry, and Smear. . . . Surely we Republicans aren't that desperate for victory." Such a course of action "would ultimately be suicide for the Republican Party," she suggested, as well as a "lasting defeat for the American people." Taking advantage of her unique status in the legislative body, Smith concluded by wondering "as a woman" about "how the mothers, wives, sisters, and daughters feel about the way in which members of their families have been politically mangled in Senate debate—and I use the word 'debate' advisedly." She knew, of course, from her own experience in 1948 what it felt like to be maligned in the political arena. Smith ended by offering her fellow senators a "Declaration of Conscience" signed by her several hand-picked Republican colleagues. It called upon Republicans and Democrats alike to stop "being tools and victims of totalitarian techniques—techniques that, if continued here un-checked, will surely end what we have come to cherish as the American way of life."[39]

McCarthy listened quietly through Smith's speech, quickly disappearing as soon as it was over. But if he felt any shame or embarrassment from the dressing down Smith delivered, he did not show it. "Snow White and the Seven Dwarfs"—so he characterized Smith and his colleagues who had joined her in signing the Declaration of Conscience. McCarthy had warned Margaret Chase Smith moments before she made her speech, "Remember, Margaret, I control Wisconsin's twenty-seven convention votes!" "For what?" Smith replied. In fact, she knew her name was being mentioned as a possible vice-presidential nominee in the upcoming 1952 presidential election. The talk was then largely a legacy of her historic success in reaching the Senate. But McCarthy was warning her to toe the line or expect retribution in any bid she might make for higher office.[40]

The national press widely reported Smith's speech, often with praise and invariably noting her singular status as the Senate's only female member. "GOP Senator Blisters Both Major Parties: Only Woman Member Blasts at Tactics in Fight on Communism," the *Hartford Courant* headlined its story. The *Baltimore Sun*'s reporter recounted the dramatic scene he observed: "The Senate was well filled when Senator Smith began to speak, and members listened attentively as she proceeded in a voice that at times was scarcely audible in the galleries." When she concluded, the *Sun* noted, Senator Tydings of Maryland admired her "stateswom-anship." The *Washington Post* in praising Smith's "magnificent declaration" paused too on its distinctive messenger. "Words that desperately needed to be said for the salvation of the country were spoken yesterday on the floor of the Senate by Senator Margaret Chase Smith of Maine," the *Post* editorial read. It observed that Senator Smith "was perhaps uniquely qualified to speak as she did—because she is a woman and a Republican, but above all because her disinterested patriotism and personal integrity are beyond question." The *Post* also lauded Smith's male colleagues who signed the declaration. The entire event demonstrated an important truth, it concluded without irony: "We need the counsel of men who are above the vulgar political battle, men who can be enlisted in the great battle for national redemption." The *New York Times* buried its lead in a story whose headline read: "Seven GOP Senators Decry 'Smear' Tactics of McCarthy." They were "led," the story disclosed in the second paragraph, "by the Senate's only woman member."[41]

McCarthy's promised retribution arrived a few months later. As ranking Republican, the Wisconsin senator succeeded in having Margaret Chase Smith replaced on the Subcommittee on Permanent Investigations. He appointed in her stead Richard Nixon, then a new senator from California, whom he claimed had more useful experience, having served on HUAC while a congressman. (Nixon had recently won election to the Senate in a race in which he had smeared his opponent, Helen Gahagen Douglas.) Smith vigorously objected to her unceremonious demotion, to no avail. McCarthy would eventually use this committee to pursue further his anticommunist probe. In fact, Smith had always disagreed less with McCarthy's concern than with his methods. She voted for the McCarran Act (1950) just three months after her Declaration of Conscience speech. It set sweeping restraints on suspected subversive organizations and individuals. In 1953, she cosponsored a bill that went further. The measure, which died in committee, would have made it possible to expatriate American citizens who embraced communism and other forms of radicalism. Where, her critics asked, was her defense of civil liberties for American communists? Her actions led journalist I. F. Stone to accuse her of "outdoing McCarthy." She certainly wanted no one to confuse her rejection of her colleague's behavior with any softening of her views on communism.[42]

Smith continued to do battle with McCarthy, however, as his star rose in a political climate he both exploited and shaped. What was remarkable about her Declaration of Conscience was how *early* it came in McCarthy's crusade. Smith confronted McCarthy less than four months after his February 1950 Wheeling speech. She did not entirely let go until McCarthy was finally repudiated by his colleagues. And even then, she held onto her anger. (When McCarthy died in 1957, Smith refused to sign a resolution drafted by other members of the Senate Government Operations Committee praising his "aggressive and courageous fight against Communism.") In 1952 she took aim at a scandalous book that Smith was convinced, correctly, as it turned out, McCarthy had stealthily abetted. The authors accused the Maine senator of being a "fellow traveler" of a female state department staffer whom McCarthy had targeted as a communist. Smith in short order filed a suit for libel against the publisher and the authors for a million dollars. She would eventually succeed in forcing them to print a retraction clearing her name. But even then the duel with Senator McCarthy was far from over. A McCarthy acolyte challenged Smith in the 1954 Maine Republican primary—her first bid for re-election to the Senate. Edward R. Murrow featured the contest in his television program "See It Now." He somberly concluded his broadcast by noting the stakes of the primary battle: "Mrs. Smith will learn the price or the reward of conscience." She won handily. Smith made sure she was present to cast her vote in the real denouement that winter. When McCarthy was finally condemned in December 1954 by the Senate for "conduct unbecoming" a member, she voted, of course, in the affirmative. Four years after her speech, Smith knew she had finally been publicly vindicated.[43]

Margaret Chase Smith had emerged by the mid-1950s as a "figure of national importance." Her stand against McCarthy, her prominence as the nation's only woman senator, her extraordinary success with those she represented, her consistent stance as a tough, even militaristic, Cold Warrior in an era of limited hot wars and heightened fears about national security, her reputation for independence and personal integrity—all these qualities garnered growing admiration. In 1954, she was the fourth most admired woman in the world, according to the Gallup Poll. Her name would appear more than twenty times in the top ten of that list. In December 1963, amid Smith's emergence as a presidential candidate, she would again appear near the top of the list—bested only by the widowed Jacqueline Kennedy, the new First Lady, Lady Bird Johnson, and Queen Elizabeth II. "Someone once said that women will begin to go places politically," one journalist wrote in a 1950 article observing the thirtieth anniversary of women's suffrage, "when they were able to beat men at their own game." Senator Smith, he added, had "consistently beaten men at the game of politics." Bernard Baruch expressed his regard more succinctly. Had a man delivered Smith's Declaration of Conscience speech, he was purported to have said, "he would be the next President of the United States."[44]

Indeed, had all things been equal, Margaret Chase Smith might well have been broadly viewed as a compelling candidate for the nation's highest office. But all things were not equal, for a great many reasons, as her decision to seek her party's nomination for president in 1964 would make starkly clear. Surely no woman in American history before her, and few after, brought such rich and deep experience in mainstream electoral politics to a run for the presidency. Smith was a widely admired, experienced senator with a national reputation for courage and integrity. Her years of experience on the House and Senate Armed Services Committees as well as on the Senate Appropriations and Aeronautical and Space Sciences Committees had added heft to her record. Not only was she well appreciated in her state, but she seemed to exemplify its great character, bringing an appealing regional aura to the national stage. As a woman who had succeeded in a man's world, she demonstrated steely determination and poise, a winning combination to be sure.

Proud of her achievements, Smith nonetheless wore them lightly in public. She chose not to make an issue of the indignities and isolation she endured as the sole woman in a male institution. There were benefits, of course, to being the only woman in a sea of men. She clearly enjoyed the attention. She made many close friends. Some senators met her presence with elaborate gestures of gallantry. She deflected moments of discomfort with humor and laughter, as when a senator looking for a place to deposit a cigar butt found the only remaining spittoon in the Chamber under her desk. But her colleagues' chivalry often came with thinly veiled condescension. And there were the hidden elements of her experience. She used a public restroom for a decade in the Senate, or took the long walk back to her office, before a lavatory for women members was finally provided. (There was a restroom for the convenience of male senators near the Senate floor.) She usually declined invitations for evening events at the White House, having never been asked if she would like to bring a male companion.

Her response to an exception to that norm was revealing and poignant. A few months into the Kennedy administration, she was invited to an evening White House reception. A month before it was to take place, her office received a call from the White House social secretary. Jacqueline Kennedy had asked her staff to convey that "since the social on April 18 at the White House will be at a late hour and there will be dancing that Sen. Smith may wish to have an escort that evening." If so, Smith's staff should "just send the name" and an invitation would be sent to the man in question. This simple act of consideration so moved the senator that she sent a personal letter to Mrs. Kennedy. "Thank you very much for your very thoughtful message with respect to an escort for me at the reception . . . which you and the President are giving," she wrote. "This is one of the most thoughtful things ever done in my twenty-five years in Washington." Her ability to look the other way stood her in good stead with those congressmen she knew only tolerated a woman in their midst. "I had a way of hearing the things I wanted to hear," she once admitted. "I ignored any discrimination. I never, never acknowledged it. Never." In sum, the personal and professional assets that Smith brought to a presidential bid would be the envy of a lesser politician—male or female.[45]

At least on the surface, the historical moment of the early 1960s also suggested that the times might be more hospitable to a woman presidential candidate. While many voters still doubted a woman's suitability for the office, a majority seemed warmer, at least in principle, to the idea. When Smith began her political career in the 1940s, only 33 percent of Americans polled agreed when asked: "If your party nominated a generally well-qualified person for president who happened to be a woman would you vote for that person?" By 1964, that number was 55 percent. John F. Kennedy had broken the barrier in 1960 imposed by his religion of Roman Catholicism. Crossing that threshold would perhaps embolden the political parties to take

risks with other candidates who had been deemed unelectable. It was certainly possible to imagine that.[46]

By the early 1960s, signs that a new women's movement was emerging likewise were in evidence. The determined efforts of activist women, especially in the labor movement, bore fruit when John F. Kennedy signed
an Executive Order in December 1961 creating a presidential commission on the status of women. Its very
appointment constituted an acknowledgment that inequality remained a stubborn reality for millions of
American women in the workplace, and in society at
large. Kennedy asked the commission to explore these
difficulties and make recommendations on how best to
remove the barriers standing in the way of women's
equality. While the group deliberated, the president
acted on a bill to prohibit wage discrimination on the
basis of sex by signing the Equal Pay Act of 1963. It
mandated that employers pay men and women equally
for comparable work. The year 1963 notably brought
the publication of Betty Friedan's *The Feminine Mystique*. Friedan's best-selling work made the case that
despite the privileged lives that middle-class American
women appeared to live, discontent was both pervasive
and subterranean among them. Their lives, for all the
surface signs of fulfillment, were constrained by values,
institutions, and mores that denied women's individuality. A "strange stirring," in the words of one historian,
was afoot. It could be felt in many aspects of American

life. Smith's candidacy for president was, in some sense, both a product and an omen of it.[47]

From the moment of her first election to the Senate, talk about Smith as a future presidential contender (or more often vice-presidential contender) could occasionally be heard. But Kennedy's election and brief presidency, the mood of the early 1960s, and the quietly brewing storm for the soul of the Republican party converged in 1963 in ways that led Smith to enter the race. Age (she was sixty-five in the fall of 1963), experience, a confidence renewed by frequent recognition, fresh bouquets of flattery, and even criticism that was sharp and newsworthy encouraged her ambitions. Her most direct answer to the question of why she decided to pursue the White House perhaps captured it best: "There was nowhere to go but the presidency," she said. She had come fully into her own, a fact that was apparent in her frequent, vocal challenges to Kennedy.[48]

In the fall of 1963, congressional debate over Kennedy's proposed Nuclear Test Ban Treaty with the Soviet Union spurred speculation about the 1964 presidential race. The proposed agreement banning the testing of nuclear weapons in the atmosphere, oceans, and in space unsettled those who believed that the Russians could not be trusted to abide by its terms. Weak inspection provisions, critics charged, would permit the United States to be hoodwinked and lured into a position of complacency on nuclear weapons. Chief among the treaty's opponents was Senator Barry Goldwater, widely assumed to be the likely Republican nominee in the 1964 contest with Kennedy. "If it means committing political suicide to vote for my country and against this treaty," Goldwater asserted in his final Senate speech urging rejection of the accord, "then I commit it gladly." Smith, as was her wont, expressed pointed reservations in the Senate debate even though she professed to remain undecided until the final hour. In the end, much to JFK's disappointment, Smith voted with Goldwater and seventeen other senators against the treaty. Despite their opposition, it was ratified by a huge margin.[49]

Her alliance with Goldwater on this issue immediately led some to muse about a Goldwater-Smith ticket. Every Republican senator "from east of the Mississippi, voted in the other side against Goldwater," the *Boston Globe* observed, with the exception, of course, of "Mrs. Smith." The outcome underscored growing divisions between moderate and liberal Republicans in the Midwest and Northeast and conservative Republicans in the West. The former were attracted to a potential Nelson Rockefeller candidacy, while the latter were drawn to Goldwater. Smith, some speculated, might allow Goldwater to smooth over liberal fears that he was an extremist. It was an idea that Senator Smith herself initially did not dampen.[50]

As would soon be routine, even the prospect of

Smith as number two on the ticket produced mockery or, as one *Washington Post* journalist would have it, good-natured ribbing. A few days after the Test Ban Treaty vote, columnist George Dixon mused about "the Barry-Maggie Ticket." He described provocatively his discomfort in commenting on the Maine senator. Smith "seems to think I write about her with tongue in cheek," Dixon observed. "This is a very uncomfortable position in which to write a whole column. Moreover, it is likely to leave you permanently protruding, like a pull over sweater you have loaned to a girl."

Smith and Goldwater both belonged, Dixon continued, "to the World's Most Exclusive Gentlemen's Club" —the United States Senate. "Skilled in military and space matters," experienced legislators, tough-minded, they shared another virtue. "Not even their most scurrilous traducers could accuse them of being too youthful," Dixon teased. Goldwater, he noted, was fifty-four. "Senator Smith," he continued, "is one of the few Senators to omit her age from the Congressional Directory but I know how old she was previous to 1900!" In truth, Dixon had landed on an interesting issue that Kennedy's election had cast in sharp relief. When he campaigned for president, many complained that at forty-three JFK lacked the gravitas to lead the country. With his election a new landmark was reached. Kennedy was not only the youngest man elected to the presidency; he was the first president born in the twentieth century.

Margaret Chase Smith, born in 1897, belonged to the nineteenth century. Dixon's column, however inadvertently, foreshadowed two themes that would dominate coverage of Smith during her six-month presidential campaign. She could not escape a preoccupation with her anomalous status as a woman venturing into a man's role nor with a fixation on the age of this potential female president.[51]

In early November on the same day that Governor Nelson Rockefeller of New York announced his bid for the 1964 Republican nomination, Smith tipped her hand that she too was considering a run for the presidency. Bill Lewis, her longtime assistant, indicated in his briefing that she would weigh the many requests she was receiving urging her to compete. Her decision would be revealed, he promised, on December 5, when she was scheduled to speak to the Women's National Press Club. The Associated Press wire story made reference to the "snow haired" Smith, who heretofore was often extolled for her attractive "silver" mane. "A trim white-haired lady of 65," the *New York Times* described the potential candidate. "As recently as two months ago," the *Times* noted, Smith had waved aside speculation that Rockefeller or Goldwater might select her as a running mate. She deemed such a possibility unrealistic. She now seemed to have arrived at "a sharp reversal of views" as she eyed the presidency. "No woman," the

Times explained, "has ever been nominated for either President or Vice President of the United States by a major political party." Victoria Woodhull, "a suffragist leader," it observed, had run on a third-party ticket.[52]

Political analysts turned themselves inside out trying to divine the meaning of a Smith campaign. Their assessments had in common an assumption that the Maine senator would not be, and indeed could not be, a serious candidate for president. One scenario imagined that Smith might be a spoiler who could prevent a clear and decisive primary win for the two male Republican front-runners in New Hampshire. Rockefeller had divorced his wife in 1962 and only recently remarried a woman, now pregnant, who had left her marriage for him. That stuck him with a "rather tarnished hat to throw in the Presidential ring," according to *Chicago Tribune* Washington Bureau Chief Walter Trohan. If Smith wound up "tossing her flowered bonnet" in she might keep Rockefeller's chances alive by preventing a Goldwater "thumping." A *Baltimore Sun* analyst suggested that Smith "might gather in some of the housewife vote that is regarded as a major threat to Governor Rockefeller." Even women journalists who had written sympathetically about Smith through the years reported that "it is considered doubtful that the country will see a woman head of state in the near or even distant future." Bill Lewis responded to such skepticism by dryly commenting that "the question of whether she will be 'a serious candidate will be decided by her and by the electorate.'"[53]

Persistent speculation that Smith was really aiming not for the presidency, as she had indicated, but to advance her prospects as a vice-presidential pick irritated the senator. In mid-November she gave an interview to a *Boston Globe* reporter and set the record straight. "I am only thinking of the Presidency," she insisted. No one, she pointed out to the reporter, runs for the vice presidency—"the presidential nominee taps his running mate." It took a seasoned woman political reporter like Mary McGrory to notice Smith's revealing choice of the Women's National Press Club as the setting to unveil her intentions. That group, McGrory noted, "has suffered much from the unkindness of men." Smith, she wrote, was "the personification of the New England virtues of attendance to business, thrift, and terseness." It would be a mistake, she suggested, to underestimate her. Republicans who "cannot believe their choice is limited to Goldwater or Rockefeller" might very well see her as "Florence Nightingale or Clara Barton, a lady with a lamp in a dark situation."[54]

President Kennedy's description of Smith as "formidable" in his mid-November news conference added luster to Smith's potential candidacy and sparked widespread media attention. It also provided an opening for two of her Senate colleagues to defend her quest for higher office. Senior Republican senator George Aiken from Vermont, a longtime friend and ally of Smith's, agreed that Kennedy would have something to worry about if he were to face her in a primary. "She not only would sweep New Hampshire but neighboring states— like a breeze, like the capable lady she is." Smith "graces her party with dignity and honor," Democratic leader Mike Mansfield warmly agreed, adding that it was "about time . . . that women in public life assert themselves and get the recognition" they deserved. Yet when George Gallup reported that recent opinion showed some people warming to the idea of a woman president, news coverage emphasized a doleful undercurrent. Women voters, the polls showed, seemed less favorable to a female chief executive than did men. The first woman elected to a state governorship (in Wyoming) certainly seemed to exemplify the feeling. Nellie Taylor Ross admired Smith but believed women in general lacked the "physical stamina" the presidency required. The Maine senator was a "lovely person," but despite her slim figure and penchant for swimming and badminton, she showed no signs of the physical strength she would need in the Oval Office.[55]

There could be no doubt that Smith's game of possum roiled the waters of presidential politics in the waning days of November 1963. On November 20 in a Rose Garden ceremony, a woman reporter from an Indiana weekly asked JFK what he would do if Margaret

Chase Smith won the Republican nomination for the presidency. "I'd run with you," he replied merrily. The *New York Times* suggested Smith's candidacy may have been a factor in a recent decision, floated purposefully to the *Times*, to deploy Jacqueline Kennedy in the upcoming campaign. The story's headline, "President's Wife to Campaign in '64—She Plans an Active Role in Drive for Re-election," conveyed a promise that would be chilling in retrospect.[56]

The death of John F. Kennedy on November 22 redrew the map for the 1964 campaign and, indeed, for the country. For Margaret Chase Smith, as for so many, it was a shocking experience. She had spent a cordial day with the president on October 19 traveling aboard Air Force One to Maine, where he received an honorary degree at the state university. After the conflict over the Test Ban Treaty, she found herself charmed by the handsome, engaging JFK, and optimistic that he was coming into his own in the presidency. They had discussed during that trip new plans to revitalize the Passamaquoddy Tidal Project, which sought to harness the power generated by the huge tides in the Bay of Fundy. She must have been thinking of that encounter, as well as his press conference comment, when she told a reporter in the immediate aftermath of Kennedy's death: "In the past few weeks, we had become very good friends and he was so generous to me only a few days ago." While other colleagues formally eulogized the slain president, Smith left a single red rose on the desk that the young John F. Kennedy had occupied when they served together in the Senate.[57]

Smith canceled all of her speaking engagements and commitments for the rest of 1963. Not until January did she keep her promise to the Women's National Press Club to announce her plans concerning a run for the presidency. In the interim, the assassination dramatically demonstrated the high stakes involved in choosing a vice president. For those who could accept the idea of a woman as *second* in command, but *not* as chief executive, recent events prompted some cooling of enthusiasm for Margaret Chase Smith. As one newspaper editorial suggested, "one of the side casualties of the assassination of President Kennedy may turn out to be the boom of Margaret Chase Smith for Vice President." Noting that "a woman Vice President is quite different from a woman President," the author concluded that the country was "not quite yet up to a woman in the White House, holding sway over Congress" and interacting with male foreign leaders. In a column published the day Smith was to make her announcement, *Washington Post* political reporters Rowland Evans and Robert Novak described her as one of "three nonserious candidates." For those who harbored such doubts, Smith's long record in the House and Senate proved less persuasive than the fact of her gender.[58]

Smith would soon be faced with another unwelcome

reality. The widespread assumption that no woman could be elected president, invoked frequently, itself became a very high hurdle for anyone who chose to make the attempt. The humiliation she would experience if the "expected crushing defeats" materialized was a powerful argument for Smith against running. Her "lack of money and organization" also posed an enormous challenge. Finally, her idiosyncratic—one might say obsessive-compulsive—"determination not to miss roll call votes" in the Senate loomed large for her. The Congress had been the focus of her life for decades, and it was in doing her business there as a senator that she felt most at home. Given these facts, her worries about a presidential run were appropriate and then some.[59]

Running for president involved a vastly different landscape than she had ever faced in Maine. By 1964, campaigns for national political office had become much more "candidate-centered" than the party-driven affairs of an earlier era. She would never have emerged as a presidential contender, to be sure, under the old conditions. But the new trend also created enormous challenges. Rather than relying primarily on political parties for funding and institutional support, individual aspirants for office focused increasingly on building their own war chests and organizations. The increasing role of mass media—television and radio, at this point —raised the cost of campaigning for national office exponentially. Expenditures for media in federal campaigns rose from an estimated $10 million in 1956 to over $60 million by 1968. Overall campaign spending doubled in the same time frame. Candidates seeking to meet these expenses benefited, obviously, from having great personal wealth or hefty donations from private sources (individuals or businesses)—both were invariably involved. Kennedy, Rockefeller, and Goldwater could draw on sizeable family fortunes. A candidate like Margaret Chase Smith had none. Not incidentally, it was one of the nation's richest presidents—Kennedy—who took early steps to explore how best to regulate the power of individual large donors. In 1961 he appointed a Commission on Campaign Costs to recommend appropriate regulations. It endorsed fuller disclosure requirements and the deployment of public funds to presidential contenders. But no reforms had been instituted by the time of the 1964 election season.[60]

The primary system also raised complex difficulties. The primary had proved to be a reform less popular in fact than in theory. It was nowhere near as important in 1964 as it would ultimately become. But it was certainly more important than it had been for much of the twentieth century. In 1960, Kennedy had used the primaries to demonstrate his national appeal to voters despite the liabilities of his youth and religion. His success underscored the primary's value to candidates who could not rely on the imprimatur of party elites who still called the shots in the final analysis. There were far fewer primaries in 1964 than there soon would be, and participation in them required significant funding. Kennedy flew from state to state in his family's airplane. (Margaret Chase Smith would wind up spending exactly $85 on the Illinois primary—the cost of her round-trip plane ticket.) It was in the nature of American politics by 1964 that a populist approach in a national election required considerable wealth to actually meet the people on the ground.[61]

Far from being unaware of these facts, Margaret Chase Smith framed her long-awaited announcement speech around them on January 27, 1964, at the Women's National Press Club. Bill Lewis drafted a speech for her with two endings—one announcing that she was in and the other that she was declining to run. (He asked Smith not to tell him of her decision in advance.) The entire appearance was cleverly crafted. As she had done with her colleagues in the House and Senate, Smith kept everyone in suspense about where she would land. She prefaced discussion of her decision with a long prologue exploring the "hate and bigotry" many believed existed in the United States. Some commentators, she noted, ascribed the Kennedy assassination to a growing climate of extremism. While acknowledging the persistence of racial prejudice and political division, she rejected the notion that the last decade had brought no progress. The emergence of a civil rights bill, which she endorsed, was itself evidence of forward movement, she claimed. She herself had felt, Smith stressed, "the whiplash" of "hatred and bigotry" during the McCarthy era. Much progress had been made from a time when even the United States Senate "was almost paralyzed by fear." She joined that narrative to a celebration of American liberty and suggested that perhaps in 1964 the time had come to "destroy any political bigotry against women."[62]

Distancing herself from unseemly personal striving and ambition, she went on to portray her interest in the American presidency as a response to an outpouring of mail urging her to run for the nation's highest office. She admitted that initially she had felt flattered but had not taken "the suggestion seriously." In time, however, the mail proved so steady and far reaching that she reconsidered. With modesty, humor, and self-effacement, Smith thus portrayed herself as a reluctant contender— intrigued, but with no burning ambition or need to exalt herself. Those who approached her emphasized, she pointed out, that her experience (a congressional career that dated to 1940) exceeded that of the other candidates. Her moderation and political independence also appealed to voters. Finally, a run, whatever its outcome, would "for the first time . . . break the barrier against women being seriously considered" for the American presidency. This argument appealed to

Smith, she stressed, because pioneering women before her had made her political career possible. She now had a chance "to give back in return that which had been given to me."[63]

In depicting her presidential run as a kind of service to others, Smith conveyed the values of virtue and selflessness that were so esteemed in nineteenth-century presidential candidates. It was also, of course, in keeping with how Smith had handled herself as a woman in politics. Smith had succeeded brilliantly in part because her reputation had been built on a rock of determination, hard work, integrity, and independence. Through most of her career, only Joseph McCarthy had accused her of craving power. And she had had the last word on that accusation. "She builds her power," one journalist perceptively noted, "by modestly declining to flaunt it. In the biographical pages of the Congressional directory, where most legislators list at some length their conquests and their triumphs, her entry—in entirety—reads thus: 'Margaret Chase Smith, Republican.'"[64]

For all these positives, there were many good reasons not to run, and Smith itemized each forthrightly. "There are those," she observed, "who make the contention that no woman should ever dare to aspire to the White House—that this is a man's world and that it should be kept that way." Others asserted that a run would be foolhardy given what would be a "certain and crushing defeat." Some believed women did not have "the physical stamina and strength to run." Her lack of a "professional political organization" and sound "financial resources" all militated against a campaign. And finally, she noted, there was the matter of her cherished roll-call record. A political campaign would take her away from her duties at the Senate. Smith kept her audience in suspense as she confessed: "I find the reasons advanced against my running to be far more impelling." Over a chorus of protest from her audience, she then concluded: "So because of these very impelling reasons against my running, I have decided that I *shall* enter the New Hampshire Presidential preferential primary and the Illinois primary." At that moment "in heaven," the *Chicago Tribune* surmised, "the first woman suffrage leaders of almost 100 years ago, Susan B. Anthony and Elizabeth Cady Stanton, must have smiled." Whatever was taking place in heaven, the crowd at the Women's National Press Club loved it. Smith had heard, she said, the same objections raised to this run countless times as she pursued previous political offices. She would look at these obstacles as challenges as she had always done. Wild applause greeted her announcement.[65]

In the closing minutes of her announcement, Smith described a set of conditions that would guide her effort. Her run in the New Hampshire primary would, she explained, "be a test in several ways." She would find out "how much support" a candidate could garner "without campaign funds and whose expense will be limited to personal and travel expense paid by the candidate." She would also test the success of "a candidate without a professional party organization of paid campaign workers." Hers would be a drive manned by "nonpaid amateur volunteers." She would test "how much support will be given to a candidate who refuses to absent herself" from the duties she had undertaken in the Senate. Her campaign in New Hampshire, in other words, would be "limited to those times when the Senate is *not* in session voting on legislation." Nor would Smith "purchase political time on television or radio or political advertisements in publications." Finally, she planned to make no campaign promises. She would run instead on her record.[66]

Each proposition Smith hoped to test had actually been a principle that had informed her previous bids for office. She had won those elections handily—in Maine. But could they propel a national presidential candidate in the new era of television, big donors, advertising, and expert-driven politics? If her audience in the Women's Press Club had doubts, there is no open evidence of it. They greeted Smith's promise to run with a roar of approval. In the flurry of excitement, it was perhaps easy to overlook the fact that her approach could not have been more out of step, for better or worse, with the direction of modern American politics.

She had succeeded in the past by appearing at least to eschew corrupting campaign influences and practices—big money, grand promises, wheeling and dealing with party bosses. (In fact, Smith had enjoyed the support of powerful men throughout her career, among them Bernard Baruch, James Forrestal, House and Senate leaders, including the now sitting president Lyndon Johnson, and others.) Her direct, independent, and simple style was what had qualified her for the moment she now inhabited. She would soon find herself caught in a paradox. The very traits that made Margaret Chase Smith an attractive presidential candidate in January 1964, should she remain loyal to them, foreclosed her chance to prevail in the race.

Smith's entry sparked hundreds of stories about the newcomer in the contest for the Republican nomination. They invariably mentioned her appearance and her age. On the day of her announcement, the *New York Times* reported: "Mrs. Smith, a trim woman with snow white hair, wore a black suit and brown alligator heels. Her only accessories were two strands of pearls and a yellow rose pinned to her lapel. Since she usually wears a red rose, she was asked if the yellow rose was of a Texas variety. 'It could be,' she smiled, 'the President is an awfully good friend of mine.'" "Trim as a model, she carries herself more like a clubwoman than a politician," another story noted. "At 66, she is an exceedingly attractive figure," another journalist reported, as he praised Smith as "slender, silver haired," sincere, and quick to laugh.

But if commentators and reporters admired her figure, they expressed reservations about her length of years. A columnist for the *Los Angeles Times* identified Smith's age as one of the biggest obstacles she faced. There was no question, Richard Wilson wrote, that Smith was a woman of "talent and ability." But, he added, "she is regarded as beyond the optimum years for the Presidency" given that she would be sixty-seven when inaugurated. At the end of a second term, Wilson pointed out, she would be seventy-five and older than Dwight Eisenhower was when his term of office ended. (He was then seventy.) "In all other respects," Wilson conceded, "Mrs. Smith has qualifications and experience for the Presidency no less than many men who have served in the office." But her age "tends to be a disqualifying factor." This was especially true given that she would be not only old but also an old woman. The optimum age for presidents, in Wilson's view, was the late forties or early fifties. Alas, at this time in life, "the female of the species undergoes physical changes and emotional distress of varying severity and duration." The author never used the indelicate term "menopause" in his article. But he underscored that the change in a woman at mid-life "is known to have an effect on judgment and behavior."[67]

The steady allusions to Smith's age were not lost on

the candidate. Two weeks after her candidacy was announced, Smith objected to the media's preoccupation with it in an NBC television appearance. "Since my candidacy was announced," she pointedly observed, "almost every news story starts off 'the 66-year-old Senator.'" "I haven't seen the age played up in the case of men candidates," she protested. Predictably enough, a *Los Angeles Times* news story about her remarks ran under the headline: "66-Year-Old Sen. Smith Hits Age Talk." *Today* show interviewer Martin Agronsky further pressed Smith on the issue when he noted that "many people consider women the weaker sex." Could Smith "stand all-night crisis conferences at the White House if she became President?" he asked. She replied by noting women's longer life expectancy compared with men's. She returned to the theme in an early campaign stop in northern New Hampshire, when she told a Rotary Club that there had been "some new reasons advanced by some of my detractors as to why I should not be running. One is my age which is referred to almost daily." In retort, she listed the ages of various male world leaders who were her senior.[68]

The nation's first and longest-serving woman senator was likewise immediately depicted as bereft of reason. The *Wall Street Journal*'s front-page coverage of her announcement offered: "Margaret Chase Smith, the lady Senator from Maine, made a powerful bid for the nation's illogical vote." "She listed four reasons why she should seek the GOP Presidential nomination, six reasons why she should not," the story continued. "She assessed the arguments against running as being far more compelling—and immediately declared she's going to do it anyhow. This courageous defiance of logic is going to prove a little difficult for other candidates to cope with." The *Los Angeles Times* welcomed Smith, in no small measure, for the novelty and excitement she would add to the race. "Let's not forget," it reminded readers, "that women have a history of coping, however illogically, with day to day problems." More often, news coverage described Smith's bid as "only a gesture" and a hopeless one at that. "Mrs. Smith knows there is no chance she will get the nomination," the *Hartford Courant* editorialized. The assumption of failure created a rather barren landscape ready to be populated by self-fulfilled expectations.[69]

Indeed, as Smith's campaign unfolded it operated on two levels—on the ground, where the Maine senator trudged the snowy, cold streets of New Hampshire, and in the twilight zone of American culture, where the prospect of a woman president produced a chaotic mix of excitement and bafflement. Reporters in various parts of the country conducted street surveys asking men and women for their reactions to Smith's candidacy. One might have imagined that some of the views expressed came out of the nineteenth century. But they seemed in some sense more primitive than the reaction to Victoria Woodhull's 1870 presidential announcement. "I wouldn't feel secure under an administration headed by a woman," offered a female receptionist. Her sentiment was shared by a male lawyer who asserted: "the country's not ready psychologically to accept a woman in the presidency." A common concern was for the welfare of the "First-Gentleman," even though Smith was a widow.

"Life will not be easy for the President's husband," Russell Baker mused in his *New York Times* column. Baker wittily sent up both his sex and the hackneyed nature of campaign politics as he speculated about the First Man. "During the pre-election campaign, he will be hauled away from his office and steered around the country in his wife's wake by a group of fat men who smell of cigars. At every airport stop, he will have to be photographed accepting huge bouquets of roses. Women reporters will badger him for his favorite recipes and advice on child care." Baker guessed "it will be easier to find good woman candidates for President than to find excellent First-Gentleman timber. The average husband would set off a national scandal before his wife's first State of the Union message arrived at Congress." "The question which Mrs. Smith's candidacy ultimately poses for womankind," Baker concluded, "is as old as a soap opera: Can this country produce a man capable of making a woman a good-wife?"[70]

In fact, Smith had such a man at her side. Bill Lewis

directed her campaign and served as her closest adviser each step of the way. They began the campaign in the small New Hampshire town of Pittsburg perched on the Canadian border where the temperature was thirty below zero. The stop proved the candidate's hardiness but turned out few voters. The campaign had no press bus, no advance team, no headquarters, no chartered planes, and no rallies. Ironically, however, reporters still braved the cold to cover the senator extensively. Suddenly "the elephant has an attractive face," as one newspaper would note of Smith and her candidacy. Smith followed in New Hampshire the formula that had won her—over and over again—a House and Senate seat in Maine. She greeted potential voters at their workplaces, talked to small clubs, shook many hands, and never asked directly for anyone to cast a ballot on her behalf.

Her fealty to her Senate duties—one of the ground rules she established for her foray into presidential politics—left her with little time in New Hampshire. She devoted only two weeks to what would certainly be her most important primary. If she could not win votes in Maine's neighboring state, where she was well known and admired by many, her credibility as a candidate would be irreparably damaged. After all, she had embarked on what an observer called "one of the toughest grinds of her career—a campaign for endorsement as the first woman candidate of a major party for President of the United States." Her lack of support among GOP leaders made the primary for Smith a very important venture. One reporter noted that "although Mrs. Smith is campaigning hard and appears sincere in her effort to nail down the Republican presidential nomination," she "laughed heartily" when one of her volunteers spied the ten-year-old son of Pittsburg's general store owner. The man looked at the boy and said "he'll live to see a woman president."[71]

Margaret Chase Smith faced her first electoral defeat in the New Hampshire primary. She garnered fewer than 3,000 votes, placing well behind winner Henry Cabot Lodge's more than 30,000 ballots, with Goldwater and Rockefeller in second and third place respectively. Lodge, who was then serving as the American ambassador to South Vietnam, scored a stunning upset. His name was not on the ballot, nor had he campaigned. But a well-organized direct mail write-in effort provided liberal and moderate Republicans with the alternative to Goldwater and Rockefeller—and to Smith—that many apparently sought. If New Hampshire was a test of the proposition that it was possible to win a presidential primary in the late twentieth century without money, a professional organization, television spots, a candidate completely devoted to campaigning, and campaign promises, the experiment was a colossal failure. Smith continued in the race but campaigned even less in Illinois and Oregon, where her name was on the primary ballot. Her presidential bid got a brief shot in the arm in April when she cut into Goldwater's margin of victory in Illinois by winning 25 percent of the vote. Women's club members had especially mobilized on her behalf in Illinois, pouring the kind of time, energy, and organization into her candidacy whose importance Smith disclaimed.[72]

When the Republican party met for its national convention in San Francisco in July, Smith watched with satisfaction as her name was placed in nomination by her old friend from Vermont, Senator George Aiken. Pressured to release her handful of delegates, she declined, thereby denying Goldwater a unanimous victory. Nor did she observe the custom that dictated candidates stay away from the convention hall during the night of nominations. Instead, in a "deep red dress," adorned with a fresh ivory rose, she watched the history she had made unfold. Signs reading "Smith for President" and "The Lady from Maine" were waved up and down as demonstrators paraded on the convention floor. A day later, a woman reporter for the *Los Angeles Times* offered a fitting elegy: "There is always a periphery story about a convention, and women are often in it," she observed. "Wednesday one woman was no longer in the periphery. She stepped out of context and into history. She was able to do what no other woman has since this country began—be formally nominated at the national convention of a major party for the office of President. She was—as most now know—Sen. Margaret Chase Smith, 66, of Maine."[73]

SHIRLEY CHISHOLM

"Shake It Up, Make It Change"

"U.S. Rep. Shirley Chisholm of New York is a woman and she's black and she doesn't stand a chance of winning the Democratic presidential primary in Florida next Tuesday"—so a journalist covering the campaign reported from Palm Beach in March 1972. The story succinctly captured a belief that seemed obvious to all but the candidate. As she traveled around the Sunshine State seeking votes, Chisholm insisted that she "could truly be president." One of eleven Democrats stumping from Jacksonville to Miami, from the Gulf Coast to the Atlantic Ocean, Chisholm battled not only her fellow Democratic contenders but the incredulity that greeted her very presence in the presidential primary. At every outdoor rally, college campus, dance hall, church, and rural outpost on her whistle-stop campaign by bus across the state, Chisholm challenged the assumption that her sex and race alone rendered her quest nothing more than a symbolic campaign. "But Mrs. Chisholm— are you a *serious* candidate?" she would be asked repeatedly throughout her ten-month race. As tiresome as the question was, she "never blamed anyone for doubting."[1]

A whole century had passed since Victoria Woodhull had imagined in the early *1870s* that the barriers to full political equality for African Americans had been erased. She hoped then that their newfound freedom might provide a springboard for women's political emancipation. Now, a century after Woodhull's presidential bid, a century after Reconstruction, and a half-century after the ratification of women's suffrage, Shirley Chisholm found herself in *1972* justifying her temerity in imagining herself to be a worthy presidential candidate.[2]

Chisholm rejected the paeans to "someday." "If not now, I say, when?" she asked when queried about her reasons for entering the presidential sweepstakes. For centuries African Americans had been counseled to wait for the fruits of a democratic nation. Patience had yielded nothing; only struggle had advanced the race. Why would it be any different for those seeking the top elective office in the land? "One of my reasons for running," Chisholm explained, "is that I want America to know that I'm sick and tired of hearing about brotherhood and the American Dream not being fulfilled at the highest level in this country." If the "helpless and the powerless" joined forces, they might yet advance the candidate who claimed to be their champion. "You never know what might happen" at July's Democratic convention in Miami, she suggested. Given the events at the party's last convention in Chicago in 1968—riots in the streets and chaos on the convention floor—that assertion, at least, was easy to accept.[3]

No one, of course, appreciated better than Chisholm herself the obstacles she faced in running for the presidency. Her entire political career had been an exercise in overcoming wild improbabilities. The first African American woman elected to Congress, Chisholm had painstakingly worked her way up from the machine-driven politics overseen by Brooklyn's 17th Assembly District Democratic Club in the 1940s. As a college student attending club meetings, she initially decorated cigar boxes for the club's annual raffle—an enterprise reserved for women. She went on to join a series of local political clubs, campaigns, and causes. And in due course, that engagement led her to a seat in the New York State Assembly. Then, in 1968, when she defeated James Farmer, a nationally known civil rights leader, Chisholm's political journey took her to Washington and a seat in the House of Representatives.[4]

When some supporters expressed concern that a bid for the White House would subject the forty-seven-year-old Chisholm to "humiliations," she had a quick rejoinder: "I can handle them. That's been the story of my life." She was, she said, "willing to accept the snubs, the snide remarks, the humiliation and abuses" for challenging the "tradition in this country—a country in which only white males can run for the Presidency. I am willing, because I understand."[5]

Courage and a rapier sense of humor would be her armature in the 1972 presidential race. Asked during an appearance at Florida Memorial, a historically black college, "what changes she would make in the White House," she replied: "It won't be the White House any longer." White and black college students greeted her with enthusiasm. Many were newly enfranchised by the Twenty-Sixth Amendment, ratified less than a year before, which lowered the voting age to eighteen. Chisholm also considered women, especially those energized by the resurgent women's movement of the period, a core constituency. Those struggling with poverty and low-wage jobs would likewise respond, she believed, to her message. Thus in the waning days of the Florida primary the congresswoman took her case to voters in the Panhandle, a region known as "real Wallace country."[6]

A depth of sentiment there favored Alabama's governor, who also sought the Democratic party's 1972 presidential nomination. George Wallace drew huge crowds throughout Florida. His record as an ardent, though now former, he emphasized, segregationist, a current opponent of school busing, and an eternal critic of the federal government "had made him," the *New York Times* reported, "the Democratic primary favorite." Chisholm hoped to mobilize a different constituency in the Panhandle—the African Americans, many of them poor, who made up a majority in a few small towns and "a large minority" in others. As her bus made its way along "dusty country roads," Chisholm was taken aback by the rural poverty she witnessed. She "knew the figures," but seeing it close at hand "made the statistics seem understated."[7]

Chisholm later claimed to have thought of the Civil War as she stood in the courthouse square to address a gathering of some three hundred people, most of them African American, in "the sleepy town of Marianna," Florida. Throughout the South she had seen statues of Confederate soldiers—one holding a rifle that "seemed almost to be pointing at me." She said of the rally in Marianna: "A feeling came over me about the court-house, a place of fear for blacks for a hundred years, where white justice had been dealt out to them." In 1934, the body of a lynched black man had been hung up in that square. "I never thought I'd live to see a black person speaking from the courthouse steps," an elderly man confided to Chisholm. However much she in-sisted that she was not a symbol, she seemed to per-sonify the wider change she sought as she made her way in the rural South seeking votes for her bid as pres-ident.[8]

When Wallace arrived by helicopter later that day, he received national press coverage as he too made a stop in Marianna. Both Chisholm and Wallace "depicted themselves as champions of the poor," one reporter noted, even though their "speeches were completely opposite." Wallace "stated that he wanted to cut federal aid programs, while Mrs. Chisholm told her audience that she favored more legislation and aid for the poor." Nonetheless, Wallace surprised the press corps when he paused to praise one of his opponents. Shirley Chisholm, he told the crowd, "says the same thing in Chicago that she says in Florida. I respect people, whether I agree with them or not, who say the same thing and don't talk out of both sides of their mouths." Chisholm privately relished the compliment.[9]

For the truth was, she shared Wallace's disdain for the Northern and Midwestern liberals who also sought the Democratic nomination. Throughout the primary they waffled, especially when confronted with questions about their stand on busing to achieve racial balance in public education. Even Hubert Humphrey, a longtime champion of civil rights who enjoyed widespread political support among African Americans, sidestepped the question. George McGovern, John V. Lindsay, and Edmund Muskie likewise "equivocated" in what Chisholm judged a "sorry performance." The primary ballot contained a nonbinding referendum asking voters whether they approved of busing schoolchildren out of their neighborhoods. Wallace vociferously opposed busing under any circumstances. Chisholm took a dim view of it as well, favoring instead the aggressive pursuit of open housing as a way to create more racially diverse schools and neighborhoods. "But in the atmosphere that pervaded Florida during the primary," she later admitted, "there was no way I could give comfort to the racists by appearing to agree with them." Busing, she allowed, was an "artificial solution" to segregated schools. Still, she believed it was better than doing nothing. "Where were you," she pointedly asked white audiences, "when for years black children were being bused out of their neighborhoods and carried miles on old rattletrap buses to go down back roads to a dirty school with a tarpaper roof and no toilets? If you believed in neighborhood schools, where were you then? I'm not going to shed any crocodile tears for you now that you've discovered the busing problem." That scolding from the former nursery school teacher was vintage Chisholm.[10]

The busing referendum fueled a large voter turnout in the March 14 Florida presidential primary, with nearly 80 percent of those participating opposing the measure. In a late campaign rally, Wallace had urged a large and boisterous crowd to send a message to his fellow Democratic candidates whose ideas were formed by "pinheaded pseudo-intellectuals." The "average man" was "fed up," and "you're going to give them the biggest jolt they ever had" on primary day, he predicted. And so they did, as Wallace won handily in every single Florida county. As expected, Chisholm trailed far behind most of the Democratic field. (Richard Nixon faced only token opposition and easily won the Republican race.) A *New York Times* story published on primary day warned with chagrin that Chisholm's campaign "imperils liberals" who would be fighting over a thin slice of the Florida electorate. Even "many black leaders," the *Times* stressed, worried that Chisholm's campaign would damage "liberal white candidates." In fact, Chisholm drew few voters in an effort marred by disorganization, poor financing, and the lack of an experienced cadre of campaign managers. It would be an all too familiar tale on "the Chisholm trail." But so would the bracing honesty, zest, and determination of the standard-bearer who showed no signs of giving up her aspirations.[11]

However long the odds, Chisholm was undoubtedly emboldened by having already cleared many high hurdles in the life she had led before the latest race. Born in Brooklyn in 1924, she had ably carried as a young girl the weight of her immigrant parents' expectations. She had learned as well the reality of their struggle to survive amid the meager opportunities and hardened discrimination they confronted in the United States. Chisholm's father, Charles Christopher St. Hill, had been born in Barbados. Although he briefly made the acquaintance of Ruby Seale there, Charles and Ruby would separately find their way to New York City in the early 1920s.

Her parents' journey resembled that of tens of thousands of other West Indians who were driven from the Caribbean by economic dislocation and the lure of greater opportunity elsewhere. Some, including Chisholm's maternal grandfather, had seized the opportunity to leave sugarcane plantations to work on the Panama Canal. The money he sent home to Barbados made it possible for Ruby Seale to leave her village for New York in 1921. Brooklyn had a well-established, vibrant West Indian community by the time Chisholm's mother and father arrived there.[12]

The couple met at a social gathering held by one of Brooklyn's Barbadian clubs. They married soon after and started their family. Their firstborn, Shirley, was followed within three years by two other daughters, Odessa and Muriel. In later accounts of her childhood, Shirley described herself as a precocious toddler who walked and talked early, adopted an imperious attitude toward her younger sisters as well as her mother, and lost no opportunity for mischief. "Even mother was almost afraid of me," she said of herself as a two-year-old. Perhaps this self-characterization served as a way for the young Shirley to understand a parental decision that would profoundly shape her upbringing. In 1928, the St. Hills decided to send their three daughters back to Barbados to live with their maternal grandmother.

"My mother," Shirley later explained, "she just didn't know what to do. So she said, this has just got to go. So I went to the islands . . . to my grandmother."

In fact, economic necessity appears to have largely dictated the family's actions. As was true of many black men in Brooklyn, Charles St. Hill had been unable to secure stable higher-wage factory work; he labored long hours for a meager salary in an unskilled job as a bakery assistant. His wife, along with so many other black women in the community, also worked to support the family. When her children were very small, Ruby St. Hill, who was a skilled seamstress, took in sewing. The St. Hills also aspired to acquire their own home in Brooklyn and to educate their children. With two working parents and in the absence of day care, they concluded that their daughters would be better off living with their grandmother until they could better provide for them in Brooklyn. Thus when Shirley was nearly four years old, her mother traveled with her children by steamship to Barbados and then on by bus to the village of Vauxhall, where Mrs. Seale resided.[13]

If Shirley remained a high-spirited and rambunctious child, she met in her grandmother "one of the few persons" in her life whom she "would never dare to defy or even question." Emmeline Seale was a tall, handsome woman with a "stentorian voice," deeply religious, stern, and loving. Her farm was home to seven children, including Ruby's three and several cousins.

Her beauty and poise deeply impressed Chisholm, who credited to her grandmother her growing self-confidence and fearlessness.[14]

The formal education she acquired in Barbados also remained a point of pride for Chisholm throughout her life. In a one-room schoolhouse, with seven grades of children crowded together, Shirley experienced a "British-style" education, notable for its long school day and its emphasis on the rigorous mastery of reading, writing, mathematics, British history, and moral discipline. School began with the "small colonials" standing "in ranks to sing 'God Save the King' and 'Rule, Brittania.'" Her mother, who stayed for six months while her daughters adjusted to their new home, especially valued the opportunity such instruction, offered by black teachers and administrators, presented to her daughters.[15]

Chisholm remembered her "winterless" childhood in Barbados idyllically. Farm chores and animals, the azure sea and sandy beaches, market days in the village, the fresh fruit and vegetables grown in her grandmother's garden, as well as the warmth and companionship of her extended family proved nurturing. She was surrounded by Barbadians from all walks of life, including an uncle who wrote for the Bridgetown newspaper. Their diverse roles made an impression on the young girl and contributed to her growing confidence and sense of possibility. Chisholm's mother would not return for her children for six years. By the time she did, in 1934, Shirley spoke with the lilt of a West Indian accent that would never leave her. The transition to life back in Brooklyn proved challenging. The St. Hills had had another daughter, Selma, in the intervening period. Their hopes for a more secure financial footing sagged amid the deprivation imposed by the Great Depression. A hard period of adjustment followed for the family.[16]

Then ten years old, Shirley remembered especially returning to the "terrible cold" of Brooklyn, which "frightened" her and her sisters. Her parents lived in a cold-water flat in Brownsville. Although a coal stove heated the kitchen, the rest of the apartment was frigid in the winter. Chisholm and her sisters sometimes remained in bed all day just to stay warm. The experience left her with a lifelong fear of cold weather. Movie theaters provided a refuge. On Saturday the St. Hill girls would sit through so many matinees for their ten cent admission that their mother would have to retrieve them when her daughters failed to come home at suppertime. Mrs. St. Hill was strict and determined to raise her girls to be "young ladies." She required attendance at three separate church services each Sunday and supervised her daughters' social activities closely.[17]

Chisholm worshiped her handsome, charismatic father. Although he had only a fifth-grade education, Charles St. Hill read voraciously, took a keen interest in the news and great pride in his labor union, the Bakery and Confectionary Workers International Union. A devoted follower of Marcus Garvey, whose black nationalist movement flourished in the 1920s, St. Hill was, his daughter later remembered, "a very proud black man." He "instilled pride in his children, a pride in ourselves, and our race that was not as fashionable at that time as it is today." St. Hill enjoyed presiding over evening gatherings of other West Indian friends in his family's kitchen. Though a teetotaler himself, he provided the whiskey as the men discussed events at home in the islands. Huddled in their beds in the next room, his daughters eavesdropped as the conversation lingered far into the night. Chisholm remembered hearing "story after story" told about the oppressive hand of British colonialism.[18]

A new home meant a new school, and for Shirley it was P. S. 84 in Brownsville, then a predominantly Jewish neighborhood. The St. Hill girls would be very much a minority in their local school, but that fact, Chisholm later said, made relatively little impression on her. She and her sisters played easily with their white classmates; the "race line" in the community to her seemed less sharply defined than it would later be. Her mother insisted that her children respect their Jewish neighbors.[19]

In 1936, the St. Hills moved to a more spacious, heated apartment in Bedford-Stuyvesant. When she ran for president in 1972, Chisholm used the example of her own neighborhood to explain how blockbusting had helped create ghettoes during the Depression era. The black population of Bedford-Stuyvesant, which had experienced enormous growth in the 1920s, doubled again during the Depression. (By the early 1940s, it would be referred to as "Brooklyn's Harlem.") Chisholm recalled hearing "racial slurs and epithets for the first time—nigger, kike, Jew bastard, black son of a bitch." "I was not used to black being used as a derogatory word," she noted. After completing elementary school, she attended junior high in Ocean Hill–Brownsville—decades later the site of a fierce battle over community control of local education and in 1968 a bitterly divisive teachers' strike when Chisholm was a candidate for Congress. As a young girl in the mid-1930s, Chisholm witnessed little "racial consciousness" or "leadership" among the black migrants from the American South, she said, despite the widespread racism and entrenched discrimination endured by African Americans.[20]

The Depression bore down especially heavily on families such as the St. Hills. Shirley's father had taken a job in a burlap bag factory that appeared to offer better prospects. But in the mid-1930s, he saw his hours and wages reduced, leaving him with a salary of about $18 a week. Her mother was now forced to work outside the home. She found employment in Flatbush as a domestic servant, and Shirley became a "latch key" child with responsibilities. She explained: "Mother had to do something she had always feared. She put a key on a string around my neck. . . . Every noon I had to walk from junior high school to P. S. 28 and collect my sisters, take them home and feed them, and return them to school. I was usually late getting back, but the teachers knew why and made allowances. Lunch was usually a glass of milk and a bun. Every Thursday Mother gave me a quarter to go to a bakery and buy whatever was marked down as stale—bread, cake, or pie, enough for the week. She told us to go straight home at the end of the day, lock the door, and not open it for anyone until she got home." Sitting in the window, the girls would wait for their mother to return. "When she came into sight," Chisholm recounted, "we always screamed out in excitement, and the landlord downstairs would always shout, 'Shut up!'"[21]

Shirley's parents were deeply committed to their children's education. Her mother, who checked her homework each school night, emphasized reading and took her daughters to the local library "every other Saturday" so that they could "check out the limit, three books each." In 1939, Chisholm earned admission to Girls' High, a well-regarded public secondary school that brought promising female students from all over Brooklyn to Bedford-Stuyvesant. By then the area itself was becoming increasingly black although the school was not. A standout at Girls' High, Chisholm received offers from two private colleges—Oberlin and Vassar—upon her 1942 graduation. Her parents urged her to attend nearby Brooklyn College, where she could live at home and benefit from free tuition. Designed to serve New York City's aspiring college students, the coeducational school had very few African American students when Chisholm attended—just sixty or so among the 10,000 enrolled at all levels.[22]

Chisholm viewed Brooklyn College as the place that "changed my life." During the war years, the campus was "alive with activity," much of it generated by student organizations and initiatives. Dubbed the "Little Red Schoolhouse" for its reputation as left-leaning, the college widened Chisholm's understanding of the world immeasurably. But it also sharpened her awareness of racism in ways that echoed the "double consciousness"—"this sense of always looking at one's self through the eyes of others"—that W. E. B. Du Bois had once described as an inescapable experience for those who were black in America. She knew coming into college that her opportunities would be limited by her race: "I was black and no one needed to draw me a diagram." It was clear, for instance, that "black students were not welcome" in the college's social clubs. In response, Chisholm and some friends "formed a sorority-like black women students' society." "We were tired of trying to get into white groups," she recalled, "and decided, 'Who needs them?'"[23]

Chisholm was still taken aback, however, and profoundly sobered by the prevalence of bigotry among those who claimed to be "progressive." In the Political Science Society, she listened as invited speakers described "my people as another breed" who needed help with their limitations. She watched as whites of lesser talents lorded it over African Americans who "were expected to be subservient even in groups where ostensibly everyone was equal." Chisholm was deeply offended when Brooklyn political boss Stanley Steingut, speaking to a black student association in which she was active, told the group that they could advance only with the guidance of white people. The assertion of this "white politician" that "black people can not lead" really "stuck in my throat," Chisholm remembered. She vowed privately to prove him wrong.[24]

Chisholm likewise bristled at the way in which women students were marginalized in campus organizations. When two white women ran on separate occasions for president of the Student Council, in defiance of its tradition of all male leadership, Chisholm campaigned energetically for them. "I painted posters, helped write slogans and speeches, helped organize rallies and spoke at them myself"—all to no avail, she noted, when "the white girls did not win." She saw clearly that as a woman and an African American, she would face twice their challenge.

Chisholm also found at Brooklyn College a supportive mentor—political science professor Louis Warsoff. An expert on legal and constitutional history, Warsoff had recently authored a book concluding that the Supreme Court had shown little interest in protecting the citizenship rights of African Americans since Reconstruction. Chisholm described Warsoff, who was blind, as "one of the first white men whom I ever really knew and trusted." The professor had a passion for Brooklyn politics and later became active in Borough Park Democratic circles. He greatly admired his student's abilities and her leadership potential. After hearing her speak in the campus debate club, he urged her to enter politics. "You forget two things," she replied. "I'm black—and I'm a woman." "You really have deep feelings about that, haven't you?" Warsoff remarked. "The conversation stuck in my mind," Chisholm admitted. "I realized that I did have deep feelings, on both scores."[25]

Chisholm's oft-quoted statement that "of my two 'handicaps,' being female put many more obstacles in my path than being black" elided the reality of her experience at Brooklyn College. "More and more people, white and black," praised Chisholm in her college years and extolled her potential. "You should do something with your life," they instructed. "But what?" was the question. As she measured her talents as a young, African American, college-educated woman against her prospects, she prepared for a career as a teacher. "There was no other road open to a young black woman," she concluded. "Law, medicine, even nursing were too expensive, and few schools would admit black men, much less a woman. Social work was not yet open to blacks in the early 1940s." Perhaps by working with children, she mused, she could "be of service to society."[26]

Chisholm graduated from college in 1946 with honors and with a fluency in Spanish that would later become a great asset to her. Nonetheless, she had difficulty finding a teaching position. Rejected again and again, she attributed the failure partly to her youthful appearance. Always a slight woman, at twenty-one she weighed only ninety pounds and at 5' 4" scarcely looked old enough to lead even an elementary school classroom. She also knew her race repeatedly barred her from positions she sought. Interviewed in the wealthy Riverdale section of the Bronx, Chisholm listened as a school administrator told her she was unqualified for the teaching post for which she was being considered. Her credentials on paper had merited the interview, Chisholm boldly pointed out to her prospective employer. The only new variable was her race. "You are not looking for someone with more administrative experience," she asserted. "You didn't know I was black." As she left the school, Chisholm vowed to herself that "if the day would ever come that I had a platform," she would make sure "white America would never forget me." Finally, the director of a Harlem child-care center hired Chisholm as a teacher's aide. Chisholm enjoyed the work so much that she decided to pursue a Master's degree in early childhood education at Columbia Teachers College.[27]

She earned her M.A. degree in 1951 and within two years rose to a position in administration, first as director of a Brooklyn nursery school. The following year she was hired to lead a large child-care center in Manhattan, where she supervised a staff of 24 and oversaw their work with 130 children, half of them Hispanic. Her fluency in Spanish proved invaluable in this setting, as it later would in politics. By 1960, Chisholm's success led to her appointment as a consultant to New York City's Division of Day Care. Within a decade, Chisholm had established herself as a dedicated and visible advocate for the city's working mothers and families.[28]

Chisholm had left Brooklyn College with a vocation. She also departed with what was, for a young female college student, an unusually intimate exposure to organized party politics. She drifted into the 17th Assembly District Democratic Club's meetings while still an undergraduate, stopping in "when there was a speaker I wanted to hear." She perhaps was encouraged to do so by Professor Warsoff. The club's political power in her Bedford-Stuyvesant neighborhood provided a stark contrast to the powerlessness black residents were expected to endure quietly.[29]

The 17th Assembly District Democratic Club that attracted Chisholm's attention resembled the many party organizations that were a fixture of New York City politics. Its Irish American leaders "ran the district" and oversaw the spoils system at the local level. They decided whom the party would advance as candidates for the available offices in each assembly district, including the district leader and state assemblyman. District captains deployed to get out the vote also helped distribute favors—the Thanksgiving turkey being the most hackneyed example—to ensure loyalty to the boss and his machine. In short, the district leader and his captains were the "community's power brokers" who "made or broke the elected officials in their area." The machine proved remarkably resilient through the decades even amid broad demographic changes. Each week members held meetings in their clubhouse, run by the district leader, where residents could raise concerns or seek assistance.[30]

In the mid-1940s the 17th Assembly District Democratic Club was overseen by the Irish American political boss Stephen Carney. Although African Americans were heavily represented in the 17th Assembly District, the Democratic Club that controlled its politics was then an "all-white (mostly Irish)" affair. Chisholm vividly remembered the feel of the meetings with Carney sitting "with his flunkies on a dais at the far end of the room, while the voters came in and took high-backed chairs to wait their turns for an audience. The blacks sat at one side, the whites on the other." African Americans, she observed, "came but they stayed in their place. . . . The blacks did not go to club nights because they felt wanted, or because they hoped to make any real inroads in the organization. They went because they needed help."[31]

Watching these hard-working people "sit and wait, evening after evening" for a chance to be heard infuriated Chisholm. "It was insulting and degrading to them; they were being treated like cattle," she asserted. "One night" at a club meeting, Chisholm marched to the front of the room, began to ascend the dais, and demanded to be heard. When two officials stood in her way, telling her to go "to the end of the line" and wait her turn, she refused. "No, this is an urgent matter," she insisted. Chisholm challenged city officials to explain why they had done so little for the people of Bedford-Stuyvesant. Why wasn't the trash collected in black neighborhoods when it was cleared regularly from the streets where white people lived? Why didn't Bedford-Stuyvesant have "adequate police protection?" Why "weren't the housing codes enforced?" As she peppered the politicians with questions, they listened politely "and they talked to me. It didn't change the system though," she ruefully admitted.[32]

Chisholm's bravado reflected a broader shift in the atmosphere of the 17th Assembly District. African American resistance to white political dominance was well under way by the time Chisholm began attending the Democratic Club meetings in the mid-1940s. An early challenge came in 1933 when Bertram Baker, a successful black accountant with West Indian roots, established a "submachine" of the 17th A.D. organization. Its goal was to increase the presence and power of African Americans as well as their access to patronage. By the time Chisholm began going to the 17th A.D. Democratic Club meetings, Baker's group had achieved only modest success in extracting patronage from the reigning white political machine. Critics would charge that Baker was too cozy with the white Democratic party, too ready to settle for the "few morsels" that fell from their table. Chisholm agreed.[33]

During her senior year in college, Chisholm made the acquaintance of Wesley McDonald Holder, another black mover and shaker in the borough who would in time change her life dramatically. An immigrant from British Guiana and a fervent follower of Marcus Garvey, Holder was a rising force in Kings County politics. He was determined to "elect black candidates to represent black communities." Chisholm would have a tempestuous relationship with Holder. But from the time of their first meeting around 1946, she viewed him as the "shrewdest" and "toughest"

167

"black political animal" around, with convictions that attracted her.[34]

Bedford-Stuyvesant was changing along with the mood of those who resided in the community. For decades, Chisholm later observed, white politicians had "exchanged gilded promises" for the votes of African Americans. But they had provided little power, patronage, or even assistance in return. By the late 1940s, the reigning white Democratic Club leaders themselves recognized that they would need to take some steps to cultivate the votes of African Americans. Their track record was one of "tokenism, a few black faces." As demeaning as that was, community activists recognized that the17th A.D. Democratic Club still controlled political futures and had patronage to give. For all her disgust with the machine's highhandedness, Chisholm decided to join the Irish pols in their clubhouse to see what she could learn.[35]

When the club assigned Chisholm to the "card party committee," she joined the domain of women, "most of them wives of members." She quickly concluded that the enterprise "exploited women." The club "lived on the proceeds of the annual raffle and card party that the women ran," but provided the committee with no funds with which to carry out its work. Chisholm was quick to point out this injustice to her fellow committee women, who agreed. They pressed their case for a budget successfully. Chisholm fast earned a reputation as a pot stirrer who was encouraging rebellion among female members. She knew she had been invited in "to be their 'good black woman in the club,' a sort of show dog." It wasn't, she offered, "what I had in mind."[36]

During these early years of teaching and dabbling in local politics, Chisholm became involved romantically with a man she had met in her senior year at Brooklyn College. It was her first relationship and it wound up deeply traumatizing her. Shirley had been "sheltered from boys and other realities" during her youth. That pattern continued for much of her time in college. Living at home and spending long "hours in the college library," Shirley claimed to have "made no new, close friends" at Brooklyn. She loved to dance and attended the occasional party. But she imagined that boys considered her a "bookworm," someone to "stay away from." She continued to attend the three church services her mother mandated every Sunday. Even in college, she was, she said, "forbidden to date."[37]

But when she took a job at a Manhattan jewelry factory during Easter vacation, "a handsome, older man" approached her in the lunchroom. Charmed by the seductive Jamaican, she spent her lunch hours in his company, and soon a romance was under way. When vacation was over, the short-term job had ended, and she had returned to school, her new companion "insisted on coming to Brooklyn to visit me at home on a Saturday." By then, the spring of 1946, the St. Hills had purchased a $10,000 property on Prospect Place. Their homeownership was an enormous accomplishment—the fulfillment of a dream for a couple who had sacrificed and "painfully saved" through year after year of exhausting low-wage labor. Their oldest daughter took great pride in her parents' "remarkable achievement."[38]

The relationship flourished despite her mother's objections to Shirley's worldly boyfriend, and within two years Chisholm was engaged. Sometime after they made a formal commitment to marry, however, Shirley learned that her intended was already married and had a family in Jamaica. The man who had swept her off her feet had been duplicitous throughout their years together. Not only had he misrepresented himself as a bachelor, but he had hidden from her his involvement in a criminal enterprise. The "racket" was "immigration fraud"—bringing "people into the country with false birth certificates and then blackmailing them." In 1948, a smuggling scheme fitting just this description hit the news when immigration officials arrested a New Yorker of Jamaican origins, a fifty-year-old salesman, as ringleader along with forty others. When Chisholm learned of her fiancé's past and his betrayal, she ended the engagement abruptly. Soon after "the Immigration and Naturalization Service arrested and deported him."[39]

This broken love affair devastated the twenty-four-year-old Chisholm, who for a time went into a deep depression. In "shock," unable to sleep or eat, she "considered suicide." Eventually, Chisholm would recall, "I groped my way back to reality." But the bitterness lingered. Her crushing romantic experience heightened Chisholm's suspicion of men. It also further reduced her willingness to display any undue deference to them.[40]

In the aftermath of her broken love affair, Shirley carried on with her work and with her studies at Columbia. There she met Conrad Chisholm, a recent Jamaican immigrant who had come to the United States "during the war years." He worked his way up from short order cook to a career as a private investigator. Shirley did all she could to discourage Chisholm's interest in her. Conrad Chisholm admired her evident "strength of character." As he put it, "she was calm, cool, and deliberate. And what she wanted, she get it. And I said, well, listen, that's kinda what I want." One of twelve children, Chisholm was a warm and nurturing man who valued home and family. "Eventually," Shirley recounted, "his calm determination and his inexhaustible sympathy got through to me. I realized that this was a different kind of man. We were married in 1949."[41]

In Conrad Chisholm, Shirley found a man who was willing to place her ambitions front and center. Like Victoria Woodhull, who relied on Colonel Blood, and

Margaret Chase Smith, who came to depend utterly on Bill Lewis, Chisholm was liberated by the selfless devotion of a male companion. As Conrad Chisholm would one day put it, "I am the wonder man behind a good woman." Once Shirley became fully immersed in politics, her husband supported her tirelessly. "Thoughtless people have suggested that my husband would have to be a weak man who enjoys having me dominate him," Shirley once explained. "They are wrong on both counts. Conrad is a strong, self-sufficient personality, and I do not dominate him. As a matter of fact, a weak man's feeling of insecurity would long since have wrecked a marriage like ours." Mr. Chisholm had no interest in the "limelight" that his wife craved. "'Take the pictures of her,'" she recalled her husband telling photographers during her campaigns. He "then ducks out of their range to stand at the side of the room, puffing his pipe."

Indeed, from the very start of their marriage, it was her husband who devoted his energy to making a home for the two of them. Shirley "couldn't boil water" when she and Conrad Chisholm married. Her husband became the "cook in my family," he recalled proudly, "and I did very well." The Chisholms would have no children; their home life thus revolved around their time together. "The private side," Conrad Chisholm would recall, "was that she was not fighting anything at home. We were just fine people together, having a little bit of tenderness that was between wife and husband. . . . She had my shoulders to cry on."[42]

In the early years of their marriage, before she sought any political office, Chisholm thrived as a working woman active in an array of civic organizations. During the 1950s, she belonged to the local chapter of the NAACP, and to the Brooklyn chapters of two groups of African American women, the Key Women of America, and the National Association of College Women. By 1958, the thirty-three-year-old Chisholm was a recognized figure in Bedford-Stuyvesant. She was honored by the Women's Council of Brooklyn that year for her "outstanding" community service. Nothing, however, absorbed her quite like politics. She tacked back and forth between the African American political insurgents in Bedford-Stuyvesant and the white Democratic political machine. Her "tenacity" and, as she put it, "determination to withstand all of the insults, humiliations and abuses that the big boys would thrust in the direction of poor people" attracted others to her.[43]

In the early 1950s, Chisholm hitched her star firmly to Wes Holder (known as "Mac"), who mounted a challenge to the authority of the Democratic party elite. After helping to elect Brooklyn's first African American judge to office, an emboldened Holder launched the Bedford-Stuyvesant Political League (BSPL)—"in effect," as Chisholm characterized it, "an insurgent political club" committed to advancing black candidates as representatives of the community in all levels of New York government. Chisholm "was in it from the start" and "gradually became Mac's protegee and one of his chief lieutenants." Promising that it would deliver "vigorous, militant Negro leadership," the BSPL ran an all-black slate of candidates in 1954 only to suffer defeat in that election season and in the following few years. The machine usually prevailed. But the league encouraged voter registration. And it held up the ideal that the community might one day break the entrenched power of the local Democratic party elite.[44]

Meanwhile, the 17th A.D. leadership realized that the district was headed for a black majority. The machine's survival depended on drawing in and securing the loyalty of African Americans. This it proceeded, somewhat haltingly, to do. Early in 1957, Chisholm was made a vice president. "I was very happy to see blacks in the club and I encouraged them too," Vincent Carney (brother of Stephen and now the machine leader) would later assert. "I could see that the population was turning." In the mid-to-late 1950s, Americans might well have imagined that the gathering momentum of the civil rights movement was a Southern phenomenon. But if so, they missed the rising tide of unrest that would come to reshape politics in Northern cities. Highly attuned to, and in fact energized by these realities, Chisholm attempted to ride the coming storm as it swept through Bedford-Stuyvesant.[45]

Although she would serve briefly on the 17th A.D. board, Chisholm would not mistake tokenism for true authority. Instead, she vowed to be someone "who moved up politically in this country." She would, by her own example, refuse to "accept any type of black control or white control that smells of exploitation." In 1958, she decided to run against her political mentor, Wes Holder, for the presidency of the organization he had founded—the Bedford Stuyvesant Political League. Her lack of deference surprised and angered Holder, who mounted a vigorous defense of his office. The night of the league election, a leaflet circulated that Holder had penned using, Chisholm accused, "vitriol for ink." In it, Holder excoriated his protégé. "For three years I've pushed Shirley Chisholm forward," Holder purportedly claimed. "Tonight, she is trying, as a reward, to push me—out." Holder prevailed and Chisholm's loss led, briefly, to her withdrawal from the political scene. It also led to a ten-year freeze in her relationship with the man from whom she had "learned politics."[46]

The hiatus was brief, however, and by 1960 Chisholm was back. She now joined an effort with other activists to overthrow entirely the white-dominated political machine that still ruled the 17th A.D. This time an African American lawyer named Tom Jones led the fight under the auspices of a new group, the Unity Democratic Club (UDC). The club's platform ad-

dressed long-neglected and pressing community concerns—raising the minimum wage, expanding employment opportunities for African American and Puerto
Rican residents, and improving schools, health care,
and housing. Most of all, members sought in political workshops and door-to-door canvassing to persuade citizens that their votes mattered. "End boss-
ruled plantations!" the UDC's campaign literature
demanded.[47]

Although the UDC failed in its first electoral challenge, by 1962 it was a different story. Its "aggressive
street corner voter registration drive" had made the
difference. Running for assemblyman and district
leader, Tom Jones won handily and in so doing de-
posed the head of the 17th A.D. Democratic Club. "The
white organization," Chisholm recounted with satisfaction, "was dead at last in Bedford Stuyvesant." The
Unity Democratic Club became the district's "official
Democratic organization." African Americans would
now play a different role in Brooklyn politics, or so it
would appear. Their leaders could command directly
the attention of county and state party leaders. The
Democratic party would seek, of course, to absorb the
insurgency in Bedford-Stuyvesant. Party officials had
no intention of losing black voters even if they had lost
the comfort of their familiar white leaders. They recognized that patronage would need to be distributed. In
1964, county leaders advanced Tom Jones for a civil

court judgeship, a seat he had coveted. That left his state assembly seat open. Chisholm saw her opportunity to finally rise to elective office.[48]

Chisholm was quick to demand support from the Unity Democratic Club to mount a campaign for the assembly seat. "I wanted it, and I told the club I felt I deserved it," she said. No one had paved a road for her. Unlike Margaret Chase Smith, she found her way in party politics not by means of a husband or a widow's mandate, but by dint of her own identity and efforts. As she put it candidly:

> By then I had spent about ten years in ward politics and had done everything else but run for office. Starting as a cigar box decorator, I had compiled voter lists, carried petitions, rung doorbells, manned the telephone, stuffed envelopes, and helped voters get to the polls. I had done it all to help other people get elected. The other people who got elected were men, of course, because that was the way it was in politics. This had to change someday, and I was resolved that it was going to start changing right then. I was the best-qualified nominee, and I was not going to be denied because of my sex.

She made this case forthrightly to her colleagues in the Unity Democratic Club.[49]

Chisholm immediately faced a flare of opposition

within the Unity Democratic Club, from county Democratic party leaders and, as she would soon find out, some voters who objected to a woman—any woman, apparently—seeking elective office. Jones himself didn't seem entirely enthusiastic about a Chisholm candidacy. From the start, he had wanted men to assume prominent leadership positions in the UDC, in part to provide "male black youth" with a positive "image." There were inevitably men in the UDC who felt they were more deserving than Chisholm of party backing for the assembly seat. Others in the club disliked Chisholm. Not surprisingly, by 1964 her long career in democratic politics had made her some enemies. In the end, Jones stuck by her. She won the backing of the UDC, and the Kings County Democratic party leaders. Her nomination was, the *Amsterdam News* reported, "a history making event in the annals of Brooklyn politics."[50]

Chisholm soon found that her sex counted on both sides of the ledger sheet—at times as a liability but in other ways as an asset. She was verbally accosted by both men and women who told her: "You ought to be home, not out here." At the same time, Chisholm could tap into an expansive network of African American women activists who had long been engaged in local politics and community service. She also stood to benefit potentially from the higher number of registered women voters than men in her district—almost

5,000 more in the 17th A.D. "Come on women of Brooklyn," an African American woman journalist wrote in her syndicated column of Chisholm's election bid. "We can definitely put her in and many others too. In unity there is strength. We have the numbers." Chisholm devoted countless hours to voter registration even as she campaigned for the state assembly.[51]

The candidate's long years of community activism, much of it in women's organizations and around issues of children and social services, helped Chisholm. As had been true of Margaret Chase Smith, she benefited tremendously from the indefatigable efforts of club women. As president of the Brooklyn Chapter of the Key Women of America, an African American civic organization, Chisholm was well placed to call out the troops. The Key Women's hard work and fundraising during the campaign—"we were actually her backbone," said one club officer—eased Chisholm's burdens as a candidate. Chisholm could scarcely afford the "mailings, posters, rallies" and a get-out-the-vote operation. The Unity Democratic Club had little money to offer; the county Democratic party "was not about to help us much," the nominee remembered. Instead, Chisholm drew on her personal savings. She made four trips to the bank during the campaign to withdraw a total of $4,000. "It is not much by modern standards," she admitted, "but I made it do." In the end, she won more than 70 percent of the primary vote and sailed to victory by an even larger margin—nearly 90 percent—in the general election.[52]

If women had constituted her campaign's "backbone," Chisholm lavished special praise on another group that she claimed to believe had cemented her victory—Bedford-Stuyvesant's growing Puerto Rican population. A day after the election she greeted her constituents in the streets of her district. Wearing a "feathered Robin Hood cap perched at a jaunty angle and trailing a beige-lined scarlet cape from her irrepressible shoulders," Chisholm, the *Amsterdam News* reported, "spouted Spanish and English felicitations" to a "milling and cheering" throng. They had "made her the first Negro woman ever elected to the State Assembly from Brooklyn," and her thanks were "effusive." She could not resist a jab at those who had opposed her. Chisholm asserted that her margin of victory would have been even larger if she "had gotten more support from the nose-in-the-air black bourgeoisie" in her district.[53]

That comment led former UDC member and African American journalist Andrew Cooper to excoriate Chisholm in a letter to the editor of the *Amsterdam News*. "Shirley's colorful and dramatic manner of dress will be a subject much discussed in the hallowed halls of our State Capitol, I am sure," Cooper asserted. "Unfortunately, the era has long since passed that saw the voting public tolerate bizarre behavior and eccentric dress in its elected officials." Chisholm had insulted and "abused" her own community by suggesting that African Americans had failed to support her. Cooper demanded that Chisholm apologize for attempting to divide "the Negro and Puerto Rican citizens of the 17th Assembly District." More typical were celebratory accounts of the strides African Americans had made in New York's 1964 election. Redistricting had indeed made a difference. Now six black assemblymen and three state senators would represent their constituents in the legislature.[54]

Chisholm established her political independence soon after she arrived in Albany. She adopted a posture that closely resembled the approach Margaret Chase Smith had taken when she won elective office. Both women transformed what others considered a weakness—their minority status as women—into a source of strength. They punished with their unpredictability male party officials whom they believed patronized them or, worse, ignored their presence entirely because they were women. That was evident in January 1965 when a political brawl erupted as two Brooklyn representatives vied for the post of assembly speaker. Stanley Steingut, who chaired the Kings County Democratic party, was a powerhouse and seemed destined to win. His close association with Chisholm's assembly predecessor, Tom Jones, led his forces to assume that the new assemblywoman's vote was in the pocket. They did nothing to court her or even include her in the ongoing deliberations. "I was a woman and a newcomer, and I was expected to accept the rules and follow tradition," Chisholm later explained. She chose to do neither, casting her vote for Steingut's opponent, Anthony Travia, who had served for years as minority leader. Travia won the speaker's post, much to Chisholm's pleasure. She was quick to warn him, however, not to take her vote for granted.[55]

Chisholm served four years in the New York State Assembly. She acquired in the process "a liberal education in how politics is run in our country—a sort of graduate course to follow my basic education in ward and county politicking." It was a trying time for her in many ways. "I did not like a great deal of what I learned," she acknowledged. Too often the horse trading among legislators involved swapping conscience and belief for party discipline and political self-interest. Chisholm had visited the state capital only three times before she joined the assembly. It was inadequate preparation for her new life in Albany. She spent her days attending committee meetings and learning the legislative process. The evenings found her alone in her room in the DeWitt Clinton Hotel. She had few invitations to join her colleagues for their frequent evenings of dining and schmoozing. One assemblyman recalled that he assumed "she preferred to take her work back to the

hotel with her at night." In fact, he was right. She disliked the "convention" atmosphere that unfolded in the
evening. She looked forward to going home to Brooklyn and her husband on the weekends.[56]

Chisholm compiled a solid legislative record while
in the New York State Assembly. She introduced fifty
bills during her four years in office and had the satisfaction of seeing nearly a fifth of them enacted. She
focused her energies on the issues most central to her
constituents—labor, education, housing, health care,
and the scourge of racial discrimination. The needs of
working women also fully engaged her. Several of the
bills she advanced touched on formative aspects of her
own life experience. She took great pride, for example,
in a bill she steered to passage designed to help disad-
vantaged youth attend college. Her efforts to improve
the lives of domestic servants—many of them poor
women of color, like her own mother—resulted in New
York State's first unemployment insurance for household workers. Chisholm's career in education sensi-
tized her to the needs of teachers and their students.
Female educators who took maternity leave were hence-
forth protected by a bill Chisholm advanced that pre-
vented them from losing the time that counted toward
their tenure. She succeeded in improving funding for
public education and day-care centers. In short, as a
legislator, Chisholm kept her promise to pursue a progressive liberal reform agenda.[57]

There could be no doubt that Chisholm's performance in the New York State Assembly resonated with voters. Redistricting forced her to run for election three times in just four years. She won re-election handily in 1965 and in 1966. In 1966, Chisholm's old critic Andrew Cooper and associates sued New York City's election commissioners for their gerrymandering of Bedford-Stuyvesant. The commission, they charged, had created "purposefully and intricately eccentric" boundaries to prevent the Bedford-Stuyvesant community from "securing Congressional representation concerned with the interests and needs of the Bedford-Stuyvesant population." The area had been divided among five different congressional districts.

In 1967, a federal district court, responding to a separate suit filed by New York's Liberal party, ruled the gerrymandering unconstitutional. New York State thus went back to the drawing board and redrew the map in a way that placed most of Bedford-Stuyvesant in a new 12th Congressional District along with parts of Crown Heights, Flatbush, Bushwick, Greenpoint, and Williamsburg. The new district would be, or so it was estimated, approximately 80 percent African American and Puerto Rican. Residents now had a chance to shape more decisively who represented them in the U.S. Congress.[58]

A political plum thus hung in the new district ripe for picking. Several prospective candidates circled around it. In December 1967, a citizens' committee in Bedford-Stuyvesant gathered to assess those likely to be in the race. After interviewing a dozen Democratic candidates, the group endorsed Shirley Chisholm, praising especially her "political independence," her record in the state assembly, and her proven ability to beat the machine. Their enthusiasm was not enough, however, to solidify support for the assemblywoman. Two African American candidates challenged Chisholm in the Democratic primary.[59]

An unexpected asset emerged when Mac Holder, Chisholm's once and future queenmaker, offered to help her in her bid. Recognizing, perhaps, that Chisholm was uniquely well positioned, if given the right direction, to become Brooklyn's first black House member, he set aside his grievances. He told Chisholm that she "could not win without him and the people in the streets." The two made amends and Holder took charge as her campaign manager. "I believe," he explained without a trace of irony, that "we can depend on Assemblywoman Chisholm to fight the Black man's unequal status."[60]

Their strategy was one Chisholm had relied on in previous elections, but now it involved even greater energy. She "tramped the streets of Williamsburg, Crown Heights, and Bedford Stuyvesant." She "ate chitlins" in black neighborhoods, "in the Jewish neighborhoods bagels and lox, in the Puerto Rican neighborhood arroz con pollo." And she made a special point of reaching out to women. "Bring your women in," she asked "every neighborhood woman leader." Chisholm unswervingly presented herself as someone who both "looked like us" and was willing to "consistently and persistently hammer away at these matters which affect the lives of the people that live in ghettoized American communities."

In the primary fight, Chisholm coined her trademark slogan: "Fighting Shirley Chisholm—Unbought and Unbossed." The phrase evoked Chisholm's storied independence. But it also captured a unique freedom that her experience as a black woman had conferred upon her. Here was a politician who had been given little assistance and less encouragement by those who distributed money and wielded power. As a result, she said, she had no debts to pay and no master to serve.[61]

Chisholm's message resonated powerfully in the late winter and spring of 1968. In that harrowing year, the liberal idealism that had launched the 1960s with the election of John F. Kennedy died an unnatural death. By then the battle against racial segregation in the American South had shifted to the rest of the country. From the Watts riot in 1965 to Detroit two years later, the impact of racial discrimination, de facto segregation, economic inequality, and the widespread poverty in American cities finally became a focal point of discussion and activism. The war in Vietnam also then bitterly divided the country. A new wave of feminism had been gathering force throughout the 1960s. By the end of the decade, the women's liberation movement would seek to radically transform the experience and place of women in American society. Scarcely a month went by throughout the year of Chisholm's 1968 campaign when the nation was not rocked by a shattering event, from the Tet Offensive in January to Martin Luther King, Jr.'s, assassination in April and then the murder of Senator Robert F. Kennedy two months later.

This was the backdrop against which Chisholm's campaign unfolded as she sought New York's 12th Congressional District seat. African American political leaders in New York State, including Chisholm, served notice to the Democratic party in February not to take their support for granted. They would not remain loyal to "the party slate at [the] national, state or local level" without "patronage, power and recognition." "If you fail to deal with us," the Council of Elected Negro Democrats warned, "you'll have to deal with our successors who'll make the Stokely Carmichaels and Rap Browns seem like conservatives." In fact, black militants worried Chisholm far less than the white Kings County Democratic establishment and, as it turned out, male African American politicians who made an issue of her sex. When Chisholm beat her two rivals in the June Democratic primary, winning nearly 46 percent of the votes cast, the *Amsterdam News* reported the former assemblywoman's victory under this head-line: "Ex-Teacher Aims at Congress Seat."[62]

James Farmer, former director of the Congress of Racial Equality and a nationally renowned civil rights leader, entered the race in March as the candidate of the Liberal party. Farmer, who lived outside the district, and indeed Brooklyn itself, jumped to front-runner status in May when he was also nominated as the Republican party's candidate. Money poured into his campaign. Chisholm's long experience in Democratic politics and her four years in the assembly seemed to suddenly shrink in significance as she faced Farmer in the general election. Bronx Borough chief Herman Badillo, a Democrat, endorsed Farmer by underscoring his "lifetime" of service to progressive causes. His praise was echoed by Governor Rockefeller when he described Farmer as a man who was "loved and respected throughout the nation"—a stature that would carry weight in Congress. Ignored, she felt, by media outlets, Chisholm called a television station one evening to complain and was told, "Who are you? A little school teacher who happened to go to the Assembly." Chisholm challenged these assumptions whenever she had the chance. "Mr. Farmer seems to feel that because he's a national figure he deserves a seat in Congress," she asserted on one occasion. "Well, let the national Government find a job for him."[63]

If some news reports seemed to dismiss Chisholm as

"a little school teacher," others asked whether she might cut too powerful a figure for the good of her community. The *Wall Street Journal* raised that question directly in its coverage of the campaign. It cited sociologist Daniel Patrick Moynihan's 1965 report which concluded, in the *Journal*'s words, that "Negro families are largely run by women," much to the detriment of black men and children. The Brooklyn contest, in the *Journal*'s view, thus turned around "a unique issue that could arise only in a Negro ghetto campaign between a man and woman: The question of whether sending a woman to Congress might tend to perpetuate the matriarchal society said to prevail in the Negro slums." Farmer's campaign seemed to think so and was attempting to "exploit the matriarch issue," the paper reported. One of the campaign's broadsides called for the black community "to get behind strong, black, proven-in-battle, masculine leadership. . . . We owe it to our children to provide for them the kind of symbol of black manhood which a man like James Farmer can give them."[64]

Chisholm was disgusted that her opponent was appealing to prejudice against advancing a woman to Congress. She later complained that Farmer "toured the district with sound trucks manned by young Dudes with Afros, beating tom-toms: the big, black, male image." She had no intention of injecting gender into the race. However, as she later recounted, she felt she had little choice: "when someone tries to use my sex against me, I delight in being able to turn the tables on him." News coverage invariably raised the gender issue, as was apparent in one lengthy *New York Times* report headlined "Farmer and Woman in Lively Bedford Stuyvesant Race." Asked during the campaign if the election of a woman might undermine African American men and families, Mrs. Chisholm, a reporter noted, "grows angry." "There were Negro men in office here before I came in five years ago," she retorted, "but they didn't deliver. People came and asked me to do something. Black women don't emasculate black men. The black men didn't deliver. I'm here because of the vacuum."

Chisholm took particular offense at "discrimination against women in politics" because they had worked so diligently "waiting in the wings" of political organizations, over so long a time, to advance men. "They do the work that the men won't do," she asserted. "I know because I have done it all." She would not be cowed now by Farmer. As she put it: "Mr. Farmer came over here from Manhattan because he thought I was going to be a pushover. I'm not afraid of him. I've licked the hell out of every man I've ever run against." She was about to do so again.[65]

Three months before election day, Chisholm underwent surgery to remove a benign tumor in her pelvis. Her physicians prescribed a period of rest and recovery. But she quickly returned to active campaigning. Holder had come up with a strategy to battle the opposition's effort to portray Chisholm as a dangerous black matriarch. Registered women voters outnumbered men 2.5 to 1 in the district, Holder learned from examining voter records. The female-headed households some saw as a weakness in the black community were also the homes of some reliable voters. Holder and Chisholm sought out women, especially the leaders of female clubs and organizations. Many joined the campaign and helped rally votes. On November 5 Chisholm, as the *Amsterdam News* put it, "walloped" Farmer 2 to 1 to become the first female African American elected to the U.S. House of Representatives. In a green knit suit, carrying a bouquet of chrysanthemums, she promised her supporters on election night that she would not be quiet in Congress. In fact, within a year she would be contemplating a run for president.[66]

Chisholm's stature as the first black woman U.S. Congress member made her a national figure overnight. Her election was covered widely in the press, which heralded her singular achievement. Her triumph owed much to broader changes in the body politic. When Chisholm was sworn into office in early January 1969, she took her place alongside nine other African Americans in the House of Representatives. Not "since the Reconstruction era," one black newspaper reported, had there been so many "black lawmakers" in the House. Others celebrated Chisholm's election as a victory for American women. "In the last 12 months," the *New York Times* observed, "women have won new rights and offices and have been admitted to places where female faces had never been seen before." Indeed, the reporter wondered whether 1968 might "well go down in history as The Year of the Woman." Although Chisholm would join nine other women in the House, Margaret Chase Smith remained the only woman in the Senate during the 91st Congress.[67]

From the start, Chisholm and a few of her African American Democratic colleagues felt enough strength in numbers to begin to caucus on an informal basis. By 1971, they had formalized their group as the Congressional Black Caucus (CBC). Although Chisholm was among the group's first members, she never felt entirely accepted by her male colleagues in the CBC. She assumed that many were jealous of the national media attention she received while others objected to her independence and outspokenness. The congresswoman also joined forces with feminists in 1971 as a founder of the National Women's Political Caucus. She fully embraced its goal of advancing women in all realms of politics and public life. But she also sought to ensure that women of color found a prominent place in the organization and that it focused on the concerns of poor women. As a congresswoman, Chisholm would not "choose" between being a woman or being African American, between feminism and the black struggle. She saw herself as a figure who bridged the divide.[68]

Chisholm claimed to have few illusions, after her experience in the New York Assembly, about what she might accomplish as a freshman congresswoman. Nonetheless, she was surprised by what she saw as the elaborate rituals and arcane customs of the House of Representatives. Her lack of patience with what she discovered became evident almost immediately. Under the "senility system," as she was to call it, "her length of service in Congress" determined her chances of getting a coveted committee assignment. Chisholm sought appointment to the Education and Labor Committee, where she felt she might best address the urgent needs of her inner-city constituents. She was amenable to other assignments. She was not prepared, however, when the Democratic leadership remanded her to the Agriculture Committee and, furthermore, to its rural development and forestry subcommittee. "Apparently all they know here in Washington about Brooklyn is that a tree grew there," she commented. "I can think of no other reason for assigning me to the House agriculture committee."[69]

Margaret Chase Smith had experienced a similar deployment to an undesirable committee when she joined Congress. And like Chisholm, she perceived the assignment as a deliberate attempt to trivialize and sideline her. But Chisholm, unlike Smith, refused to knuckle under the decision. She first complained to the Speaker of the House, John McCormack, who attempted to educate her. "Mrs. Chisholm," he said, "this is the way it is. You have to be a good soldier." She had been a "good soldier" for "all my forty-three years," Chisholm replied. If the Speaker didn't intervene to change her committee she would "have to do my own thing." "Your what?" she recalled the nearly eighty-year-old Speaker replying. "It means I will do what I have to do, regardless of the consequences," the new congresswoman explained. Chisholm then took the matter to the Democratic caucus, where she demanded reassignment to a committee where she might be able to better help "the predominantly black and Puerto Rican people who elected me, many of whom are unemployed, hungry and badly housed." The lack of African American representation in Congress, she argued, made it imperative that the leadership place its few black members on committees where they could do some good. Chisholm's defiance yielded results. She was reassigned to Veteran Affairs—not ideal, in her view, but, as she put it, "there are a lot more veterans in my district than there are trees." When a House colleague said of her rebellion, "You've just committed political suicide," Chisholm was unfazed. The prediction, she said, "sort of made me feel at home." "Brooklyn Lady No Farmer—But She Can Raise Cain," read one newspaper headline reporting on her insubordination.[70]

Given the workings of the House and her junior place within it, Chisholm soon concluded that there were "children in my district" who would "not live long enough" for her to bide her time courting colleagues to support progressive new legislation. In 1969, existing laws prohibiting racial discrimination were not being enforced. Current social programs were vulnerable to being dismantled. Improving implementation of current statutes and policies, she decided, ought to be a chief objective. Indeed, Chisholm claimed that she could be most effective as a "voice" rather than "as a lawmaker, an innovator in the field of legislation." She made her constituents, however, her first priority. To ensure that their needs were addressed as expeditiously and thoroughly as possible, she appointed Mac Holder to run her Brooklyn office. Chisholm staffed her Washington office initially entirely with young women, half of them African American. While their energy and commitment impressed her, she wanted to reward those who typically did "most of the work to make a congressman look good" at "substandard pay" and with "little hope of advancing." "In my office," she promised, things "would be different."[71]

Chisholm was good to her word when she delivered her maiden speech before Congress in March 1969. She lambasted President Nixon for unveiling his plans to build an Anti-Ballistic Missile system the same day cuts to the District of Columbia's Head Start Program were announced. She vowed to vote against every single appropriation bill that came before the House if it contained any funding for the Department of Defense. Decrying the "monstrous waste" and "shocking profits in the defense budget," as well as spending in the service of a "senseless war," the congresswoman called for a redirection of national resources "for people and peace." "At this time, gentlemen," she lectured her colleagues in the House, "the business of America is WAR and it is time for a change." As she left the chamber that day she heard one colleague say in a stage whisper, "You know, she's crazy!" Such remarks registered but left Chisholm undeterred. "The one great fear in the capital," she reported to the Federation of Jewish Women's Clubs six weeks after she was sworn into Congress, "is that some day the women of this country will band together and fight for justice and freedom on every level. We have got to make this happen."[72]

In fact, Chisholm's record as a legislator went far beyond her self-appointed role as agitator. "Shake it up, make it change," she urged those unhappy with "the system." As a freshman congresswoman, she took her own advice. She sought to enlarge federal support for social and economic welfare through an array of initiatives, many building on existing programs. Among the bills she helped cosponsor were measures that sought an expanded jobs program, increased affordable housing, protection for the rights of organized labor, health insurance coverage for household workers, expanded day-care centers, welfare reform, and a rise in the minimum wage. She lobbied for an extension of the Voting Rights Act and fought efforts to dismantle the Office of Economic Opportunity, the federal agency at the heart of Lyndon Johnson's Great Society program.

Her resolute support for the core demands of modern feminism remained a touchstone. In a 1970 speech to the National Organization for Women, she asserted that the "harshest discrimination I have encountered in the political arena is anti-feminist, both from males and from brain-washed Uncle Tom females." The comment made headlines. Like Margaret Chase Smith, Chisholm backed the Equal Rights Amendment, delivering her first remarks to Congress in its favor just four months after taking office. As the amendment made its way (again) through the House, she joined feminist leaders who argued that protective labor legislation served as a barrier to women's economic advancement.[73]

The repeal of restrictive laws criminalizing abortion became an important cause for Chisholm, who also allied herself visibly with prochoice advocates and organizations. Her stance proved controversial, not only among those who opposed reproductive rights but also among some in the black community who considered abortion and contraception a barely concealed effort at genocide. Chisholm acknowledged "a deep and angry suspicion among many blacks that even birth control clinics are a plot by the white power structure to keep down the numbers of blacks." "But I do not know," the congresswoman asserted, "any black or Puerto Rican *women* who feel that way." She judged such accusations "male rhetoric, for male ears."[74]

To say that by 1970 Chisholm was widely known for her candor would be an understatement. She was outspoken in her support for feminism, direct in calling attention to racism and its many manifestations, frequently critical of continued American involvement in the Vietnam War, blunt in her denunciations of the Nixon administration, and enthusiastic in her vision of a new political coalition made up of young people, African Americans, Puerto Ricans, women, poor people, and Native Americans. Such positions, as well as her entire persona, made Chisholm a very popular speaker on college campuses. In the first year alone of her congressional term, she spoke at more than forty colleges and universities. Chisholm welcomed the energy and idealism of these audiences. They were a tonic for the frustration and isolation she endured in the House of Representatives.

The idea of running for the presidency first occurred to Chisholm, she would later claim, in a question and answer session with college students. Invariably her campus lectures would end with a student asking if she would run for president in 1972. She would deflect such queries by pointing to what she felt was the obvious: "You must understand, whatever my ability to handle the job, and regardless of your belief in me, I am black and I am a woman." On this occasion a white male student challenged her: "Well, when are we going to break this tradition?" His question, she later said, "stayed with me for some reason." As she mused about the interaction, she could find her way to only one appropriate answer—"never, if we don't start now." "The germ of the decision," she recounted, "began there."[75]

In fact, Chisholm was a shrewd observer, as she had been for decades, of trends in American political life that she believed were redefining the Democratic party. With that transformation might come new possibilities for women and minority candidates to rise to higher office. The election of 1968 and the defeat of Hubert Humphrey, she believed, told the story. Despite a strong civil rights record, Humphrey failed to energize African American and other minority voters. They were not alone in their disillusionment. Humphrey's association with the Johnson administration's conduct of the Vietnam War had also turned off younger voters. "Their absence was decisive," Chisholm believed, "because the old alignments" of the Democratic party were changing. "The South was no longer solid, and the coalition that had made the Democrats a majority party for more than half a century," she observed, "was crumbling." The signs had been evident before the 1968 election. But after it, Chisholm wrote in 1970, "there could be no doubt."

Nor was it simply a matter of traditional voters sitting out the election. "The white middle and working class voting blocs" that had been the backbone of Democratic urban political machines had fled to the suburbs. There they were "working as hard" as they could, Chisholm charged, to create barricades against incursions from "black and brown immigrants from the metropolis." President Nixon, she warned, was pursuing a "Southern strategy" by setting aside desegregation in order to curry votes for the Republican party in Dixie. The New Deal coalition of blue-collar workers, African Americans, unions, Southerners, and urban ethnics that had put FDR, Truman, and Kennedy in office would soon be no more.[76]

Vowing that Nixon's "southern strategy will be his Vietnam," Chisholm foresaw a re-energized Democratic party if it rose to the challenge it now faced. Soul searching in the highest reaches of the party after 1968 led a year later, in fact, to new rules governing procedures, primaries, and selection of delegates. These decisions would have an enormous impact, or so many hoped, on how the party chose its nominee for president. The changes now mandated that delegates sent to the national convention by state Democratic parties must include "reasonable" numbers of minority groups, women, and young people. What "reasonable" meant was a matter of debate. But the door was opened for the party itself to enforce the standard on state party delegations. Eventually, the party recommended that the delegations reflect the proportion of each group in individual state populations. If state conventions would no longer handpick delegates, primaries emerged as a favored substitution for the old methods. Chisholm was at least modestly encouraged by these developments. They were, she believed, "little short of a revolutionary change—on paper." The new rules would likely bring more women and minority delegates to the 1972 Democratic convention.

This change made possible, Chisholm hoped, a "new politics" that would need "new men and women" as candidates. Expanding participation in the party would mean little if the "habitual pattern of delegating power: a few white men lead, everyone else follows," survived the rules change. As the country's first African American congresswoman, Chisholm was one of the most visible representatives on the national stage of the wave battering the Democratic party's gates. She had endured the ancien regime, triumphed despite it, and welcomed the prospect of a more open party. It is hardly surprising that she might imagine that she could play a part in the Democrats' efforts to reclaim the presidency in the next campaign.[77]

Others, of course, harbored the same expectation. In the fall of 1971, several male African American leaders, often of widely diverging political beliefs, began to meet quietly to plot their own strategy. Some, such as Washington, D.C., House delegate Walter Fauntroy, Georgia House member Julian Bond, and Manhattan Borough president Percy Sutton, were elected officials. Others, like Vernon Jordan and the Reverend Jesse Jackson, had emerged from the civil rights movement to lead notable organizations—in Jackson's case, the Chicago-based Operation Breadbasket (soon to be Operation Push). A key figure was black nationalist Amiri Baraka, who at that time saw the wisdom of amassing black political strength to influence organized electoral politics, perhaps through a third party. At an important, well-attended, and closed September meeting in Northlake, Illinois, discussion coalesced around two possible approaches to the coming election. Bond urged presidential primary runs by African American native sons or "daughters" in states with large black voting blocs. Such an approach might attract a healthy turnout of black voters and permit the accumulation of black delegate slates. At the convention those delegates, in turn, would increase African American leverage over the platform and the eventual nominee. Others argued that it would be better to mobilize behind one black presidential candidate, again with the goal of exerting force on the Democratic party. All agreed, in any case, with Baraka's idea of holding a large political convention of African Americans in Gary, Indiana, in March 1972.[78]

Chisholm declined to attend the Northlake meeting, sending her "chief political operative, Thaddeus Garrett," in her place. She later gave various reasons for her absence—usually emphasizing her expectation that the meeting would be unproductive and contentious. "I said to myself," she later recounted, "I don't have time for this foolishness. I knew what they were going to do." She anticipated that the men would emerge from endless heated discussion with "no plan, no unity and nothing agreed on except to hold more meetings." She also expected them to be hostile to her own presidential ambitions, which had begun taking shape in the summer of 1971.[79]

The first meeting of the National Women's Political Caucus in Washington, D.C., may have played a role in quickening Chisholm's thoughts about a presidential candidacy. The July gathering attracted national media attention with feminist leaders Gloria Steinem, Bella Abzug, Betty Friedan, and Chisholm herself in attendance. The goal of the organization was to increase women's political power, most notably by enlarging their representation in government. The caucus further issued a demand that women constitute 50 percent of all delegates to the 1972 Republican and Democratic national conventions. Friedan predicted such success for the endeavor that "it will not be a joke by 1976, the 200th anniversary of our Republic, that a woman might run for President." Her comment, and the launch of the caucus, led to a flurry of news stories speculating about the prospect of a female president. Even *Women's Wear Daily* chimed in with a squib entitled, "Lady Prez? Yez Yez! By '76, Trio Sez." "There may be a Bella Abzug, a Shirley Chisholm, or a Betty Friedan in the White House by 1976," it ventured. Chisholm delivered a tart rejoinder to news reports that President Nixon and his advisers had joked about the caucus meeting, laughing at a news photograph of Steinem, Friedan, Abzug, and Chisholm sitting together. They looked, one administration official opined, like a "burlesque." "We will indicate to them in 1972 what can happen when women get together," Chisholm told the *Amsterdam News.*[80]

Two weeks later, Chisholm announced publicly that she was "seriously considering" a run for president in 1972. After delivering a speech at a National Welfare Rights Organization meeting in Providence, Rhode Island, she told reporters that she had supporters "in very strategic positions in about 27 states" who were testing the waters for a Chisholm candidacy. How her campaign developed would depend, she asserted, on "what happens with the coalitions we are making in an effort to change the Democratic party." If things came together favorably, her bid might have a chance. And if the Democrats rejected her or advanced a candidate uninterested in the most compelling issues of the day, Chisholm offered that there was always the possibility of a third-party run. Described variously as "fiery" and a "pepperpot" in news coverage, Chisholm faced from that very first day skepticism that hers could be anything more than a symbolic campaign. The *Hartford Courant*'s headline "Black Woman May Run for President" captured the source of the incredulity. A Gallup poll released just days after Chisholm set out the bait, however, offered her some encouraging news. When asked if they would vote for a woman president, 66 percent of those surveyed answered affirmatively. And for the first time in the Gallup polls, a higher percentage of women than men endorsed the idea of a woman president. Indeed, support among women for a female president had risen by 18 percent in just two years. Overall enthusiasm for a woman president had more than doubled since the question was first posed in 1937.[81]

Chisholm was far less certain in July about a presidential run than her bold statements suggested. *She* was testing the waters at the Providence press conference. The reality, she later explained, was that she had "no money to finance a campaign" and could not countenance attempting to raise funds if it "would all be wasted." For all the encouragement she was receiving from women, college students, and average citizens, she noted, "I knew what I would be getting into. Into debt, for one thing." She also "knew, as my would-be supporters did not, what a controversy my candidacy would stir up in the black community, between blacks and other groups, and within the Democratic Party."[82]

Signs of discord surfaced immediately. Her colleague in the Congressional Black Caucus Representative John Conyers of Michigan began publicly promoting Mayor Carl Stokes of Cleveland for president in mid-September. The goal of such a campaign, he stated, would be to "create a black caucus with increased bargaining power at the 1972 Democratic National Convention." Conyers called upon all black Democrats to rally around the mayor, despite Stokes's repeated statements that he had no interest in being a candidate.

After the September Northlake meeting, Conyers went further. He revealed that he shared the discomfort other attendees felt that Chisholm was more likely to be "the candidate of women" than "the candidate of blacks." As another "male politician" put it, "when the deal goes down and she has to negotiate away something, is it going to be the interests of blacks or the interests of women that are hurt?" (It is unclear what the issue was thought to be that might fundamentally divide *all* African Americans and *all* women or how African American women figured in the syllogism.) Some "black politicians," the *Washington Post* reported, were very direct in stating that they believed Chisholm's sex alone disqualified her—at least for this election. "In this first serious effort by blacks for high political office," one asserted, "it would be better if it were a man."[83]

Thad Garrett, Chisholm's staff assistant, forcefully rebuked such comments, as did Representative Ron Dellums of California, her colleague in the Congressional Black Caucus and an early supporter. Rejecting the notion that Chisholm could be either black *or* a woman in her loyalties, Garrett emphasized: "She is a black woman, of the black experience, and from one of the blackest districts in the country, Bedford-Stuyvesant. She can do nothing but be black in her dealings." Dellums likewise rejected any talk that Chisholm's sex disqualified her. On the contrary, he maintained, "she could have a dramatic effect on the politics of the country," though he suggested that her run would be most effective in laying the groundwork for a ticket in 1976 "that could win." (By December Dellums was promising to support Chisholm for president "until hell freezes over.") Garrett underscored the seriousness of Chisholm's intentions: "Our goal right now is 1600 Pennsylvania Ave., and nothing less." If her critics thought their doubts would discourage the candidate, they did not know the congresswoman very well. By late September, she announced that she would enter the race officially on New Year's Day—and run in several primaries—if she had raised $100,000 by then.[84]

Tensions over Chisholm's candidacy among some

African American activists continued to be publicly aired after her preliminary announcement. Members of the Congressional Black Caucus, it was reported in October, were steering clear of "either supporting or opposing her." Her "bid," one male politician confessed off the record to the *Wall Street Journal,* "has left male egos bleeding all over the floor." An appearance by Chisholm at a Black Expo that Operation Breadbasket organized in Chicago ratcheted up the strain. The congresswoman, invited to speak at a "women in politics" workshop, overheard a group of well-dressed, "middle aged" African American men, whom she took to be "politicians," mutter about her as she passed by. "There she is—that little black matriarch who goes around messing things up," she remembered them saying. Chisholm rewarded the comment with a "hard stare," saving her fury till she reached the podium. There she lit in to her "black brothers, who I know are not going to endorse me." She went on to say that she neither expected their support nor solicited it, having "learned too much for too long in my dealings with politicians, black and white." "Prisoners of their traditional attitudes," "wounded in their male egos," and victims of "male vanity at work," such men, she charged, "would never endorse me." The only endorsements that mattered to her, Chisholm went on to say, were those "coming from just plain people." Although she ended her remarks on a conciliatory note—"Brothers, black women are not here to compete or fight with you"—she had defiantly staked out her independence.[85]

Worries that Chisholm would be driven by blind loyalty to her sex, or for that matter to her race, might have been assuaged had anyone examined closely her decision to back Senator Harold Hughes of Iowa, a white male, over Patricia Harris, an African American, for an important post on the Democratic National Committee (DNC) that fall. Hughes had been a prime mover in efforts to liberalize the rules of the party after 1968. In October, the senator sought election as chair of the all-important credentials committee, which would adjudicate how those key rules were enforced at the national convention. Larry O'Brien, chair of the DNC, seeking to leash the reform wing of the party, promoted Harris, a prominent Washington attorney with ties to Hubert Humphrey, for the post instead. Chisholm not only supported but nominated Hughes, stressing that the matter involved "not personalities" but whether the DNC would in fact carry out its promised reforms. Almost unanimously, white Southerners voted for Harris, a preference that led a *Boston Globe* reporter to suggest that "when the Southern regulars vote for a black candidate . . . it can only mean one thing: That they believe she can be controlled in some manner by the regulars." Chisholm accused the DNC "establishment" of advancing Harris as a "ploy to embarrass black committeemen." To those who criticized her support for a white male over an African American female, Chisholm had this comment: "They don't understand power. God gave me a brain and I'm using it." She was, nonetheless, gracious in defeat when Harris prevailed over Hughes and took pains to explain that she believed Harris would serve honorably.[86]

The prospect of a presidential campaign daunted Chisholm despite her bravado. She knew, she would later write, that "I could not win." Her effort was hamstrung from the outset by the crushing burden imposed in financing a national campaign. In her previous runs for state office, and even in her congressional battle, Chisholm had compensated for her paltry war chest "by sheer effort." She had "beaten a better-known and well-financed Republican candidate" when she bested Farmer. And she had done it by enlisting a dedicated cadre of volunteers, many of them women, and by pounding the pavement. "Translating that approach into a campaign for national office was obviously ridiculous," she admitted.[87]

Truer words were never said. In 1972, modest legislative changes signed into law by President Nixon set ceilings on the amount an individual presidential candidate could "personally" devote to his or her own campaign ($50,000) and the amount the campaign could expend on media coverage ($6 million). But the new law did not curb the cost of national elections. It only made more apparent, through new disclosure rules, how the costs of presidential races continued to career out of control. The McGovern and Nixon campaigns together would spend "over $100 million in the general election"—twice as much as their predecessors had paid out four years earlier. Furthermore, nominees needed vast sums of money just to make it to the convention: the front-runners in 1972 were expected to spend at least $1 million each in the primaries. The new reform rules of the Democratic party had encouraged a proliferation of presidential primaries. The number of such contests in both major parties soared, with more than twenty-three held in the 1972 race. Stretching from March to June, arrayed across the country, the primaries only augmented the financial drain on candidates.[88]

By the time Shirley Chisholm formally announced her run for president in late January 1972, she had nowhere near the $100,000 she hoped to have raised. Most of the contributions that flowed in from her supporters were in amounts of less than $10. When she began, she had "no idea what a bare-minimum campaign would cost," but with "filing fees, buttons and bumper stickers, postage, plane tickets, motels," she guessed that "a quarter of a million dollars was the rock-bottom amount I needed." In the end, Chisholm would spend almost $300,000 in a presidential run for which she raised under $120,000. It was a campaign, she later said, that "I would operate on my American Express card." A national media drive was "not even worth considering," she decided. "There was no way I would ever raise the millions that it would take." Instead, Chisholm would "leave fund-raising and spending to local groups in each state and city. They would be responsible for everything." Her campaign headquarters would rely on volunteers primarily and whatever national funds could be raised. These realities helped dictate Chisholm's choice of primaries. She would eventually choose Florida, Georgia, North Carolina, Massachusetts, New Jersey, Michigan, and California as among her best bets.[89]

Chisholm's formal entry into the race came on January 25, 1972, in an auditorium at Bedford-Stuyvesant's Concord Baptist Church. Among those crowded around the candidate on the stage were her old supporters and friends, Mac Holder and the staff of her Brooklyn congressional office, Manhattan Borough president Percy Sutton, Ron Dellums, Betty Friedan, and of course her husband. Conrad Chisholm looked over her protectively, as he would throughout his wife's campaign. In her forthright and engaging manner, Chisholm made a case for herself before the whirring television cameras. As she outlined her commitments to economic and social justice, she emphasized that she ran to be the candidate of all Americans. Chisholm also hoped to "repudiate the ridiculous notion that the American people will not vote for a qualified candidate simply because he is not white or because she is not a male. I do not believe that, in 1972, the great majority of Americans will continue to harbor such narrow and petty prejudices."[90]

That assertion did little to stanch the ink that would soon be spilled raising just those notions. A few days before her announcement an African American newspaper asked Chisholm if she really believed she was qualified to be president of the United States. "I am tremendously qualified," she answered without skipping a beat. "I am the only candidate not tied to corporate, banking, labor, or other big interests in this country. I am the only one supported by the common people. I am literally and figuratively a dark horse." The *New York Times* underscored her latter observation when it noted that she came into the race with "at least two strikes against her—her sex and her race."[91]

Chisholm would be surprised to learn that those strikes appeared to figure prominently even in the calculations of a few putative supporters as they surveyed the emerging candidates. Chisholm joined a crowded field in the primary race. Some fourteen other contenders would vie for the Democratic nomination, including another woman, Representative Patsy Mink of Hawaii. Liberals in Oregon had persuaded Mink to allow her name to appear on the primary ballot. She agreed, in part as a way of "establishing the right of women to aspire to the presidency" and to use her campaign to make the case for an end to the Vietnam

War. (Mink withdrew from the race in May.) Among the male front-runners were George McGovern, Hubert Humphrey, Edmund Muskie, George Wallace, and John V. Lindsay (now a Democrat). Feminists who had championed her bid in principle, much to Chisholm's dismay, sat on the fence once she entered the race.

No one seemed to irritate her more than Bella Abzug, fellow veteran of New York politics, colleague in the House of Representatives, and cofounder of the National Women's Political Caucus. After insisting upon appearing next to Chisholm when she repeated her official announcement at a Washington press conference, Abzug declined to endorse the candidate. "It was a letdown, and also bewildering," Chisholm later confessed. "If she intended to sit on the fence, why did she ask to appear with me when I made my announcement for the Presidency?" At a National Organization for Women meeting a few weeks after Chisholm declared her candidacy, Abzug entertained the crowd with visions of the White House under a Chisholm administration. But she again offered, a *New York Times* reporter noted, "no concrete endorsement" of the candidate she celebrated.

When Betty Friedan introduced Chisholm to the crowd on that same occasion, she repeated an odd remark that she had made a month earlier at the Bedford-Stuyvesant announcement event. "We will settle for no less than the Vice Presidency," Friedan said. The remark was not lost on the candidate. "I want to make unequivocally clear," Chisholm sternly began when she reached the stage, "that I am running for the Presidency of the United States. I don't want half-baked endorsements, I want whole-hearted people," she continued. "If you are going to be with me in a half-hearted fashion, don't come with me at all." Friedan would run as a Chisholm delegate from New York. But her hesitance reflected her loyalty to Eugene McCarthy, who was considering entering the race. Friedan later told Chisholm that she would campaign for her but wanted to campaign for McCarthy in states where the two were not competing against each other. Chisholm told her to choose. "Such a double endorsement," Chisholm explained, "would only enhance the problems I was having in being taken seriously as a candidate." Abzug "never offered to campaign for me," Chisholm bitterly recalled, "in Florida, North Carolina or even New York."[92]

Gloria Steinem also seemed to have trouble, or so Chisholm felt, getting fully behind the woman presidential candidate she lavishly praised. When the two women appeared on a Chicago television program the day before Chisholm officially entered the race, Steinem celebrated the prospect of her campaign. But she added: "I'm supporting both Shirley and McGovern. I don't think that's a conflict of interests. I feel he's the best white male candidate." This wasn't Chisholm's first exposure to Steinem's "hybrid endorsement." But it was the last she was going to tolerate. "Gloria," she said, "you're supporting either George McGovern or Shirley Chisholm. I don't mind if you are supporting George. If he is your candidate, so be it, but don't do me any favors by giving me this semi-endorsement. I don't need that kind of help." Eventually, Steinem "settled down in my corner," Chisholm noted. Steinem recently has described watching Chisholm deliver a televised speech she wrote for the candidate as "her proudest moment" in organized politics.[93]

Far more difficult for Chisholm to manage were the tensions among some of her most enthusiastic supporters. Although she saw herself as the leader of a new coalition politics, it proved difficult at times to make the ranks coalesce. "All of these different segments," Chisholm explained, "blacks, women, Chicanos and Puerto Ricans, were involved in a political campaign for the first time and they wanted to be number one in the campaign wherever I went in the country." Conflict between white women deeply involved with feminism, and indefatigable in their efforts to assist Chisholm, and equally committed African American volunteers especially vexed the candidate. "I had to spend time with them, trying to smooth things out, and with the feminists, trying to convince them that there was more to the campaign than their concerns," she recalled regretfully.[94]

These tensions would persist to the very end of

the campaign. Just three weeks before the Democratic National Convention the *Amsterdam News* criticized Chisholm for permitting Betty Friedan a prominent role in the campaign. Running as a Chisholm delegate in the Harlem/Westside 19th Congressional District, the newspaper claimed, Friedan had "insisted that she had a message for the women of Harlem and that she wanted to campaign there." African American Chisholm delegates on the slate "were equally insistent that the sisters uptown didn't need Betty's message." Friedan had "persisted" and "wore everyone down." Thus "on the last Saturday before" the June 20 New York primary, a press release touting Friedan's "journey to Harlem" promised a "Traveling Watermelon Feast." "Yes," the *News* reported, "Betty Friedan was coming to Harlem, band and all and to distribute watermelon to the natives. One of the sisters on the slate had to be restrained when she heard about this. She was on her way to Betty's house to straighten her out once and for all. . . . Well, the watermelons and Betty never got to Harlem." Such strife among the various groups committed to her exhausted Chisholm and weakened, she believed, the entire endeavor.[95]

It was a campaign that could not afford to be weakened. The strategy of placing so much responsibility on local groups to raise funds and organize events was midwifed by necessity. But chaos ruled without a highly experienced professional campaign staff coordinating the disparate parts of the operation. Lizabeth Cohen, an idealistic Princeton University junior who served as an intern in Chisholm's Washington headquarters, vividly recalls the air of anxiety and tension in the office. Running on a shoestring budget while short-staffed and trying to do advance work for a candidate who was on the road and not always easy to reach magnified the inevitable strains in any campaign. Chisholm admitted that "local jealousies and rivalries thrived" amid the confusion. Disasters—events canceled at the last minute, no-shows, and "chores left undone"—multiplied. While other candidates blew through Florida, for example, in "a six-car train," "a cavalcade of buses," or "a chartered airplane," Chisholm "went place to place in commercial airliners and volunteers' automobiles." Like Margaret Chase Smith, Chisholm also placed her duties in the House first. Throughout the primaries, she "tried to campaign without cutting seriously into the time" she spent in Washington "taking care of Congressional business." She would find, as did Smith, that her conscientiousness yielded few rewards in the presidential race.[96]

Despite these enormous liabilities, Chisholm pressed on, determined to take her message to those who hungered for a candidate who took clear stands, spoke directly, and conveyed the raw authenticity that the airbrushed politics of the media age had washed away. She baffled supporters in May after a would-be assassin shot George Wallace at point-blank range during a campaign appearance in Laurel, Maryland. Chisholm visited Wallace in the hospital to express her concern and sympathy. The gesture attracted widespread media attention and puzzled, to say the least, those who had followed Wallace's career as one of the most vitriolic segregationists of his day. Chisholm wanted to convey, in part, her belief that it was important in a democracy to respect contrary opinions without "impugning the motives" and "maligning the character" of one's opponents. To view it any other way, Chisholm argued, was to encourage "the same sickness in public life that leads to assassinations." Chisholm likewise refused to "disavow" the Black Panther party's endorsement of her candidacy. "The Black Panthers are citizens of the United States," she said, "and they have a right to endorse whomever they decide to endorse." In fact, she welcomed their support, expressing her admiration that such "an oppressed group" would wish to engage in the political process given the "meaningless platforms and empty promises" they had rightfully come to expect.[97]

The warmth and enthusiasm of the throngs she attracted carried Chisholm and convinced her she was making headway. But the energy of the crowds did not produce a similarly robust vote on election days. She trailed in primary after primary, winning a preferential but nonbinding "beauty contest" in New Jersey but no delegates there or in North Carolina, where she placed third but failed to meet the threshold required to secure delegates. She gathered two handfuls of delegates in Massachusetts and Minnesota but was "crushed" in Michigan, where George Wallace won handily. Sheer determination seemed to take Chisholm all the way to the final June California primary. It turned out to be one of the more bizarre chapters in her presidential campaign. She scored a victory outside the voting booth when she challenged the major television networks that excluded her from a series of debates between front-runners McGovern and Humphrey. Chisholm's campaign complained to the Federal Communications Commission without success that the congresswoman was being denied equal time. Four days before the primary, a Federal Appeals Court ordered the networks to rectify the mistake.[98]

As she campaigned in California, Chisholm became the victim of a dirty trick engineered by high officials in the Nixon administration. Donald Segretti, operating, he claimed, with the approval of Nixon White House appointments secretary Dwight Chapin, drew up a fake press release on stolen Humphrey campaign stationery. The goal of this, and similar though less extreme phony documents, was purportedly to "discredit front-running Democratic candidates." Chisholm was scarcely a front-runner in the final days of the primary season, and the depravity of the release was extreme, even by the standards employed by miscreants in the Nixon administration. Her status as a target perversely suggested that she had, indeed, achieved some success as a presidential candidate in garnering attention for the issues she sought to advance.

The release alleged that Chisholm, dressed "as a transvestite in men's clothing" and "hostile and aggressive," had been committed to a Virginia mental institution in the early 1950s after being diagnosed as schizophrenic. The physician who purportedly presided over her commitment "wrote that Rep. Chisholm makes facial grimaces, talks and gestures to herself, exhibits inexplicable laughter and weeping, and at times has an abnormal interest in urine and feces which she smears on walls and herself." Further contending that Chisholm remained under "periodic" psychiatric care, the document warned "the voters of the nation" so that they could make "an intelligent and meaningful choice . . . Black voters should be made aware of these facts as her strongest appeal is to them." Although none of the media outlets to which the press release was sent ever published its claims, it was widely circulated. When Chisholm learned of the document, she was extremely distraught by its cruelty and broke down in tears. Not until the Watergate investigations in the fall of 1973 would the press release be traced to the Nixon White House.[99]

Chisholm later charged that the press release had

further damaged her campaign. But she had come into California limping from a long, grueling, and uphill battle. She placed third in the primary and would have been entitled to twelve delegates but for the "winner take all" rule that governed the primary. "After more than six months of campaigning in eleven states," she had amassed only 28 delegates. Some "452 black delegates and alternates" would attend the convention in 1972—then the largest number of African Americans participating in the history of the Democratic party. Chisholm herself had never attended a national convention until the one in which her name was placed in nomination as president. Most African American delegates were, in the end, committed to George McGovern. During the convention, however, the release of Humphrey's black delegates to Chisholm and further horse trading resulted in her gaining additional support. Indeed, she would go on record as having accrued more delegate votes (just over 151) than any woman candidate until Hillary Clinton beat her record in 2008.[100]

That year a Washington correspondent for *The Nation* drew a straight line from Chisholm to Clinton. Chisholm, John Nichols wrote, "paved the way for Hillary Clinton and Barack Obama." Perhaps, he continued, "Clinton can now pave the way for the woman who will actually be both the Democratic nominee and the president." In fact, neither Chisholm nor any other female candidate could "pave the way" to the presidency. Institutional, political, and structural impediments required far more than a brave test candidate. Chisholm considered her "greatest achievement" that she "had the audacity and nerve to make a bid for the presidency of the United States." But she was, nonetheless, a realist about the enduring obstacles. When asked in 2002, less than three years before her death, how she wanted history to remember her, she replied: "not as the first black woman to have made a bid for the presidency of the United States." Instead, she hoped to be remembered as "a black woman who lived in the twentieth century and who dared to be herself. I want to be remembered as a catalyst for change in America."

Certainly Chisholm believed women's quest for the presidency would continue. "Brothers and sisters, at last I have reached this spot!" she exclaimed the night she was nominated for president in 1972. She would never run for president again. But she hoped, she later reflected, "in a broad sense, my campaign will continue. In fact, it is just beginning."[101]

EPILOGUE

2016

"I learned a lot from losing"—so Hillary Clinton would reflect several years after her defeat in the 2008 race for the Democratic party's presidential nomination. Her vantage point—four eventful years as secretary of state in her one-time rival's administration—had undoubtedly recast her perspective on the "painful end" to her historic presidential campaign. The journey through the primaries had been "grueling, heated, long and close." Indeed, less than 1 percent separated the votes cast for the defeated Clinton from those in favor of the winner, Barack Obama.

Clinton could take satisfaction in the many firsts she had achieved. She had transformed eight years as First Lady into a foundation for a remarkable political career. Campaigning for a United States Senate seat from New York in 2000 while her husband was still president, she breezed to victory in the Democratic primary and went on to beat her Republican rival decisively. She earned the respect of her colleagues and the loyalty of many constituents during her first Senate term. She won re-election easily. By 2008, just eight years after leaving the White House as First Lady, she had become a creditable presidential candidate in her own right. Indeed, she was the putative front-runner when she entered the 2008 presidential race. She piled up more votes in the primaries than any woman who had ever run for president—arguably more, in fact, than any male candidate of either party had *ever won* since such races began. It was not enough. Looking back, Clinton remembered how she had ended the campaign—"disappointed and exhausted."[1]

Neither state was apparent when Clinton conceded the race in June 2008. Surrounded by legions of her supporters, gathered under the vaulted ceiling of the National Building Museum, Clinton spoke of her gratitude, the campaign's achievements, and of its legacy. Each vote cast for her, she consoled the crowd, had made a difference. American democracy's "highest, hardest glass ceiling"—the one that kept American women from the presidency—now had "18 million cracks in it." "The light," she vowed, "is shining through like never before, filling us all with the hope and the sure knowledge that the path will be a little easier next time." That sentiment had also consoled Clinton's predecessors, Margaret Chase Smith and Shirley Chisholm. Victoria Woodhull too had imagined she would clear the way for future female presidential candidates. But here it was, nearly a century and a half later. Surely it was fair to ask: how much had changed?[2]

The answer—everything and nothing—was evident in Clinton's 2008 campaign. Clinton's bid alone, while still unusual, was evidence of change. In the decades after Shirley Chisholm's run, several women entered presidential races. Most Democratic and Republican aspirants crashed early between the Scylla of inadequate fundraising and the Charybdis of weak party support. Those who ran as third-party candidates struggled for recognition and legitimacy on the national stage. That stage was still firmly occupied by the two major political parties, however weakened they appeared to be by the candidate-centered dynamics and privately funded organizations that drove modern races.

For most women, and most men for that matter, financing remained *the* insurmountable hurdle to a presidential run. As primary contests proliferated, and the costs of technologically sophisticated, media-saturated, and professionally managed campaigns soared, it became ever more difficult to amass a war chest sizeable enough to sustain a long race. Doubts that they could ever prevail in a general election made this obstacle especially difficult for female candidates. Donors often considered them a poor bet—"unelectable" in the parlance of party politics. And why wouldn't they? No woman, of whatever merits, had yet managed to mount an aggressive, well-funded, and highly competitive race for a major party's nomination, however one understood the obstacles that stood in their way.

Several women after Chisholm found this out the hard way. Colorado Representative Patricia Schroeder's three-month campaign in 1987 had felt like a walk on a "high wire without a net." Then in her eighth congressional term, Schroeder sat on the powerful House Armed Services Committee throughout and was recognized for her expertise on defense. She also earned a reputation as the "forceful doyenne of American liberals." Nonetheless, her late entry into a crowded field of Democratic candidates invited pundits to deploy an irresistible sobriquet, one that had also once been applied to Margaret Chase Smith—she too was "Snow White" among "the Seven Dwarfs." As a congresswoman, Schroeder sought to advance "women's issues," including reproductive rights, expanded provisions for child care, workplace equity, the ERA, and improvements in women's health care, among other causes. Her identification with such concerns led her to be asked often as a presidential candidate if she planned to "run as a woman." She would reply: "Do I have a choice?" In the end, she found it impossible to mount an effective campaign for a more tangible reason. "The bottom line is, the money's not there," she concluded before leaving the race.[3]

In 2000, Republican Elizabeth Dole, who showed much promise in early polls, arrived at a similar verdict. Her opponents, George W. Bush and millionaire Steve Forbes, held a "75 to 1, or 80 to 1 cash advantage," Dole observed. "I can handle 2 to 1, or even 10 to 1, but not 80 to 1," she admitted as she ended her campaign. She spoke eloquently and pointedly about the overwhelming disadvantage at which "inadequate funding" placed a presidential campaign—limiting staff hires, curtailing communication, and restricting travel. "Wherever you go," Dole explained, "you find yourself answering questions not so much about guns in the classroom, or China in the World Trade Organization, but money in the bank and ads on the airwaves." (Dole had taken a strong, and controversial, stance in favor of gun control.) It was a disappointing outcome for a woman with a "glittering resume," including posts as secretary of labor and secretary of transportation in two presidential administrations. Dole, who credited women especially with supporting her campaign, expressed the customary hope that she "had paved the way for the person who will be the first woman president."

The metaphor of "paving the way" ill suited the realities. Echoing Schroeder's precise language a decade earlier, Dole had described the most intractable barrier she faced: "the bottom line, money." Political action committees dedicated to advancing women in electoral politics, including Emily's List, founded in 1985, and the Wish List, created in 1992, would make a critical difference for aspiring women candidates. But neither was then focused on presidential politics. Four years after Dole's run, former senator Carol Moseley Braun, the first African American woman elected to the Senate, would cite "name recognition and funds" as the Achilles heel of her brief 2004 presidential candidacy. So prodigious was the burden of fundraising that one reporter speculated, presciently, after Elizabeth Dole abandoned the 2000 race: "the woman who does make the history she sought to forge will have to begin the walk to 1600 Pennsylvania Avenue many years, rather than many months, before Election Day."[4]

Nonetheless, the entry of such women into the arena, as Victoria Woodhull, Margaret Chase Smith, and Shirley Chisholm all had hoped, did indeed dent the appearance of mainstream presidential politics as an exclusively male domain. Women presidential candidates, though unsuccessful, were no longer exotic by the time Hillary Clinton joined the 2008 race. Their presence, in a sense, evolved predictably from women's growing visibility in national politics and public life. Presidential ambitions are most often nurtured as politicians rise in elective office. Over the last century, most presidents have emerged from the vice presidency, the Senate, or governorships. Women have enjoyed full voting rights for less than a hundred years in the United States. They thus entered the presidential pipeline slowly. Today women remain far behind men in their representation in American politics. Yet when Hillary Clinton began her campaign for the presidency, she occupied a vastly different political landscape than had her earliest predecessors.

The contrast with the political world inhabited by Shirley Chisholm just thirty-six years earlier captures the story. In 2008, Clinton had seventeen women colleagues in the United States Senate; nine women served as their states' governors. Nearly eighty women held seats in the House of Representatives. Shirley Chisholm, by contrast, was one of just a dozen women in the House in 1972; Margaret Chase Smith was the only woman in the Senate when Chisholm entered the presidential race. There were then no women governors. Both Democrats and Republicans took measures in the 1970s and thereafter to increase women's presence within each party's apparatus, as delegates and in leadership positions. These were not acts of charity. Women themselves exerted increasing pressure on the parties to address the lack of diversity.[5]

Their demands gained force in no small measure from the gender gap that began to be apparent from the 1980 presidential election. Until that point, no dramatic differences consistently divided women's and men's voting preferences for a specific candidate. But in 1980 a gender gap emerged in male and female re-

231

sponses to Ronald Reagan, with men 8 percent more likely to vote for the California governor than women. That discrepancy would persist in subsequent elections. Indeed, from 1980 to 2012 a gender gap ranging from a low of 4 percent (1992) to a high of 11 percent (1996) would be evident in presidential elections. More women than men also identified themselves as Democrats than Republicans over a similar period. These trends influenced both major political parties to cultivate women voters. Although uneven in their effects, such efforts involved an appeal to women voters and a recognition of their centrality in the electorate. Public resistance to the idea of a woman president, if the polls could be believed, also declined sharply over the same period—years in which the women's movement did much to alter expectations and realities.[6]

Hillary Clinton's 2008 bid for the presidency thus reflected very modern developments. Indeed, as a young woman Clinton had herself lived through the sea change in women's experience that drove these broader trends. A graduate of Wellesley College (1969) and of Yale Law School (1973), she belonged to a generation of privileged young women whose lives would be transformed by the modern women's movement. Unwilling to accept the constraints they believed had defined the lives of their mothers and grandmothers, they held high aspirations for their own lives and for the advancement of their sex. As commencement speaker at her college graduation, Clinton, College Government president and leader of the College Senate, unabashedly gave voice to her classmates' dream of seeking "human liberation." The goal of education, she offered, was "a liberation enabling each of us to fulfill our capacity" for action and creativity.[7]

Clinton would soon pursue the engaged life she idealized as a college student. After law school, she worked for the Children's Defense Fund and served as a staff member on a House advisory committee appointed to investigate President Nixon's impeachment. When she moved to Arkansas for Bill Clinton, she became a law professor, directing a legal aid clinic that helped indigent clients and supervising students who were assisting prisoners. She was one of two women on the law faculty at the University of Arkansas. As her husband pursued his political ambitions, she joined an Arkansas law firm, advancing to senior partner. She remained a visible advocate for children's welfare, and was a cofounder of an Arkansas child advocacy group. She stayed active professionally while the wife of a sitting governor. The *National Law Journal* judged her one of the country's 100 most influential lawyers in 1988 and 1991. Early in her husband's first term as president, a British journalist wrote that "by any yardstick Hillary Clinton is a remarkable woman." Her "talents," he asserted, "would have made her a leading candidate for Attorney General in a Democratic administration headed by anyone other than her husband." Though the claim was hyperbolic, it reflected widespread recognition of her professional accomplishments.[8]

Yet for all her achievements, Clinton came to national attention initially because of her husband. This was the other side of the equation—one that invoked a far more traditional aspect of women's political experience. Indeed, it reached back to the widow's (or at times wife's or favored daughter's) mandate that through marriage catapulted women such as Margaret Chase Smith over high hurdles into national politics. Hillary Clinton brought an impressive resume to the White House when she entered as First Lady. But she arrived and became familiar to the American public first as the wife of the president, not as a political figure in her own right. No woman who got anywhere in a major political party advanced without the support of powerful men. But marriage as an entry point to American political life remained both an advantageous and a perilous route for women, as Clinton herself would discover.

The tension quickly became apparent in Bill Clinton's race for the 1992 Democratic party's presidential nomination. By all accounts, the Arkansas governor was proud of his wife's achievements. "I had always believed she had as much (or more) potential to succeed in politics as I did," Bill Clinton remembered of their early years together. He often praised her talents. Indeed, he suggested that if he won the presidency, voters would benefit from having two Clintons in the White House. An early reference to the pair as a team surfaced in January 1992, just three months into Clinton's primary race. Rumors about the governor's sexual indiscretions were already roiling the campaign. In an effort to rebut these claims, Clinton advanced, one journalist noted, "his attractive and powerful-speaking wife to the forefront of his campaign" at a stop in Bedford, New Hampshire.

At the Bedford Town Hall gathering, Mrs. Clinton forthrightly admitted that the couple had had their difficulties. But she asked: "Is anything about our marriage, which has lasted for 16 years in the fishbowl of a very small state, and gone through eight elections, is anything about it as important to the people of New Hampshire as whether they have the chance to keep their own families together in this recession?" The question played well and the crowd "constantly interrupted" the candidate's wife with "echoing cheers and applause." "Several of them commented as they left the hall that maybe the Clinton family was running the wrong candidate," the journalist reported. After his wife's remarks, Bill Clinton memorably offered, "'Now you know why my slogan is, "Buy one Clinton, and get another one free."'" Mrs. Clinton reiterated the comment in mid-March when the couple spoke at her former suburban Chicago high school. "People call us two-for-one," she said, likening herself and her husband to a "blue plate" special.[9]

Critics soon seized on this self-description to attack both Clintons and to cast (further) doubt on the Arkansas governor's suitability for the White House. If there is any office that appears more solitary in its essence than the American presidency, one would be hard-pressed to find it. Unsurprisingly, even a feint at the idea of sharing its awe-inspiring power and responsibility, whatever the gender politics, fueled a ready backlash. (Jimmy Carter ran into a similar buzz saw when he supported his wife's desire to sit in on cabinet meetings.) Noting that Mrs. Clinton's assertiveness made her a "polarizing" figure, one high-ranking Republican official elaborated on the vulnerability: "It's not that she's an accomplished modern woman. It's just that she's grating, abrasive and boastful. There's a certain familiar order of things, and the notion of a co-equal couple in the White House is a little offensive to men and women."

The flames were fanned when Hillary Clinton responded to charges impugning her integrity leveled by former California governor Jerry Brown, also a candidate in the Democratic race. In a mid-March televised debate, Brown suggested that Hillary Clinton's legal work in Arkansas involved conflicts of interest and ethical violations. Governor Clinton angrily rejected the charge, adding that Brown was not fit to share a stage with his wife. A day later, when a reporter suggested to Mrs. Clinton that she ought to have paid more attention to appearances, she responded tartly. "I suppose I could have stayed home and baked cookies and had teas," she replied, "but what I decided to do was fulfill my profession, which I entered before my husband was in public life."[10]

The "tea and cookies" comment dropped a depth charge into the already turbulent waters of the campaign. It made irresistible copy, sparked widespread media coverage, and fed persistent suspicion among some about Hillary Clinton. To her critics, Mrs. Clinton exemplified professional women of unbridled ambition and callous indifference who had denigrated women who devoted their energies full time to their families. Other detractors pounced upon the comments as further evidence that Mrs. Clinton herself harbored political aspirations, hungered for power, and planned to use the White House as a base of operations. Was she "Lady Macbeth in a black preppy headband" or simply a First Lady who hailed from a new generation?[11]

Much press and air time was devoted to debating the question. As a professional woman, Mrs. Clinton had a past that was accessible to those intent on investigating it. When the Clintons themselves invoked the "two for one" idea, they opened the door, in the eyes of some, for the press to scrutinize the potential future First

Lady as minutely as the candidate—her husband. Mrs. Clinton would later remember "the 'buy one, get one free' comment" as a sobering episode in the primary race. "I hadn't had enough exposure to the national press corps," she admitted, "to fully appreciate the extent to which the news media was a conduit for everything that happened on a campaign." She understood that she "represented a fundamental change in the way women functioned in our society," regardless of what role she might or might not play in a Bill Clinton presidential administration. Letters "demonizing" Hillary Clinton "as a woman, mother and wife" poured forth; the criticism, she recalled, was "venomous."[12]

The concerns were not allayed when five days after his inauguration President Clinton appointed his wife to lead an initiative to overhaul the American health care system. The decision created an uproar, with the new president learning, as he put it, "when it came to the First Lady's role, it seemed Washington was more conservative than Arkansas." "This is a test of the national psyche," the *New York Times* editorialized. "Millions of citizens will feel threatened by Mrs. Clinton's assertiveness. Others will have questions about the propriety of an unelected, unsalaried person with no formal portfolio exercising authority by virtue of marriage." According to the *Washington Post,* Hillary Clinton had been "carrying a heavy burden over the last year" because she was "the quintessential transitional figure." She stood in the crosshairs of an ongoing argument about women's roles that had unfolded over thirty years, it asserted, and that had left many uncomfortable with the uncertainties change had produced. Although other First Ladies made their influence felt in their husband's administrations, most did so privately and informally. No one before Mrs. Clinton had been officially appointed to such a central policy position. Quoting an Arkansas business leader who judged Mrs. Clinton "as smart as a treeful of owls," the *Wall Street Journal* reported that the rest of the country was not so enthusiastic. Nearly half of those polled opposed her involvement in "major policy decisions."[13]

The Clinton administration's health care initiative sparked a fierce debate, as had every previous effort to reform the American health care system. Critics denounced the Clinton plan, "Hillarycare," as some opponents dubbed it, in the same terms that others had characterized the Truman administration's efforts—as "socialized medicine." Charges that the task force was conducting its deliberations in secrecy heightened public concern about the endeavor and its chairwoman. When Mrs. Clinton toured the country making the case for the new legislation her task force formulated— a bill over 1,300 pages long—she was met by crowds of protesters. So angry was the mood, and so pointed was the enmity toward Clinton herself at these demonstrations, that she agreed to the Secret Service's insistence that she wear a bullet-proof vest. The bill gained little traction in Congress and the initiative was dead by the midterm elections. Its failure, and thus Clinton herself, were widely blamed for contributing to the catastrophic losses the Democrats suffered in the House of Representatives. That same year, Special Prosecutor Kenneth Starr began a far-ranging and widely reported investigation of the Clintons' role in a failed Arkansas land investment company, the Whitewater Development Corporation. As it spun out, the inquiry further damaged Mrs. Clinton's standing with the public. In January 1996, she "received the lowest rating of any First Lady in modern history."[14]

Ironically, she would more than regain that lost esteem amid the 1998 impeachment proceedings against her husband. When Starr's investigation uncovered a relationship between the president and a White House intern, the Clintons' marriage once again became a focus of embarrassing public and political attention. It was an excruciating chapter in the Clinton presidency, and a wrenching experience, both would attest, for the couple personally. The Clinton presidency and marriage survived it. Indeed, Mrs. Clinton's stoicism and steadfastness during what she later described as "the most devastating, shocking, and hurtful experience of my life" earned widespread admiration. Nearly 70 percent of Americans viewed her favorably in late December 1998 after the president was impeached in the

House of Representatives. She was then the woman Americans admired most in the world, according to the Gallup Poll. (The "four least liked news figures" in 1998 were Saddam Hussein and three women tied to Bill Clinton and his impeachment—Linda Tripp, Paula Jones, and Monica Lewinsky.) Although approval of Mrs. Clinton had moderated by the end of her husband's presidency, she remained very popular, with nearly 60 percent of the public rating her favorably. Women especially admired the First Lady, as had been true throughout her husband's term of office.[15]

In a widely viewed *60 Minutes* television interview in the 1992 campaign, Hillary Clinton memorably insisted that she was not "some little woman standing by my man like Tammy Wynette." Yet at the political nadir of her husband's presidency Clinton had done just that. Throughout her years as First Lady, Hillary Clinton remained an outspoken advocate of women's and children's rights, as she traveled the world on behalf of the administration. She also remained committed to her "domestic policy agenda," an array of concerns that included improving early childhood education, widening access to child care, supporting family and medical leave, and advancing women's and children's economic security, which she pursued more quietly after the original health care initiative blew up. Given those commitments, critics harboring wildly diverging views of feminism deemed her apparent willingness to forgive her husband hypocrisy. In the end, however, her personal resilience and her decisions as a wife and mother, while in the highly visible role of First Lady, apparently most burnished her credentials with the public. On the surface, it was a startling turnabout for a woman who had entered the arena of national politics as an avatar for a new generation. But her experience reflected, in some measure, the complexities that accompanied the grown-up lives of women, and men, across generations, or so most Americans appeared to believe.[16]

For all that she had endured, Hillary Clinton did not seem eager to leave political life when she and her husband neared the end of their White House years. On the contrary, in 1999, she began to mull a run for political office. She set her sights on retiring New York senator Daniel Patrick Moynihan's seat. Many close friends and advisers discouraged her from this undertaking. Among other challenges, she would face a "spouse problem." Some believed her husband would inevitably loom over her candidacy, making it impossible for her to establish her own political identity. Clinton herself recognized that "a fine line would have to be drawn between asserting myself as a candidate in my own right and taking advantage of the President's support and advice."

In fact, the line inevitably proved porous. Her high national profile and unique situation conferred extraordinary advantages, of course. From the moment she announced her plan to pursue a race, the First Lady became, the *New York Times* observed, "the center of the kind of attention that is unheard of in a race for the United States Senate—or even in the early days of a race for President." She was able to draw on a deep bench of Clinton loyalists—Democratic party power brokers, political experts, operatives, and donors—amassed over her husband's two campaigns for the White House and an eight-year presidential administration. At the six-month mark, the national Democratic party had already poured some $3 million into Clinton's New York Senate race—far more than it had deployed to any other senatorial candidate.[17]

But Clinton also faced a ferocious national effort by Republicans determined to block her advance. The prospect of Mrs. Clinton's election to the Senate served as a rallying cry. "It's going to take more than a village to defeat Hillary Clinton," the chairman of Alabama's Republican Committee exhorted donors. "Let's rid our nation once and for all of Bill and Hillary Clinton. We must get them out of our lives and into the Democrat's scrapbooks forever." Calls to "pillory Hillary" tapped a deep reservoir of anti-Clinton sentiment among conservatives. Opponents pointed to a trail of scandals that had dogged the First Lady and the president. From "Travelgate" (charges that cronyism prompted the Clintons to terminate White House Travel Office employees) to Whitewater to impeachment, there was no shortage of material. Nor was the strategy new to Mrs. Clinton's race for the New York Senate; both Clintons had been similarly invoked to rally the Republican base for nearly a decade. However, a "scary" new prospect now loomed on the horizon for those determined to derail a Clinton victory—"Imagine four years from now—'Hillary for President.'" A New York State Republican party leader who welcomed the national interest of anti-Clinton groups in the local race noted, "We feel she is only coming up here to run for President."[18]

Clinton won the Senate election, however, by focusing intently on New York. She campaigned especially hard in the cities, towns, and rural areas upstate, where she did surprisingly well in an area traditionally seen as conservative. Her issues-oriented approach appealed to voters, many of whom expressed little interest in the relentless press attention to the Clinton administration scandals. "One of the odd advantages I had," Mrs. Clinton later reflected, "was that everyone already thought they knew everything about me, good or bad. [Republican opponent Rick] Lazio's attacks were old news." It was, indeed, an unexpected payout from eight years of scrutiny, much of it negative, while her husband occupied the White House. The public needed no introduction to Mrs. Clinton. She also carried with her the cachet of her status as First Lady. New Yorkers who had never met a senator never mind the wife of a sitting president came out to greet her. On election day, Clinton drew handsomely on the loyalty of traditional Democratic voters. The unions mobilized on her behalf. African Americans turned out and gave her 90 percent of their votes. The huge statewide vote for Al Gore in the presidential race boosted Clinton as well.

In the end, she benefited especially from the enthusiasm of women. A gender gap had accompanied Mrs. Clinton through much of her career as a national political figure before she ever ran for any office. Women liked her more than men, and nowhere was this more true in the fall of 2000 than in New York. Exit polls indicated that women made up 54 percent of the voters—and 60 percent of them cast their ballots for Clinton. "Dinner party evidence"—the often "passionate denunciations of the first lady by professional women at social events in Manhattan"—proved spurious. In the end, these voters largely came home, as did women upstate, who voted for Clinton over Lazio by 55 percent to 43 percent. There was no consensus among pundits about why women were drawn to Clinton. Perhaps, one journalist speculated, she was never as disliked as media accounts repeatedly suggested. Some women had certainly taken umbrage when Representative Lazio whipped out a sheet of paper during a televised debate and demanded that Clinton sign a pledge to forgo soft campaign money. A retired nurse interviewed after the election seemed to speak for other working women when she decried Lazio's action. "He shoved this thing in her face and I got very offended. . . . I felt if she were a man he wouldn't have done that." It was possible, according to one account, that despite the extraordinary trajectory of her life other women identified "with her struggles" and could see "some of themselves in her."[19]

The day after she won the Senate race, Hillary Clinton began, as the *New York Times* described it, a "remarkable transition." She emerged from a "quarter-century of derivative power as a political spouse to a potent force in her own right." Clinton herself felt the shift profoundly. "After eight years with a title but no portfolio," she later wrote, "I was now 'Senator-Elect.'" Speculation about a presidential run in her future began immediately. At her first postelection news conference, Clinton was asked if she planned to run for president four years hence. She "briskly" dispatched the question with a negative. Gore's defeat in the 2000 race, however, inevitably heightened expectations that she would emerge as "perhaps the most important Democrat in the country." In fact, she kept her promise to remain in her position as New York's senator for her entire term, winning re-election handily in 2006.[20]

Hillary Clinton came into the Senate with floodlights upon her. But although she was the "celebrity senator," she refused to behave like a celebrity among her colleagues. She "aggressively avoids the spotlight and intentionally holds back," one Southern senator observed. That approach earned her the warmth and regard of many in the chamber. Unlike the rebellious and outspoken Shirley Chisholm, she also took pains to conform to the hierarchical rules of the institution and to earn by compliance with tradition the respect of senior members and the public. Her posture more closely resembled the approach of Margaret Chase Smith, at least to outward appearance. Clinton did not, however, follow the Maine senator's storied political independence and stance toward her party. Smith had carved out a place for herself in the Senate and the Republican party as an unpredictable force despite outward signs of decorum and cooperation. Senator Clinton worked hard and paid close attention to the concerns of her varied New York constituents. She also cultivated alliances across the aisle even as she invested thoroughly, both literally and figuratively, in the Democratic party. In 2002, her generous donations of time and money to Democrats running for re-election won her loyalty, admiration, and indebtedness. Within two years of leaving the White House as First Lady, Senator Clinton had become "her party's single best fundraising draw, a source of advice to candidates, a partisan cheerleader . . . and the only Democrat, other than perhaps her husband, who can pack a room."[21]

Clinton's willingness to compromise and modify her own positions while in the Senate would give rise to harsh criticism from progressives who felt betrayed by her move to the center. She had characterized herself as a "new Democrat" during the New York Senate campaign, underscoring her identification with fiscal responsibility and her support for the economic well-being of the middle class. To conservatives and their arch-enemies alike she appeared a chameleon, quick to adopt whatever camouflage best suited her political purposes. She remained a "polarizing figure" nationally as Republicans continued to invoke her as the exemplar of all that had been wrong with the Clinton administration and the Democratic party more generally. But she retained strong support among Democrats and among women. Even women who identified themselves as Republicans or independents viewed her more favorably than did men in their respective political camps.[22]

Senator Clinton's 2002 vote authorizing President George W. Bush to use military force in Iraq proved especially controversial. It would come back to haunt her in the 2008 Democratic primary campaign when support for the war that ensued had withered. Clinton joined roughly half of her Democratic colleagues in the Senate, and a heavy majority overall, in backing the Iraq War resolution. But she broke with more liberal members of her party, including Senator Ted Kennedy, who rejected the measure as rash and ill-advised. Some speculated that Clinton had presidential ambitions in mind when she endorsed the Iraq War. *New York Times* columnist Maureen Dowd explicitly accused Clinton of that calculation shortly before the October 2002 Senate vote. Citing a recent *USA Today* poll indicating that 40 percent of women did not expect to see a woman elected president within the next decade and 14 percent doubted that it would ever happen, Dowd posed the following question: "Are those 14 percent unaware of the Clintonian relentlessness of the junior senator from New York?" Clinton's verbal support for President Bush's threats of military action against Saddam Hussein, Dowd suggested, were "the latest sign that she is running for president in 2008." Senator Clinton, Dowd continued, "knows that any woman who hopes to be elected president cannot have love beads in her jewelry case."[23]

Like Margaret Chase Smith before her, Clinton demonstrated support for American military intervention, a robust defense, and an array of heightened national security measures. Both women sought assignment to and served on the Senate Armed Services Committee. In so doing, they sharply distinguished themselves from the pacifist associations that had historically clung to women in public life. Their experience and commitments likewise addressed, at least in theory, whatever potential doubts existed among the public about a woman's capacity to serve as commander in chief. When vice-presidential nominee Geraldine Ferraro was asked on *Meet the Press* in 1984 whether she was "strong enough to push the nuclear button," she seized the opportunity to expose the assumption that women lacked suitability for the responsibilities of the American presidency. "I don't know if I were not a woman," Ferraro replied, "whether or not I would be asked questions like 'Are you strong enough to push the button.'"[24]

By 2007, public opinion polls indicated that at least in the case of Hillary Clinton such concerns had been assuaged. Clinton scored higher by a wide margin than either Barack Obama or John Edwards when queried about each candidate's potential to excel as commander in chief. She had then emerged as a leading figure— the Democratic front-runner by most accounts—in the impending 2008 presidential race.[25]

Clinton owed that status to a remarkable convergence of forces that made her uniquely well situated to come within striking distance of the presidency. Less radical than Woodhull, she had nonetheless been supported in her aspirations by a women's movement whose origins reached back into the nineteenth century. She had benefited from the challenges Shirley Chisholm and other dedicated feminists, civil rights activists, and radicals of her era had posed to the Democratic party. She had parlayed the traditional role of First Lady into a long, and admittedly turbulent, courtship with the American people, who came to know her as the bright, embattled, and ultimately resilient wife of an enduringly popular, despite his many difficulties, two-term president. She had then shown the mettle to compete for national office in a political climate in which she was variously bloodied, mocked, and celebrated. Her access to money, power, and patronage was unrivaled for a female candidate in the twentieth century. It was still not enough in 2008. But in defeat, she joined her opponent's administration. And in so doing, she gained experience in a cabinet post that had led six previous secretaries of state—Thomas Jefferson, James Madison, James Monroe, John Quincy Adams, Martin Van Buren, and James Buchanan—to the presidency.

The 2008 contest between Hillary Clinton and Barack Obama, in some sense, brought the story of women's quest for the American presidency full circle from its origins during Reconstruction. When Barack Obama entered the presidential race in February 2007, he was the only African American serving in the United States Senate. As the twentieth century closed, only four black senators had preceded him since Hiram Revels (R-Mississippi) broke the color barrier in 1870 during Reconstruction. It was a year after Revels' election, when Victoria Woodhull had described "the spirit of this age" of Reconstruction as one of "unbounded emancipation." She imagined an ongoing revolution that would extend the voting rights newly conferred on African American men to all American women.

Another half-century would pass before Woodhull's

dream of women's voting rights would be realized. The vindication of political liberties guaranteed to African Americans would take much longer. Less than fifty years before Obama's race for the presidency, African Americans were still being systematically denied the right to vote in various parts of the country. A century after Reconstruction, an act of Congress—the Voting Rights Act of 1965—was required to remove constraints against the exercise of this basic democratic freedom. Complaints of voter suppression would arise in the 2008 election.[26]

If the promise of equality had proved elusive, both the Clinton and the Obama candidacies were testaments to the imperfect fruits of a long struggle. Like Shirley Chisholm, Obama was the unlikely offspring of an old Democratic urban political machine that once controlled party politics. Chisholm had been more radical; he would be triumphant. Nonetheless, neither Obama nor Clinton would have even been in the running were it not for the challengers who had preceded them. Among those relegated to the margins of party politics were women and men who refused to accept such limitations in a democracy. Sweeping movements over many decades had made both Obama's and Clinton's candidacies possible. Perhaps for that reason, neither standard-bearer would fully satisfy their varied constituencies. Some feminists complained in

2008 that although they wanted to see a woman president, they wanted someone other than Hillary Clinton. Through a long primary fight, a general election, and two terms as president, Barack Obama would still be buffeted by criticism on all sides for doing too much or too little for racial minorities. His election in 2008, nonetheless, was a watershed in the nation's turbulent, dramatic, moving, and still incomplete lurch toward racial progress.

Hillary Clinton stepped down as secretary of state in the winter of 2013. In April 2015, more than a year and a half in advance of the 2016 election, she announced her candidacy for the presidency. Although most Democrats greeted her run enthusiastically, her entry into the race reignited her opponents. Some progressives within her own party gravitated to Vermont senator Bernie Sanders. A crowded field sought the Republican party's nomination, including the conservative former Hewlett Packard executive Carly Fiorina, who like the radical Victoria Woodhull nearly a century and a half earlier emphasized her business acumen in making the case for her candidacy. All zeroed in on Clinton as the likely Democratic standard-bearer. They found unity at least in their full-throated opposition to the former secretary of state.

In the early months of the campaign, Clinton's admission that she maintained and used a private email

server while in the State Department unleashed renewed suspicions that built on an array of long-
standing accusations. Among the latter was the charge
that through a lack of oversight while secretary of state,
she had opened the door to the tragic deaths of the
American ambassador to Libya and three other Americans in Benghazi during a terrorist attack on September 11, 2012. Although an official report criticized State
Department practices and policies, it assigned no direct blame to Clinton herself. The secretary publicly
accepted responsibility for the diplomats' fate. Conservative House Republicans mounted an ongoing investigation that joined the email controversy to her tenure
at the State Department and the Benghazi tragedy. A
probe of tens of thousands of Clinton's emails ensued.
Her most vociferous critics charged that Clinton was
reckless, duplicitous, and perhaps even criminal in her
behavior as secretary of state. At a late October congressional hearing, she appeared in the House for
the second time to answer questions amid admission
by some Republican members that their inquiry was
driven in large part by the former secretary's bid for the
presidency. Clinton coolly dismissed their claims in a
grilling that lasted nine hours and left her, in the view
of most commentators, largely "unscathed." Some suggested, in fact, that conservative Republicans on the
committee had provided Clinton with an opportunity
to appear presidential.[27]

EPILOGUE: 2016

Would Clinton's renewed campaign for the presidency result in victory this time? Only time would tell. But there could be little doubt that no woman in American history had ever come closer. The quest was now a political contest.

NOTES
ACKNOWLEDGMENTS
INDEX

NOTES

Prologue

1. "Iron My Shirt," *New York Times,* January 7, 2008, available at http://thecaucus.blogs.nytimes.com/2008/01/07/iron-my-shirt/; "Sexist Hecklers Interrupt Hillary: 'Iron My Shirt!'" *Huffington Post,* March 28, 2008, available at http://www.huffingtonpost.com/2008/01/07/sexist-hecklers-interrupt_n_80361.html; "Postfeminism and Other Fairy Tales," *New York Times,* March 16, 2008, WK 1; "Hillary's Back," *Pittsburgh Post Gazette,* January 11, 2008, B7.

2. "A Woman President?" Presidential Gender Watch 2016, Center for Women and American Politics, available at http://presidentialgenderwatch.org/polls/a-woman-president/. There is a wide literature, across an array of fields, addressing women and the American presidency as well as women and electoral politics more broadly. Among the key studies are Jill Norgren, *Belva Lockwood: The Woman Who Would Be President* (New York: New York University Press, 2007); Erika Falk, *Women for President: Media Bias in Nine Campaigns,* 2nd ed. (Urbana: University of Illinois Press, 2010); Jo Freeman, *We Will Be Heard: Women's Struggles for Political Power in the United States* (Lanham, Md.: Rowman & Littlefield, 2008); Eleanor Clift and Tom Brazaitis, *Madam President: Shattering the Last Glass Ceiling* (New York: Scribner, 2000); Nichola D. Gutgold, *Paving the Way for Madam President* (Lanham, Md.: Lexington Books, 2006);

Anne E. Kornblut, *Notes from the Cracked Ceiling: What It Will Take for a Woman to Win* (New York: Broadway, 2011); Lori Cox Han and Caroline Heldman, *Rethinking Madam President: Are We Ready for a Woman in the White House?* (Boulder: Lynne Rienner Publishers, 2007); Marianne Schnall, *What Will It Take to Make a Woman President?* (Berkeley: Seal Press, 2013); Kristina Horn Sheeler and Karrin Vasby Anderson, *Woman President: Confronting Postfeminist Political Culture* (College Station: Texas A & M University Press, 2013); Janet M. Martin, *The Presidency and Women: Promise, Performance, and Illusion* (College Station: Texas A & M Press, 2003); Deborah Jordan Brooks, *He Runs, She Runs: Why Gender Stereotypes Do Not Harm Women Candidates* (Princeton: Princeton University Press, 2013); Jennifer L. Lawless and Richard L. Fox, *It Still Takes a Candidate: Why Women Don't Run for Office* (Cambridge: Cambridge University Press, 2010); Kristin A. Goss, *The Paradox of Gender Equality* (Ann Arbor: University of Michigan Press, 2013); Sue Thomas and Clyde Wilcox, *Women and Elective Office: Past, Present, and Future* (New York: Oxford University Press, 2014).

3. Harriet Beecher Stowe, *My Wife and I: Or Harry Henderson's History* (New York: J. B. Ford and Company, 1872), pp. 262–263. For an in-depth assessment of the gender dynamics of Hillary Clinton's 2008 run see Rebecca Traister, *Big Girls Don't Cry: The Election That Changed Everything for American Women* (New York: Free Press, 2010).

4. James T. Havel, *U.S. Presidential Candidates and the Elections: A Biographical and Historical Guide,* vol. 1, *The Candidates,* and vol. 2, *The Elections, 1789–1992* (New York: Macmillan, 1996). I am indebted to Nadia Fajood for her analysis of this data.

Victoria Woodhull

1. "The Correspondence between the Victoria League and Victoria C. Woodhull," in Madeleine B. Stern, ed., *The Victoria Woodhull Reader* (Weston, Ma.: M & S Press, 1974), no page numbers. According to Woodhull biographer Lois Beachy Underhill, Woodhull herself was the driving force in organizing the Victoria League and the Equal Rights Party for which she served as nominee. See Lois Beachy Underhill, *The Woman Who Ran for President: The Many Lives of Victoria Woodhull* (Bridgehampton, N.Y.: Bridge Works Publishing Co., 1995), pp. 163–167. On nineteenth-century political nomination practices, see Gil Troy, *See How They Ran: The Changing Role of the Presidential Candidate* (Cambridge, Ma.: Harvard University Press, 1996), pp. 17–18 and Chapters 4 and 5.

2. "Correspondence between the Victoria League and Victoria C. Woodhull"; Victoria C. Woodhull, Letter to the Editor, "The Coming Woman," *New York Herald,* April 2, 1870, p. 8; Morton Keller, *Affairs of State: Public Life in Nineteenth Century America* (Cambridge, Ma.: Harvard University Press, 1977), Chapter 1; Kate Masur, *An Example for All the Land: Emancipation and the Struggle over Equality in Washington, D.C.* (Chapel Hill: University of North Carolina Press, 2010), Chapter 5 esp.; Eric Foner, *Reconstruction: America's Unfinished Revolution, 1863–1877* (New York: Harper and Row, 1988), pp. 255–256; Ellen C. DuBois, "Outgrowing the Compact of the Fathers: Equal Rights, Woman Suffrage, and the United States Constitution, 1820–1878," *Journal of American History,* vol. 74, no. 3 (December 1987), pp. 844–847.

3. On the fate of Reconstruction, see Foner, *Reconstruction;* Kenneth M. Stampp, *The Era of Reconstruction, 1865–1877* (New York: Vintage, 1965); Steven Hahn, *A Nation under Our Feet: Black Political Struggles in the Rural South from Slavery to the Great Migration* (Cambridge, Ma.: Harvard University Press,

2005); Masur, *An Example for all the Land;* Douglas R. Egerton, *The Wars of Reconstruction: The Brief, Violent History of America's Most Progressive Era* (New York: Bloomsbury, 2014); and Garrett Epps, *Democracy Reborn: The Fourteenth Amendment and the Fights for Equal Rights in Post–Civil War America* (New York: Holt, 2007).

4. Woodhull has been the subject of several recent biographies including Underhill, *The Woman Who Ran for President;* Barbara Goldsmith, *Other Powers: The Age of Suffrage, Spiritualism, and the Scandalous Victoria Woodhull* (New York: Harper Collins, 1999); Mary Gabriel, *Notorious Victoria: The Life of Victoria Woodhull, Uncensored* (Chapel Hill: Algonquin Books, 1998); Myra MacPherson, *Scarlet Sisters: Sex, Suffrage, and Scandal in the Gilded Age* (New York: Twelve, 2014); as well as a muckraking account published in 1929 by Emanie Sachs entitled *The Terrible Siren: Victoria Woodhull, 1838–1927* (New York: Harper Bros., 1928). See also Amanda Frisken's excellent study of Woodhull and the culture of late nineteenth-century America: Amanda Frisken, *Victoria Woodhull's Sexual Revolution: Political Theater and the Popular Press in Nineteenth-Century America* (Philadelphia: University of Pennsylvania Press, 2004). Underhill, *The Woman Who Ran for President* does develop her presidential run at length. Woodhull's life presents tremendous difficulties of reconstruction for the historian. For penetrating discussions of the challenges see Frisken, *Victoria Woodhull's Sexual Revolution,* pp. 9–15; and Helen Lefkowitz Horowitz, "A Victoria Woodhull for the 1990s," *Reviews in American History,* vol. 27, no. 1 (March 1999), pp. 87–97.

5. On the frivolous nature of her presidential run, see, for example, Eleanor Flexner, *Century of Struggle: The Woman's Rights Movement in the United States* (Cambridge, Ma.: Harvard University Press, 1975), p. 147; Aileen S. Kraditor, *Ideas of the*

Woman Suffrage Movement, 1890–1920 (New York: W. W. Norton, 1981), p. 114; Richard Brookhiser, "The Happy Medium," *New York Times Book Review,* March 29, 1998, p. 11.

6. Theodore Tilton, *Victoria C. Woodhull: A Biographical Sketch* (New York: The Golden Age, 1871), pp. 3–6; Underhill, *Woman Who Ran for President,* pp. 11–19; Goldsmith, *Other Powers,* pp. 13–16, 18–19, 25–27.

7. Tilton, *Victoria C. Woodhull,* pp. 3–6, 8–12; Underhill, *Woman Who Ran for President,* 15–19; Goldsmith, *Other Powers,* Chapters 1 and 2. Woodhull's description of her visit by angels is quoted from Goldsmith, *Other Powers,* p. 25.

8. Underhill, *The Woman Who Ran for President,* pp. 156–157; Goldsmith, *Other Powers,* pp. 48–49; Morton Keller, *Affairs of State,* p. 249; Ann Braude, *Radical Spirits: Spiritualism and Women's Rights in Nineteenth-Century America* (Bloomington: Indiana University Press, 2001), pp. xix–xxi, 2–4, and passim.

9. "Declaration of Sentiments and Resolutions, Women's Rights Convention, Held at Seneca Falls, 19–20 July 1848," *The Elizabeth Cady Stanton and Susan B. Anthony Papers Project,* available at http://ecssba.rutgers.edu/docs/seneca.html.

10. Underhill, *The Woman Who Ran for President,* pp. 22–26; Tilton, *Victoria C. Woodhull,* pp. 12–16. Woodhull's comment to Lucretia Mott quoted in Goldsmith, *Other Powers,* p. 52.

11. Tilton, *Victoria C. Woodhull,* 16–24; Underhill, *The Woman Who Ran for President,* pp. 35–38. For Colonel Blood's appearance see the daguerreotype of Blood available at http://collections.mohistory.org/resource/141832.html. The date of Woodhull and Blood's marriage, as well as the location and dates of their travels, remains contested. For varying accounts see "Autobiographical notes, fragments regarding Victoria Woodhull Martin," Box 1, Folder 2, Victoria Woodhull–Martin Papers, 1870–1962, Special Collections Research Center, Southern Illinois University, Carbondale [hereafter Woodhull-Martin

Papers, *SIU*]; Underhill, *The Woman Who Ran for President,* pp. 38–39; MacPherson, *Scarlet Sisters,* pp. 24–26; Goldsmith, *Other Powers,* pp. 80–109.

12. Tilton, *Victoria C. Woodhull,* pp. 22–23; Underhill, *The Woman Who Ran for President,* pp. 30–34; Goldsmith, *Other Powers,* 67–68, 80–82; MacPherson, *Scarlet Sisters,* pp. 18–22.

13. Underhill, *The Woman Who Ran for President,* pp. 43–49; MacPherson, *Scarlet Sisters,* pp. 34–39; Tilton, *Victoria C. Woodhull,* pp. 11–12, 27; "The Great Will Contest," *New York Tribune,* October 16, 1878, p. 4; Goldsmith, *Other Powers,* pp. 157–162.

14. "Autobiographical notes, fragments regarding Victoria Woodhull Martin," Box 1, Folder 2, Woodhull-Martin Papers, *SIU;* "National Conventions—1869," Chapter 22, *History of Woman Suffrage,* vol. 2, *1861–1876,* ed. Elizabeth Cady Stanton, Susan B. Anthony, and Matilda Joslyn Gage (Rochester, N.Y.: Privately published, 1881), pp. 345–348; Ellen C. DuBois, "Outgrowing the Compact of the Fathers," pp. 844–848. The January 1869 meeting was sponsored by the Universal Franchise Association. Ann D. Gordon, ed., *The Selected Papers of Elizabeth Cady Stanton and Susan B. Anthony,* vol. 2, *Against an Aristocracy of Sex, 1866 to 1873* (New Brunswick: Rutgers University Press, 2000), p. 208, n. 1. The language of the Fifteenth Amendment is available at https://www.law.cornell.edu/constitution/amendmentxv. For an excellent study of the nineteenth-century suffrage struggle see Suzanne Marilley, *Woman Suffrage and the Origins of Liberal Feminism in the United States, 1820–1920* (Cambridge, Ma.: Harvard University Press, 1996).

15. "National Conventions—1869," *History of Woman Suffrage,* p. 355.

16. "National Conventions—1869," *History of Woman Suffrage,* pp. 353–355, 346–347.

17. "Victoria Woodhull," *The Revolution,* February 11, 1869, p. 86. This news report of the *New York World* reporter "Alpha,"

date stamped January 28, 1869, was reprinted in *The Revolution*. See also the discussion of these events in Underhill, *The Woman Who Ran for President,* Chapter 5.

18. "Autobiographical notes, fragments regarding Victoria Woodhull Martin," Box 1, Folder 2, Woodhull-Martin Papers, *SIU.*

19. "The Queens of Finance. A New Phase of the Woman's Rights Question," *New York Herald,* January 22, 1870, p. 10; "The Queens of Finance: The Palace of the Female Sovereigns of Wall Street," *New York Herald,* February 5, 1870, p. 8; Underhill, *The Woman Who Ran for President,* pp. 56–76; MacPherson, *The Scarlet Sisters,* pp. 38–39. On Woodhull's net worth in contemporary dollars, see John J. McCusker, "How Much Is That in Real Money? A Historical Price Index for Use as a Deflator of Money Values in the Economy of the United States," *Proceedings of the American Antiquarian Society,* vol. 101, part 2, October 1991, pp. 297–373. My thanks to economic historian Winifred Rothenberg of Tufts University for assistance in interpreting this data. For a lively account of Woodhull and Claflin's activities on Wall Street see MacPherson, *The Scarlet Sisters.*

20. "The Great Will Contest," *New York Tribune,* October 16, 1878, p. 4. The investor, Miss Susan King, offered her remarks in court testimony during a contest over the recently deceased Vanderbilt's will.

21. "The Lady Brokers Driving the Bull and Bears of Wall Street," *New York Telegraph,* February 18, 1870, reproduced in Goldsmith, *Other Powers,* p. 192; "Women in Wall Street," *Evening Post,* Feb. 7, 1870, p. 2.

22. "Wall Street Aroused—The Female Brokers," *New York Times,* February 6, 1870, p. 8; "Women in Wall Street," *Evening Post,* Feb. 7, 1870, p. 2; "The Lady Bankers of Broad Street," *New York Herald,* February 7, 1870, p. 6; "The Queens of Finance— The New Furore in Wall Street," *San Francisco Bulletin,* Feb. 19, 1870, p. 3. For stories of a similar tone see, for example, "Female

Stock Brokers," *Schenectady Reflector,* Feb. 10, 1870, p. 2; "New York Financial—The Female Brokers," *Cincinnati Daily Enquirer,* February 8, 1870, p. 4; "Mrs. Woodhull and Mrs. Claflin," *Idaho Statesman,* March 3, 1870, p. 2.

23. "Carrying the War into Africa," *The Revolution,* March 24, 1870, p. 188.

24. Tilton, *Victoria C. Woodhull,* p. 24; Underhill, *The Woman Who Ran for President,* Chapter 7; Stern, *Victoria Woodhull Reader,* pp. 3–4; Timothy Messer-Kruse, *The Yankee International: Marxism and the American Reform Tradition, 1848–1876* (Chapel Hill: University of North Carolina Press, 1998), pp. 109–110; Goldsmith, *Other Powers,* pp. 210–211. On prevailing nineteenth-century sexual ideas see esp. Helen Lefkowitz Horowitz, *Rereading Sex: Battles over Sexual Knowledge and Suppression in Nineteenth-Century America* (New York: Vintage, 2002). On Woodhull and the free-love issue see also Helen Lefkowitz Horowitz, "Victoria Woodhull: Free Love in the Feminine, First-Person Singular," in Susan Ware, ed., *Forgotten Heroes: Inspiring American Portraits from Our Leading Historians* (New York: Free Press, 1998); Helen Lefkowitz Horowitz, "Victoria Woodhull, Anthony Comstock, and Conflict over Sex in the United States in the 1870s," *Journal of American History,* vol. 87, no. 2 (September 2000); Ellen C. DuBois, "Feminism and Free Love," unpublished article provided by the author.

25. "The Coming Woman," *New York Herald,* April 2, 1870, p. 8; Troy, *See How They Ran,* Chapter 4; "A Woman's Rights Woman for the Next Presidency," *New York Herald,* April 3, 1870, p. 6. On Train's involvement with Stanton and Anthony see Goldsmith, *Other Powers,* pp. 136–137.

26. Tilton, *Victoria C. Woodhull,* p. 28; *New York Herald,* April 2, 1870, p. 8; Troy, *See How They Ran,* Chapter 4. *Hartford Courant* on Greeley quoted in Troy, *See How They Ran,* p. 76.

27. Tilton, *Victoria C. Woodhull,* p. 28; *New York Herald,* April 2, 1870, p. 8; Troy, *See How They Ran,* pp. 5–6, Chapter 11.

The reprinted version of Woodhull's letter to the *Herald* in Stern, *Victoria Woodhull Reader,* comes from Woodhull's later book entitled *The Argument for Women's Electoral Rights* (1887). Woodhull apparently revised her original letter for publication as that version does not reflect accurately her letter of April 2, 1870. I have used the original printed version from the newspaper in my quotations. For the range of presidential candidates see James T. Havel, *U.S. Presidential Candidates and the Elections: A Biographical and Historical Guide,* vol. 2, *The Elections* (New York: Macmillan Library Reference USA, 1996).

28. "The Coming Woman," *New York Herald,* April 2, 1870, p. 8.

29. "The Coming Woman," *New York Herald,* April 2, 1870, p. 8.

30. "The Coming Woman," *New York Herald,* April 2, 1870, p. 8.

31. "The Coming Woman," *New York Herald,* April 2, 1870, p. 8; Keller, *Affairs of State,* pp. 191–194.

32. "The Coming Woman," *New York Herald,* April 2, 1870, p. 6.

33. "A Woman's Rights Woman for the Next Presidency," *New York Herald,* April 3, 1870, p. 6; Underhill, *The Woman Who Ran for President,* pp. 80–85; "A Female Philippic: Victoria C. Woodhull on 'The Tendencies of Government,'" *New York Herald,* April 16, 1870, p. 5; Editorial, *Chicago Tribune,* May 6, 1870, p. 2. On the authorship of Woodhull's essays see also Frisken, *Victoria Woodhull's Sexual Revolution,* pp. 10–11; Stern, *Victoria Woodhull Reader,* pp. 1–5; Goldsmith, *Other Powers,* pp. 213–214. Hiram Revels served as a U.S. senator from Mississippi for thirteen months during Reconstruction. He was the first African American senator. Thomas Downing, "the oysterman," died in 1866. He had been a wealthy African American restaurateur whose eponymous establishment was located on Broad Street in New York City. His son George Downing was an African Amer-

ican activist and hotel owner. Egerton, *The Wars of Reconstruction*, p. 279; "Downing's Oyster House," *Mapping the African American Experience,* available at http://maap.columbia.edu /place/1. Koopmanschap was a Dutch immigrant involved in securing Chinese contract labor for employment in California. In 1869, he attracted attention for a speech he delivered to Southern planters suggesting Chinese workers be hired to replace the now emancipated slave laborers. See Lucy M. Cohen, *Chinese in the Post–Civil War South: A People without a History* (Baton Rouge: Louisiana State University Press, 1984), pp. 69–70.

34. "That Distinguished Brace of Patriots," *Jackson Citizen Patriot,* April 12, 1870, p. 2; "A Woman in the Ring for President," *Mobile Register,* April 21, 1870, p. 2; *Weekly Alta California,* April 23, 1870, p. 4.

35. "Another Candidate for the Presidency," *Albany Argus,* April 5, 1870, p. 2; "Mesdames Woodhull and Claflin," *Columbus Daily Sun,* June 9, 1870, p. 2.

36. "To the Press," *Woodhull & Claflin's Weekly,* vol. 1, no. 1 (May 14, 1870), pp. 1, 8; Messer-Kruse, *Yankee International,* pp. 109–110; Michael E. McGerr, *The Decline of Popular Politics: The American North, 1865–1928* (New York: Oxford University Press, 1986), pp. 14–22, Chapter 5; Underhill, *The Woman Who Ran for President,* pp. 86–88.

37. *Woodhull & Claflin's Weekly,* vol. 1, no. 1 (May 14, 1870); "Magazines, &c.," *New York Herald,* May 15, 1870, p. 6; "The Lady Brokers of Wall Street," *New York Herald,* May 18, 1870, p. 6; *Leavenworth Bulletin,* May 26, 1870, p. 1; "Woodhull and Claflin's Weekly," *Patriot,* May 28, 1870, p. 2; "The New Paper," *Coldwater Sentinel,* June 3, 1870, p. 3.

38. "Universal Government," *Woodhull & Claflin's Weekly,* August 6, 1870, p. 8; Stephen Pearl Andrews, "The Pantarchy," in *Woodhull & Claflin's Weekly,* August 27, 1870, p. 5; "What Is Prostitution?" *Woodhull & Claflin's Weekly,* August 13, 1870,

p. 10; "Femininity," *Cleveland Plain Dealer,* September 10, 1870, p. 2; "New York Letter," *Albany Argus,* August 27, 1870, p. 2; *Idaho Statesman,* September 13, 1870, p. 2; "Something about Ourselves," *Woodhull & Claflin's Weekly,* November 19, 1870, p. 9. On Andrews the "pantarch" see Madeleine B. Stern, *The Pantarch: A Biography of Stephen Pearl Andrews* (Austin: University of Texas Press, 1968).

39. "Startling Annunciation!" *Woodhull & Claflin's Weekly,* November 19, 1870, p. 8.

40. DuBois, "Outgrowing the Compact of the Fathers," pp. 852–853; "Startling Annunciation!" *Woodhull & Claflin's Weekly,* p. 9; Underhill, *The Woman Who Ran for President,* pp. 55–56.

41. "Startling Annunciation!" *Woodhull & Claflin's Weekly,* p. 9.

42. DuBois, "Outgrowing the Compact of the Fathers," pp. 853–854; Paulina Wright Davis, *A History of the National Woman's Rights Movement* (New York: Journey-Men Printers' Co-Operative Association, 1871), pp. 82–95; Underhill, *The Woman Who Ran for President,* pp. 94–101; Woodhull's memorial is available at http://hdl.loc.gov/loc.rbc/rbpe.12801400. The text of the Fourteenth and Fifteenth Amendments is available at https://www.law.cornell.edu/constitution/overview.

43. Stanton, Anthony, and Gage, *History of the Woman Suffrage Movement,* vol. 2, p. 443, note 1, and 442–458; "Reflections and Incidents—The Washington Convention," *The Revolution,* January 19, 1871; DuBois, "Outgrowing the Compact of the Fathers," pp. 856–858; Lisa Tetrault, *The Myth of Seneca Falls: Memory and the Women's Suffrage Movement, 1848–1898* (Chapel Hill: University of North Carolina Press, 2014), pp. 56–68; History, Art and Archives, U.S. House of Representatives, "The First Woman to Address a Congressional Committee," available at http://history.house.gov/HistoricalHighlight/Detail.

44. *New York Times* report quoted in "The Suffrage Movement South," *Hartford Daily Courant,* January 14, 1871, p. 2; Su-

san B. Anthony to Victoria Claflin Woodhull, February 4, 1871, in Gordon, *Selected Papers of Elizabeth Cady Stanton and Susan B. Anthony,* p. 415.

45. Isabella Beecher Hooker to Susan B. Anthony, March 11, 1871, in Jeanne Boydston, Mary Kelley, and Anne Margolis, *The Limits of Sisterhood: The Beecher Sisters on Women's Rights and Women's Sphere* (Chapel Hill: University of North Carolina Press, 1988), pp. 207–208; "The Washington Convention," *The Revolution,* January 12, 1871.

46. "Enfranchisement of Women," *New York Herald,* January 12, 1871, p. 3; "Mrs. Woodhull," *New York Tribune,* January 12, 1871, p. 4; "The Annual Convention of Female Suffragists," *Boston Herald,* January 12, 1871, p. 2.

47. "Woman Suffrage Before Congress," *New York Tribune,* January 12, 1871, pp. 1, 4; *Daily Republican,* January 13, 1871, p. 4; *Cincinnati Daily Enquirer,* January 14, 1871, p. 4.

48. "Woman's Right to Speculate," *New York Times,* February 22, 1871, p. 2; "Wall Street Aroused," *New York Times,* February 6, 1870, p. 8.

49. "A Bustle Unbecoming to the President," *Chicago Republican,* April 10, 1871, p. 2; *Jackson Daily Citizen,* June 10, 1870, p. 3; *Critic-Record,* November 3, 1870, p. 4.

50. Underhill, *The Woman Who Ran for President,* pp. 114–116; "The Cosmo-Political Party," *Woodhull & Claflin's Weekly,* January 28, 1871, p. 1. See also various issues throughout the spring of 1871 of *Woodhull & Claflin's Weekly,* starting with the January 28, 1871, edition.

51. "Mrs. Woodhull and the Poodles of the Press," *Woodhull & Claflin's Weekly,* March 25, 1871, p. 4.

52. "Labor Reform," *New York Times,* May 9, 1871, p. 8; "A Lecture on the Great Social Problem of Labor & Capital," in Stern, *Victoria Woodhull Reader;* Messer-Kruse, *Yankee International,* pp. 106–112.

53. "SOILED LINEN—Woodhull, Claflin & Co.—Family

Matters in a Police Court—A Weak Minded Mother with Strong Minded Daughters?" *Wooster* [Ohio] *Republican,* May 4, 1871, p. 5; *Alexandria Gazette,* May 6, 1871, p. 2; "Scandalous Developments about the Noted Wall Street Firm Woodhull, Claflin & Co.," *Cincinnati Commercial Tribune* , May 6, 1871, p. 1; "Mrs. Woodhull in Trouble," *Cincinnati Daily Enquirer,* May 6, 1871, p. 1.

54. "Scandalous Developments," *Cincinnati Commercial Tribune,* May 6, 1871, p. 1; "SOILED LINEN," *Wooster* [Ohio] *Republican,* May 4, 1871, p. 5; "Mrs. Woodhull in Trouble," *Cincinnati Daily Enquirer,* May 6, 1871, p. 1.

55. *Providence Evening Press,* May 6, 1971, p. 3; "THE WOODHULL CLAFLIN FAMILY," *Chicago Republican,* May 8, 1871, p. 2.

56. Isabella Beecher Hooker to Susan B. Anthony, March 11 [and 14], 1871, in Boydston, Kelley, and Margolis, *The Limits of Sisterhood,* pp. 206–207.

57. Elizabeth Cady Stanton to Lucretia Coffin Mott, April 1, 1871, in Gordon, *The Selected Papers of Elizabeth Cady Stanton and Susan B. Anthony,* vol. 2, pp. 427–428.

58. Elizabeth Cady Stanton to Lucretia Coffin Mott, April 1, 1871, in Gordon, *The Selected Papers of Elizabeth Cady Stanton and Susan B. Anthony,* vol. 2, pp. 428–429; Susan B. Anthony to Martha Coffin Wright, March 21, 1871, in Gordon, *The Selected Papers of Elizabeth Cady Stanton and Susan B. Anthony,* vol. 2, p. 425.

59. *Cincinnati Commercial Tribune,* May 11, 1871, p. 4; "BUSTED: The Cosmo-Political Party Gone to Smash and Woodhull & Clafflin Disgraced," *Atlanta Constitution,* May 10, 1871, p. 1.

60. "Mrs. Woodhull and Her Critics," *New York Times,* May 22, 1871, p. 5. On Woodhull's imprisonment see Horowitz, "Victoria Woodhull, Anthony Comstock, and Conflict over Sex in the United States in the 1870s." There is a wide literature on the

Beecher Tilton scandal. See, for example, Richard Wightman Fox, *Trials of Intimacy: Love and Loss in the Beecher Tilton Scandal* (Chicago: University of Chicago Press, 1999); Debby Applegate, *The Most Famous Man in America* (New York: Doubleday, 2006); Horowitz, *Rereading Sex;* as well as the previously cited biographies of Victoria Woodhull.

Margaret Chase Smith

1. President's Office Files, 1961–1963, Series 5, Press Conferences, Box 61, November 14, 1963, p. 7, John F. Kennedy Presidential Library, Boston, Massachusetts (hereafter JFKL); Press Conference, November 14, 1963, White House Audio Recordings, 1961–1963, JFKL; "Why No Female Political House Cleaning?" *Dallas Morning News,* August 27, 1963, p. 3; "Some Are Saying Smith in '64," *Dallas Morning News,* September 24, 1963, p. 2. On the *Dallas Morning News* and the Kennedy administration see Bill Minutaglio and Steven L. Davis, *Dallas 1963* (New York: Twelve, 2013), pp. 101–110, 127–132, 162–164.

2. "Sen. Smith's Candidacy—No Laughing Matter," *Boston Globe,* November 17, 1963, p. 4; Smith's Republican colleague quoted in Maxine Cheshire, "What Is Maggie Up To?" *Saturday Evening Post,* April 18, 1964, p. 31; "Margaret Chase Smith," *Biographical Directory of the United States Congress, 1774–Present,* available at http://bioguide.congress.gov/scripts/biodisplay .pl?index=S000590; "Women in Congress," in *Guide to U.S. Elections,* 6th ed., vol. 2 (Washington, D.C.: CQ Press, 2010), pp. 910–913. In 1960, Maurine Neuberger prevailed in a special Senate election in Oregon to finish out the term of her deceased husband. She won a general election that year, as well, and served from 1961 until her retirement in 1967. "Maurine Brown Neuberger," *Biographical Directory of the United States Congress,*

1774–Present, available at http://bioguide.congress.gov/scripts /biodisplay.pl?index=N000052.

3. "Smith, Margaret Chase," *History, Art & Archives, U.S. House of Representatives,* available at http://history.house.gov /People/Detail/21866 (July 09, 2015); Richard K. Donahue, recorded interview by John F. Stewart, March 8, 1967, p. 90, John F. Kennedy Library Oral History Program, JFKL.

4. Margaret Chase Smith quoted in Janann Sherman, *No Place for a Woman: A Life of Senator Margaret Chase Smith* (New Brunswick: Rutgers University Press, 2000), p. 4; Jo Freeman, *A Room at a Time: How Women Entered Party Politics* (Lanham, Md.: Rowan and Littlefield Publishers, 2000); Nadia L. Farjood, "Careers, Communities and Coattails: The Routes of Forty-Four Women to the Senate Chamber," Senior Honors Thesis, Harvard University, 2013.

5. Sherman, *No Place for a Woman,* pp. 8–17.

6. Sherman, *No Place for a Woman,* pp. 16–17; Patricia L. Schmidt, *Margaret Chase Smith: Beyond Convention* (Orono: University of Maine Press, 1996), pp. 25–26; Patricia Wallace Ward, *Politics of Conscience: A Biography of Margaret Chase Smith* (Westport: Praeger, 1995), pp. 9–13.

7. Pamela Neal Warford, "Margaret Chase Smith Oral History," Schlesinger Library, Radcliffe College, p. 33; Margaret Chase Smith, Diary, Tuesday, January 20 [no year given, but her ancillary activities as well as a 1920 calendar suggest 1920], Margaret Chase Smith Library, Skowhegan, Maine [hereafter MCSL]; Margaret Chase Smith Diary, Tuesday, January 13 [1920], MCSL; Margaret Chase Smith Diary, Sunday, January 11, [1920], MCSL; Margaret Chase Smith Diary, Wednesday, January 7 [1920], MCSL. Pamela Warford's oral history of Smith was published as Pamela Neal Warford, ed., *Margaret Chase Smith: In Her Own Words* (Skowhegan: Northwood University Margaret Chase Smith Library, 2001).

8. Smith quoted in Warford, *Margaret Chase Smith,* p. 8;

Sherman, *No Place for a Woman,* pp. 16–27; Schmidt, *Margaret Chase Smith,* pp. 41–43; Ward, *Politics of Conscience,* pp. 19–26.

9. Smith quoted in Warford, *Margaret Chase Smith,* p. 21; Sherman, *No Place for a Woman,* pp. 18–21; Ward, *Politics of Conscience,* pp. 23–25; Gregory P. Gallant, *Hope and Fear in Margaret Chase Smith's America: A Continuous Tangle* (Lanham: Lexington Books, 2014), pp. 21–22, 35–36. On the role of early twentieth-century women's clubs see especially Theda Skocpol, *Protecting Soldiers and Mothers: The Political Origins of Social Policy in the United States* (Cambridge, Ma.: Harvard University Press, 1995), and Karen J. Blair, *The Clubwoman as Feminist: True Womanhood Redefined, 1868–1914* (New York: Holmes and Meier, 1980).

10. Sherman, *No Place for a Woman,* pp. 27–36; Ward, *Politics of Conscience,* pp. 32–38; "Clyde Harold Smith," *Biographical Directory of the United States Congress, 1774–Present,* available at http://bioguide.congress.gov/scripts/biodisplay .pl?index=S000523; "Clyde Harold Smith," *History, Art & Archives, U.S. House of Representatives,* available at http://history .house.gov/People/Detail/21788.

11. Margaret Chase Smith quoted in Sherman, *No Place for a Woman,* p. 31; Gallant, *Hope and Fear,* pp. 13–15, 20, 33–35; Schmidt, *Margaret Chase Smith,* pp. 79–85; Wallace, *Politics of Conscience,* pp. 12–14, 31–32.

12. Sherman, *No Place for a Woman,* pp. 38–41; Gallant, *Hope and Fear,* pp. 11–13; John A. Kolmer, M.D., to Benjamin B. Foster, M.D., December 21, 1938, Clyde H. Smith File, MCSL; Notes on Symptom and Complaints, Clyde H. Smith File, MCSL; Clyde H. Smith to Benjamin B. Foster, M.D., January 17, 1939, Clyde H. Smith File, MCSL; Clyde H. Smith to John A. Kolmer, M.D., January 17, 1939, Clyde H. Smith File, MCSL; "Dr. Dicken's Statement," handwritten notes dated April 6, 1940, Clyde H. Smith File, MCSL; "Syphilis—Fact Sheet," *Centers for Disease Control and Prevention,* December 16, 1914, avail-

able at http://www.cdc.gov/std/syphilis/stdfact-syphilis-detailed
.htm; John Parascandola, *Sex, Sin, and Science: A History of Syphilis in America* (Santa Barbara: Praeger, 2008).

13. Smith's 1938 Navy Day remarks quoted in "Statement of Margaret Chase Smith," May 24, 1940, Smith Social Activities, Armed Services Committee Folder, MCSL; and Margaret Chase Smith, "July 1940 Luncheon of Kennebec Co. Republican Women's Club Held at Lake View Arms, Winthrop," Smith Social Activities, Armed Services Committee Folder, MCSL. For details on the Navy Day speech and Chase Smith's divergence from her husband see Sherman, *No Place for a Woman,* pp. 39–40; Gallant, *Hope and Fear,* pp. 24–25; Schmidt, *Margaret Chase Smith,* p. 108; Eric R. Crouse, *An American Stand: Margaret Chase Smith and the Communist Menace, 1948–1972* (Lanham: Lexington Books, 2013), p. 5.

14. Sherman, *No Place for a Woman,* pp. 38–42; "Margaret Chase Smith Oral History," prepared by Pamela Neal Warford, Schlesinger Library, Radcliffe College, 1991, pp. 40–41.

15. Mae Ella Nolan quoted in "Mae Ella Nolan," *History, Art & Archives, U.S. House of Representatives,* available at http://history.house.gov/People/Detail/18986; Alice Roosevelt Longworth quoted in Carol Felsenthal, *Princess Alice: The Life and Times of Alice Roosevelt Longworth* (New York: St. Martin's Press, 1988), p. 167; Farjood, "Careers, Communities and Coattails," pp. 40–48; Freeman, *A Room at a Time,* pp. 232–234; "The Widow and Familial Connections," *History, Art & Archives, U.S. House of Representatives, Office of the Historian, Women in Congress, 1917–2006,* available at http://history.house.gov/Exhibitions-and-Publications/WIC/Historical-Essays/No-Lady/Widow-Familial; "Hattie Wyatt Caraway," *History, Art & Archives, U.S. House of Representatives,* available at http://history.house.gov/People/Detail/44589.

16. "Mrs. Smith Goes to Washington," *Christian Science Monitor,* May 17, 1940, p. 13; "Mrs. Smith Goes to Washington,"

Daily Boston Globe, June 2, 1940, C2; Sherman, *No Place for a Woman,* pp. 44–45.

17. Smith's primary opponent and the *Portland Sunday Telegram* columnist quoted in Sherman, *No Place for a Woman,* p. 46; her primary fight is covered in excellent detail on pp. 45–47.

18. "5 of 8 Women in Congress Are Isolationists," *New York Herald Tribune,* July 14, 1940, p. 1. On women and the peace movement see Jane Addams, *Women at the Hague: The International Congress of Women and Its Results* (Urbana: University of Illinois Press, 2003); Harriet Alonso, *Peace as a Women's Issue: A History of the U.S. Movement for World Peace* (Syracuse: Syracuse University Press, 1993); Linda Schott, *Reconstructing Women's Thoughts: The Women's International League for Peace and Freedom before World War II* (Stanford: Stanford University Press, 1997); Roland Marchand, *The American Peace Movement and Social Reform, 1889–1918* (Princeton: Princeton University Press, 1973); Frances Early, *A World without War: How U.S. Feminists and Pacifists Resisted World War I* (Syracuse: Syracuse University Press, 1987).

19. Margaret Chase Smith, Remarks to D.A.R., Poland Springs, June 29, 1940; Notes from *Lewiston Journal,* June 7, 1940; Transcript of *Portland Press Herald,* May 25, 1940, "Mrs. Smith Urges Defense Preparations Immediately"; Margaret Chase Smith, Remarks, Farmington, Maine, May 30, 1940, all in "Smith, Social Activities" Folder, Armed Services Committee File, MCSL; Robert Dallek, *Franklin Roosevelt and American Foreign Policy, 1932–1945* (New York: Oxford University Press, 1995), Chapters 9 and 10.

20. Margaret Chase Smith notes on 1940 election in Campaign Diary, MCSL; Report of the Standing Committee on Election Results, State of Maine, July 2, 1940, in Campaign Diary, MCSL; "House General Elections, Maine, 1932–1940, All Dis-

tricts," in *CQ Voting and Elections Collection (Web site)* (Washington, D.C.: CQ Press, 2003); Warford, *Margaret Chase Smith,* p. 29; Sherman, *No Place for a Woman,* pp. 45–52.

21. Gregory P. Gallant discusses this legal document and its terms in *Hope and Fear,* pp. 33–34; "Margaret Chase Smith Oral History," p. 43.

22. "Senator White Warns of Peril in Nazi Win," *Daily Boston Globe,* November 16, 1941, B32; Gannett quoted in Sherman, *No Place for a Woman,* p. 50; Sherman, *No Place for a Woman,* pp. 47–53; Gallant, *Hope and Fear,* pp. 48–64.

23. Senate staff member quoted in Cheshire, "What Is Maggie Up To?" p. 31; Sherman, *No Place for a Woman,* pp. 50–57.

24. Smith quoted in "Norma Beatty Interview," Margaret Chase Smith Presidential Nomination File, MCSL; Sherman, *No Place for a Woman,* pp. 58–66; Jo Freeman, "What's in a Name? Does it Matter How the Equal Rights Amendment Is Worded?" available at http://www.jofreeman.com/lawandpolicy/eraname .htm; Gallant, *Hope and Fear,* pp. 51–52; Cheshire, "What Is Maggie Up To?" p. 32.

25. Sherman, *No Place for a Woman,* pp. 58–72; Gallant, *Hope and Fear,* pp. 52–65.

26. Smith quoted in Sherman, *No Place for a Woman,* p. 96; Schmidt, *Margaret Chase Smith,* pp. 148–153; Cheshire, "What Is Maggie Up To?" p. 32; Gallant, *Hope and Fear,* pp. 54–55; Sherman, *No Place for a Woman,* pp. 61, 74–75, 95–97, 80–81.

27. *New York Times,* quoted in Sherman, *No Place for a Woman,* p. 84; "Sen. White to Retire in 1948; Rep. Smith Out for Maine Seat," *Daily Boston Globe,* June 2, 1947, p. 16; Sherman, *No Place for a Woman,* pp. 73–76, 78–89; Gallant, *Hope and Fear,* pp. 82–85.

28. Smith quoted in Sherman, *No Place for a Woman,* p. 83; "Sleeping Giantess Stirs," *Washington Post,* August 13, 1947, p. 12; "Maine Candidate for U.S. Senator Baked Bean Champ,"

Daily Boston Globe, June 15, 1947, p. 1; Sherman, *No Place for a Woman,* pp. 80–87; Elaine Tyler May, *Homeward Bound: American Families in the Cold War Era* (New York: Basic Books, 1988).

29. "Maine GOP Nominates Mrs. Smith for Senator," *Christian Science Monitor,* June 22, 1948, p. 5.

30. Brewster quoted in Gallant, *Hope and Fear,* p. 84; the CIO quoted in Sherman, *No Place for a Woman,* p. 85; "Mrs. Smith Victor over Three Men in Maine Senate Primary Race," *New York Herald Tribune,* June 22, 1948, p. 1; Sherman, *No Place for a Woman,* pp. 85–86. See Gallant, *Hope and Fear,* pp. 84–87, for a detailed examination of the smear campaign.

31. "Say Margaret Smith Could Be President," *Daily Boston Globe,* June 23, 1948, p. 1; "Women Hail Smith Victory in Maine," *Christian Science Monitor,* June 23, 1948, p. 7; "Women Organize to Sway Congress: Senate Debut of Margaret Chase Smith Sharpens Their Interest in Legislation," *New York Times,* January 3, 1949, p. 20; "Two N.E. Senators among 28 Proposing Equal Rights Law," *Christian Science Monitor,* January 15, 1949, p. 4.

32. "Margaret Smith Wants Juliana to End Warfare," *New York Herald Tribune,* January 4, 1949, p. 5; "Political Royalty Takes Over from Glamor Girls in Capital," *Daily Boston Globe,* January 2, 1949, C21.

33. "Woman Lays GOP Defeat to Leaders," *Los Angeles Times,* January 9, 1949, p. 31; "Margaret Smith Analyzes Defeat of Republicans," *New York Herald Tribune,* January 9, 1949, p. 7; Smith's views of government as protector of the public interest quoted in Gallant, *Hope and Fear,* p. 99.

34. "Senator Margaret Smith Appeals to Queen Juliana to Halt Fighting," *New York Times,* January 4, 1949, p. 3; Gallant, *Hope and Fear,* pp. 136–137, and Chapter 4; Rhodri Jeffreys-Jones, *Changing Differences: Women and the Shaping of American Foreign Policy, 1917–1994* (New Brunswick: Rutgers University Press, 1994), Chapter 7; Crouse, *An American Stand;*

John Gaddis, *Strategies of Containment: A Critical Appraisal of American National Security Policy during the Cold War* (New York: Oxford University Press, 2005).

35. David Oshinsky, *A Conspiracy So Immense: The World of Joe McCarthy* (New York: Free Press, 1983), p. 158; "Joseph McCarthy, Speech at Wheeling, West Virginia, 1950," available at http://wps.prenhall.com/wps/media/objects/108/110880/ch26_a5_d2.pdf; Robert Griffith, *The Politics of Fear: Joseph R. McCarthy and the Senate* (Amherst: University of Massachusetts Press, 1987).

36. Margaret Chase Smith, *Declaration of Conscience* (New York: Doubleday and Co., 1972), p. 9; Sherman, *No Place for a Woman,* pp. 104–111; Oshinsky, *A Conspiracy So Immense,* pp. 158–163.

37. Smith, *Declaration of Conscience,* pp. 4–12.

38. Smith, *Declaration of Conscience,* pp. 12–14.

39. Smith, *Declaration of Conscience,* pp. 15–18.

40. Smith, *Declaration of Conscience,* pp. 12, 21.

41. "GOP Senator Blisters Both Major Parties: Only Woman Member Blasts at Tactics in Fight on Communism," *Hartford Courant,* June 2, 1950, p. 2; "Seven GOP Senators Repudiate McCarthy: Party Warned to Avoid Seeking Political Gain by 'Exploitation of Fear,'" *Baltimore Sun,* June 2, 1950, p. 1; "Four Horsemen," *Washington Post,* January 2, 1950, p. 20; "Seven GOP Senators Decry 'Smear' Tactics of McCarthy," *New York Times,* June 2, 1950, p. 1.

42. I. F. Stone, "An Old Police State Custom," *I. F. Stone's Weekly,* vol. 2, no. 2 (February 1, 1954), p. 4, available at http://www.ifstone.org/weekly/IFStonesWeekly-1954feb01.pdf; Sherman, *No Place for a Woman,* pp. 132–133; Smith, *Declaration of Conscience,* pp. 21–61; Oshinsky, *A Conspiracy So Immense,* pp. 215–217.

43. Murrow quoted in Sherman, *No Place for a Woman,* p. 135; Government Operations resolution quoted on p. 143; see

also discussion on pp. 133–140, 142–143; Smith, *Declaration of Conscience,* pp. 38–61; Oshinsky, *A Conspiracy So Immense,* pp. 215–217.

44. Dorothy Thompson, "The Maine Woman Senator's Declaration," *Daily Boston Globe,* June 9, 1950, p. 24; "Women in Politics Begin New Chapter," *Boston Globe,* June 25, 1950, A2; "Mrs. Kennedy Remains Most Admired Woman," *Hartford Courant,* December 25, 1963, p. 30; Smith, *Declaration of Conscience,* p. 19; Sherman, *No Place for a Woman,* p. 112.

45. Margaret Chase Smith to Jacqueline Kennedy, March 28, 1961, Kennedy Administration Folder, Correspondence File, MCSL; Office Staff Note to Margaret Chase Smith, March 20, 1961, Kennedy Administration Folder, Correspondence File, MCSL; Smith comment on discrimination quoted in Sherman, *No Place for a Woman,* p. 55; "Washington Scene . . . A Great Comeback," *Washington Post,* December 4, 1963, A21; Sherman, *No Place for a Woman,* pp. 93–94, 165–166.

46. "Barack Obama, Hillary Clinton Again Top Most Admired List," Gallup Poll, December 27, 2011, available at http://www.gallup.com/poll/151790/barack-obama-hillary-clinton-again-top-admired-list.aspx; "Long Term Gallup Poll Trends: A Portrait of American Public Opinion through the Century," Gallup Poll, December 20, 1999, available at http://www.gallup.com/poll/3400/longterm-gallup-poll-trends-portrait-american-public-opinion.aspx.

47. Cynthia Harrison, *On Account of Sex: The Politics of Women's Issues, 1945–1968* (Berkeley: University of California Press, 1988), pp. 87–88, 103–105, 111–116, 134–137; Stephanie Coontz, *A Strange Stirring: The Feminine Mystique and American Women at the Dawn of the 1960s* (New York: Basic Books, 2011).

48. Smith quoted in Schmidt, *Margaret Chase Smith,* p. 300; Sherman, *No Place for a Woman,* pp. 168–182.

49. "Goldwater Repeats 'No' on Ban Pact: Arizonan Says He

Accepts Political Risk of Opposing Treaty," *Washington Post,* September 20, 1963, A1.

50. "Senate Vote Linked to '64," *Boston Globe,* September 25, 1963, p. 19.

51. "Washington Scene: The Barry-Maggie Ticket," *Washington Post,* September 30, 1963, A15.

52. "Woman Senator Will Announce Decision Dec. 5," *Boston Globe,* November 8, 1963, p. 15; "Sen. Goldwater Mum on His Own Decision," *Chicago Tribune,* November 8, 1963, p. 2; "Mrs. Smith Weighs Primary Tests," *Christian Science Monitor,* November 8, 1963, p. 14; "Sen. Margaret Smith May Enter Primaries," *Los Angeles Times,* November 8, 1963, p. 2; "Margaret Chase Smith Weighs Drive for the Vice Presidency," *New York Times,* November 8, 1963, p. 1.

53. Walter Trohan, "Report from Washington," *Chicago Tribune,* November 9, 1963, N3; Thomas O'Neill, "Politics and People: The Long Haul," *Baltimore Sun,* November 8, 1963, p. 14; "Mrs. Smith Weighs Primaries: Many Supporters," *Christian Science Monitor,* November 9, 1963, p. 1.

54. "Top Spot or None, Mrs. Smith Says," *Boston Globe,* November 14, 1963, p. 15; Mary McGrory, "Sen. Smith—Holds Lamp in Dark," *Boston Globe,* November 15, 1963, p. 19.

55. "Chivalry Isn't Dead; Accolades to Sen. Smith," *Hartford Courant,* November 15, 1963, B8; George Gallup, "Woman Still Opposed for U.S. Presidency," *Washington Post,* November 15, 1963, A21; "Presidency Not for Women, She Says," *Los Angeles Times,* December 12, 1963, C18.

56. "Answer to Sen. Smith," *Washington Post,* November 21, 1963, C1; "President's Wife to Campaign in '64: She Plans an Active Role in Drive for Re-election," November 15, 1963, p. 21.

57. Smith, *Declaration of Conscience,* pp. 309–310; "N.E. Pays Tribute to President," *Boston Globe,* November 23, 1963, p. 21; Sherman, *No Place for a Woman,* pp. 79–80, 181–182; "All Activity at a Halt in Washington," *Chicago Tribune,* November 23,

1963, p. 9; "Red Rose Marks Kennedy's Senate Desk," *Chicago Tribune,* November 26, 1963, A6.

58. "Mrs. Smith's Bonnet," Library Exhibits Documents and Files, Newspapers, MCSL; "Inside Report . . . The 'Undecideds,'" *Washington Post,* January 27, 1964, A13.

59. Smith, *Declaration of Conscience,* pp. 362–363.

60. Anthony Corrado, "An Overview of Campaign Finance Law," in Paul S. Harrison, ed., *Guide to Political Campaigns in America* (Washington, D.C.: Congressional Quarterly Press, 2005).

61. Gil Troy, *See How They Ran: The Changing Role of the Presidential Candidate* (Cambridge, Ma.: Harvard University Press, 1996), pp. 202–205, 215–221.

62. Smith, *Declaration of Conscience,* pp. 362–368.

63. Smith, *Declaration of Conscience,* pp. 368–370.

64. "Try for White House by Mrs. Smith Roils GOP Primary Outlook," *Wall Street Journal,* January 28, 1964, p. 1.

65. Smith, *Declaration of Conscience,* pp. 362–372; "Sen. Smith Tosses Bonnet in G.O.P. Ring for Presidency," *Chicago Tribune,* January 28, 1964, p. 1.

66. Smith, *Declaration of Conscience,* pp. 371–372.

67. "Margaret Chase Smith Seeks Presidency," *New York Times,* January 28, 1964, p. 1; "Senator Margaret Smith Enters Presidential Race," *Baltimore Sun,* January 28, 1964, p. 1; "A Chic Lady Who Fights: Margaret Chase Smith," *New York Times,* January 28, 1964, p. 17; "Try for the White House by Mrs. Smith," *Wall Street Journal,* January 28, 1964, p. 1; "Obstacles in Sen. Smith's Path," *Los Angeles Times,* February 4, 1964, A5.

68. "66-Year-Old Sen. Smith Hits Age Talk," *Los Angeles Times,* February 7, 1964, p. 6; "Mrs. Smith Says Her Age Is No Bar to Presidency," *New York Times,* February 7, 1964, p. 14; "Mrs. Smith Visits N.H. Folks," *Boston Globe,* February 11, 1964,

p. 4; "Sen. Smith Seeks Votes in Frigid New Hampshire," *Chicago Tribune,* February 11, 1964, p. 6.

69. "Try for White House by Mrs. Smith," *Wall Street Journal,* January 28, 1964, p. 1; "Here's Something New in American Politics," *Hartford Courant,* January 29, 1964, p. 14.

70. "He's Not Ready to Say 'Ma'am' to President," *Washington Post,* January 29, 1964, D3; Russell Baker, "Observer," *New York Times,* January 30, 1964, p. 28.

71. "N.H. Voters Warm Up to Visit by Mrs. Smith," *Christian Science Monitor,* February 11, 1964, p. 6; "The Elephant has an Attractive Face," Newspaper clipping in vol. 301, June 1964–July 1964, Presidential Campaign, MCSL; "Mrs. Smith Visits N.H. Folks," *Boston Globe,* February 11, 1964, p. 4; "Sen. Smith Braves Cold to Seek Primary Votes," *Los Angeles Times,* February 11, 1964, p. 3.

72. Sherman, *No Place for a Woman,* pp. 192–199.

73. "Sen. Smith—A Step into History," *Los Angeles Times,* July 16, 1964, C1.

Shirley Chisholm

1. "U.S. Rep. Shirley Chisholm Campaigns 'For Real' in Florida," *Hartford Courant,* March 10, 1972, p. 21.

2. Shirley Chisholm, *The Good Fight* (New York: Harper and Row, 1973), p. 2.

3. "Shirley Chisholm Interview," Part 1, p. 3, Shola Lynch Transcripts, Box 9, Folder 7, Shirley Chisholm '72 Collection, Archives and Special Collections, Brooklyn College Library, Brooklyn, New York (hereafter SCC); "U.S. Rep. Shirley Chisholm Campaigns 'For Real' in Florida," *Hartford Courant,* March 10, 1972, p. 21; "Shirley Stimulates Black Fla. Voters," *Chicago Daily Defender,* March 15, 1972, p. 6. For an outstanding analysis of Chisholm's political career, see Anastasia Cur-

wood, "Black Feminism on Capitol Hill: Shirley Chisholm and Movement Politics, 1968–1984," *Meridians,* vol. 13, no. 1 (2015).

4. Shirley Chisholm, *Unbought and Unbossed* (Washington, D.C.: Take Root Media, 2009), pp. 46–51.

5. Chisholm, *The Good Fight,* pp. 34, 83.

6. "Mrs. Chisholm Isn't Kidding—She's Off and Running," *Baltimore Sun,* March 12, 1972, A9; Chisholm, *The Good Fight,* p. 67.

7. "Florida Expects Record Turnout in Primary Today," *New York Times,* March 14, 1972, p. 1; "Shirley Stimulates Black Fla. Voters," *Chicago Daily Defender,* March 15, 1972, p. 6; Chisholm, *The Good Fight,* pp. 67–68.

8. "Shirley Stimulates Black Fla. Voters," *Chicago Daily Defender,* p. 6; Chisholm, *The Good Fight,* p. 69. Chisholm remembered the Confederate statue as being in Marianna, but there is no statue of a standing soldier meeting that description in the town. She may have conflated her memory of the visit to Marianna with her glimpse of another such statue, perhaps in Jacksonville, where she also visited and where a Confederate statue of similar description stands.

9. "Shirley Stimulates Black Fla. Voters," *Chicago Daily Defender,* p. 6; "Wallace Lauds Rep. Chisholm," *Washington Post,* March 12, 1972, A1; Chisholm, *The Good Fight,* pp. 63–64.

10. Chisholm, *The Good Fight,* pp. 62–63; "Wallace Lauds Chisholm," *Washington Post,* A1.

11. "Wallace Lauds Chisholm," *Washington Post,* A1; "Chisholm Appeal Divides Blacks; Imperils Liberals in Florida Race," *New York Times,* March 14, 1972, p. 30; "After Florida Loss . . . Shirley Heads for Wisconsin," *Chicago Daily Defender,* March 16, 1972, p. 2; Chisholm, *The Good Fight,* pp. 56–57; "When Florida Counted: 1972," *Tampa Tribune,* June 22, 2008, available at http://www.tbo.com/special_section /life/2008/jun/22/tr-when-florida-counted-1972-ar-159375.

12. Chisholm, *Unbought and Unbossed,* p. 23; Barbara Wins-

low, *Shirley Chisholm: Catalyst for Change, 1924–2005* (Boulder: Westview Press, 2014), pp. 5–8; Damani Davis, "Ancestors from the West Indies: A Historical and Genealogical Overview of Afro-Caribbean Immigration, 1900–1930s," National Archives and Records Administration, *Prologue,* Fall / Winter 2013; Craig Steven Wilder, *A Covenant with Color: Race and Social Power in Brooklyn* (New York: Columbia University Press, 2000), pp. 150–152, 123–126.

13. Chisholm, *Unbought and Unbossed,* pp. 23–25; "Shirley Chisholm Interview," Part 1, p. 34, Shola Lynch Transcripts, Box 9, Folder 7, SCC; Winslow, *Shirley Chisholm,* pp. 8–10. On the pervasiveness of racial discrimination in employment in early twentieth-century Brooklyn see Wilder, *A Covenant with Color,* pp. 152–158.

14. Chisholm, *Unbought and Unbossed,* pp. 25–29; "Shirley Chisholm Interview," Part 1, p. 32, Shola Lynch Transcripts, Box 9, Folder 7, SCC.

15. Chisholm, *Unbought and Unbossed,* pp. 25–29; Winslow, *Shirley Chisholm,* pp. 10–12.

16. Chisholm, *Unbought and Unbossed,* pp. 26–29; Winslow, *Shirley Chisholm,* p. 12. For more on Chisholm's identification with her West Indian roots, see Tammy L. Brown, "'A New Era in American Politics': Shirley Chisholm and the Discourse of Identity," *Callaloo,* vol. 31, no. 4 (Fall 2008).

17. Chisholm, *Unbought and Unbossed,* pp. 30–31, 35.

18. Chisholm, *Unbought and Unbossed,* pp. 32–34.

19. Chisholm, *Unbought and Unbossed,* pp. 34–35; Jeffrey Gerson, "Building the Brooklyn Machine: Irish, Jewish and Black Political Succession in Central Brooklyn, 1919–1964," PhD. diss., City University of New York, 1990, p. 67.

20. Chisholm, *Unbought and Unbossed,* pp. 36–37; Wilder, *Covenant with Color,* pp. 195–197; Gerson, "Building the Brooklyn Machine," p. 170; "Shirley Chisholm Speaks Out," Presidential Campaign Position Paper, No. 8, Box 5, Folder 26, SCC.

21. Chisholm, *Unbought and Unbossed*, p. 37.

22. Winslow, *Shirley Chisholm*, pp. 21–22; National Visionary Leadership Project, "Interview with Shirley Chisholm," Part 9, available at http://www.visionaryproject.org/chisholmshirley/#2; Chisholm, *Unbought and Unbossed*, pp. 40–41.

23. Chisholm, *Unbought and Unbossed*, pp. 40–44; "Student Voices: Brooklyn College Oral Histories on World War II and the McCarthy Era—Phyllis LeShaw," available at http://oralhistory.ashp.cuny.edu/pages/farmLabor/flITIPolitics.html; W. E. B. Du Bois, *The Souls of Black Folk* (New York: Bedford Books, 1997), p. 38; "Shirley Chisholm Interview," Part 1, p. 31, Shola Lynch Transcripts, Box 9, Folder 7, SCC.

24. Chisholm, *Unbought and Unbossed*, pp. 40–42; National Visionary Leadership Project, "Interview with Shirley Chisholm," Part 8.

25. Chisholm, *Unbought and Unbossed*, p. 43; Louis A. Warsoff, *Equality and the Law* (New York: Liveright Publishing Co., 1938); "Warsoff and Schupler Debate to a Standstill—Still No Decision," *Brooklyn Daily Eagle*, April 9, 1952, p. 11.

26. Chisholm, *Unbought and Unbossed*, pp. 20, 41–45.

27. Chisholm, *Unbought and Unbossed*, pp. 41, 45; Winslow, *Shirley Chisholm*, pp. 25–28; Chisholm, *The Good Fight*, p. 65. Chisholm's experience in Riverdale quoted in Winslow, *Shirley Chisholm*, p. 26.

28. Chisholm, *Unbought and Unbossed*, pp. 45, 61–65; Winslow, *Shirley Chisholm*, pp. 25–28.

29. Chisholm, *Unbought and Unbossed*, pp. 46–47.

30. Gerson, "Building the Brooklyn Machine," pp. 74–77; Jason Sokol, *All Eyes Are upon Us: Race and Politics from Boston to Brooklyn* (New York: Basic Books, 2014), pp. 139–141.

31. Chisholm, *Unbought and Unbossed*, pp. 46–47. Chisholm described *Vincent* Carney as the district leader when she first attended the 17th A.D. Democratic Club meetings, but his brother *Stephen* held that post in the period when she was a

college student. Gerson, "Building the Brooklyn Machine," pp. 199–200. Professor Anastasia Curwood suspects that Chisholm may have actually become a regular attendee at the 17th A.D. meetings later than Chisholm remembered, when Vincent Carney was in charge. This may account for the confusion in *Unbought and Unbossed*. Private email communication to the author from Anastasia Curwood, October 29, 2015.

32. Chisholm, *Unbought and Unbossed*, pp. 47–48, 55.

33. Gerson, "Building the Brooklyn Political Machine," pp. 183–215, 230; Chisholm, *Unbought and Unbossed*, p. 49.

34. Chisholm, *Unbought and Unbossed*, pp. 48–49.

35. Chisholm, *Unbought and Unbossed*, pp. 48–54.

36. Chisholm, *Unbought and Unbossed*, pp. 49–51; Gerson, "Building the Brooklyn Machine," pp. 181–182.

37. Chisholm, *Unbought and Unbossed*, pp. 38–41, 44, 61–63.

38. Chisholm, *Unbought and Unbossed*, pp. 61–62, 45.

39. Chisholm, *Unbought and Unbossed*, p. 62. For details on the criminal enterprise that seems to match what Chisholm describes in her memoir see "Suspect in Alien Smuggling Jailed," *Afro-American*, October 30, 1948, p. 6; "Smuggling Drive Nets 42 Arrests," *Baltimore Sun*, October 13, 1948, p. 1; "Expose BWI Smuggling Plot: Mount Vernon Resident Is Facing Charge," *New York Amsterdam News*, October 16, 1948, p. 1; "Deport Jamaican After Work in Smuggling Ring," *Los Angeles Sentinel*, June 30, 1949, A2. There is no way to know for certain, however, if this operation involved Chisholm's fiancé.

40. Chisholm, *Unbought and Unbossed*, p. 63.

41. "Conrad Chisholm Oral History," Shola Lynch Transcripts, Box 8, Folder 3, SCC; Winslow, *Shirley Chisholm*, pp. 27–28; Chisholm, *Unbought and Unbossed*, pp. 63–64.

42. "Conrad Chisholm Oral History," Shola Lynch Transcripts, Box 8, Folder 3, SCC; Chisholm, *Unbought and Unbossed*, pp. 63–64.

43. "Shirley Chisholm Oral History," Ralph J. Bunche Oral

History Collection, May 2, 1973, Moorland-Spingarn Research Center, Howard University, Washington, D.C., p. 2 (hereafter "Chisholm Oral History," MSRC); Chisholm, *Unbought and Unbossed*, pp. 53, 56; "Women's Council Fetes Six at Breakfast," *New York Amsterdam News*, February 8, 1958, p. 19; Linda Perkins, "The National Association of College Women: Vanguard of Black Women's Leadership and Education, 1923–1954," *Journal of Education*, vol. 172, no. 3 (1990).

44. "Chisholm Oral History," MSRC, p. 2; Sokol, *All Eyes Are upon Us*, pp. 141–142; Gerson, "Building the Brooklyn Machine," pp. 230–241; Chisholm, *Unbought and Unbossed*, pp. 51–52.

45. Gerson, "Building the Brooklyn Machine," pp. 254–264; "King's Diary: Inside Brooklyn," *New York Amsterdam News*, January 19, 1957, p. 19.

46. "King's Diary: Inside Brooklyn," *New York Amsterdam News*, January 19, 1957, p. 19; "Chisholm Oral History," MSRC, pp. 2–3; Gerson, "Building the Brooklyn Machine," pp. 283–285; Sokol, *All Eyes Are upon Us*, pp. 141–143; Chisholm, *Unbought and Unbossed*, pp. 55–57, 65–66.

47. Gerson, "Building the Brooklyn Machine," pp. 309–321; Chisholm, *Unbought and Unbossed*, pp. 65–67; Sokol, *All Eyes Are upon Us*, pp. 140–143.

48. Chisholm, *Unbought and Unbossed*, pp. 67–69; Gerson, "Building the Brooklyn Machine," pp. 328–329; Joshua Guild, "To Make That Someday Come True: Shirley Chisholm's Radical Politics of Possibility," in Dayo F. Gore, Jeanne Theoharis, and Komozi Woodard, eds., *Want to Start a Revolution? Radical Women in the Black Freedom Struggle* (New York: New York University Press, 2009), pp. 252–253.

49. Chisholm, *Unbought and Unbossed*, pp. 68–69.

50. Chisholm, *Unbought and Unbossed*, pp. 70–71; Gerson, "Building the Brooklyn Machine," pp. 333–337, 352; Sokol, *All*

Eyes Are upon Us, p. 143; "First Brooklyn Negro Woman Running for the Assembly," *New York Amsterdam News,* May 9, 1964, p. 33.

51. Chisholm, *Unbought and Unbossed,* pp. 70–71; Julie A. Gallagher, *Black Women and Politics in New York City* (Urbana: University of Illinois Press, 2012), pp. 104, 164–165; "Bessie Allison Buchanan," Jessie Carney Smith, ed. , *Notable Black American Women,* Book II, (Farmington Hills, Michigan: Thomson Gale,) pp. 73–75; Marjorie D. Ison, "Across the Brooklyn Bridge," *New Pittsburgh Courier,* May 9, 1964, pg. 7; Marjorie Drexel Ison, "Across the Brooklyn Bridge," *New Pittsburgh Courier,* September 26, 1964, p. 6.

52. Club woman quoted in Gallagher, *Black Women and Politics,* p. 165; Marjorie Drexel Ison, "Across the Brooklyn Bridge," *New Pittsburgh Courier,* May 30, 1964, p. 7; Chisholm, *Unbought and Unbossed,* pp. 70–71; "State and City Tally for President, Senator and Other Offices; Local Judiciary Vote," *New York Times,* November 5, 1964, p. 23.

53. "The Lady Is also First," *New York Amsterdam News,* November 7, 1964, p. 27.

54. "Letter of the Week," *New York Amsterdam News,* December 5, 1964, p. 29; "6 in Assembly, 3 in Senate," *New York Amsterdam News,* November 7, 1964, p. 1.

55. Chisholm, *Unbought and Unbossed,* pp. 73–77; Sokol, *All Eyes Are upon Us,* p. 144.

56. Chisholm, *Unbought and Unbossed,* pp. 79–80; Winslow, *Shirley Chisholm,* pp. 48–49.

57. Chisholm, *Unbought and Unbossed,* pp. 78–81; Gallagher, *Black Women and Politics,* pp. 166–167.

58. Chisholm, *Unbought and Unbossed,* p. 82; Sokol, *All Eyes Are upon Us,* pp. 145–146; Cooper v. Power, 260 F. Supp. 207 (1966); *Wells v. Rockefeller,* 273 F. Supp. 984 (1967); Gallagher, *Black Women and Politics,* p. 167; Guild, "To Make That Some-

day Come," p. 253; "The 40th Anniversary of Cooper v. Power," *Brooklyn Eagle,* May 4, 2007, available at http://50.56.218.160 /archive/category.php?category_id=4&id=12674.

59. Chisholm, *Unbought and Unbossed,* pp. 82–85; Gallagher, *Black Women and Politics,* pp. 167–169; Guild, "To Make That Someday Come," pp. 253–255.

60. Chisholm, *Unbought and Unbossed,* pp. 82–85; "Holder Chisholm Coordinator," *New York Amsterdam News,* March 23, 1968, p. 58.

61. Chisholm, *Unbought and Unbossed,* pp. 82–86; Gallagher, *Black Women and Politics,* pp. 167–169; Guild, "To Make That Someday Come," pp. 253–255; "CNC Picks Shirley Chisholm for Congress," *New York Amsterdam News,* December 30, 1967, p. 19; "CNC Blasts Off Chisholm Campaign," *New York Amsterdam New,* January 27, 1968, p. 21.

62. "Elected Democrats Issue an Ultimatum," *New York Amsterdam News,* February 3, 1968, p. 1; "Ex-Teacher Aims at Congress Seat," *New York Amsterdam News,* June 22, 1968, p. 23.

63. "'Black Power Logical,' Hatcher: Says Du Bois Robeson Real Black Heroes[,] Farmer's Chances Are Good," *New Pittsburgh Courier,* June 1, 1968, p. 3; "Farmer's Candidacy Backed by Badillo," *New York Times,* October 1, 1968, p. 33; "Governor Endorses James Farmer Race," *New York Times,* October 7, 1968, p. 40; Chisholm, *Unbought and Unbossed,* pp. 87–88; "Negroes in Congress: Black House Members Will Add to Their Ranks in the Next Few Weeks," *Wall Street Journal,* October 22, 1968, p. 18.

64. "Negroes in Congress," *Wall Street Journal,* October 22, 1968, p. 18; Christopher Jencks, "The Moynihan Report," *New York Review of Books,* vol. 5, no. 5, October 14, 1965, p. 39.

65. Chisholm, *Unbought and Unbossed,* pp. 87, 91–92; "Negroes in Congress: Black House Members Will Add to Their Ranks in the Next Few Weeks," *Wall Street Journal,* October 22,

1968, p. 18; "Farmer and Woman in Bedford Stuyvesant Race," *New York Times,* October 26, 1968, p. 22.

66. Chisholm, *Unbought and Unbossed,* pp. 88–92; Winslow, *Shirley Chisholm,* pp. 65–70; "Freshman in Congress Won't Be Quiet," *New York Times,* November 6, 1968, p. 25; "Rep. Shirley Chisholm Goes to Washington," *New York Amsterdam News,* January 11, 1969, p. 23.

67. "Record Nine Congressmen to Answer Roll Call on Jan. 3," *Afro-American,* January 4, 1969, p. 6; "1968: For Women, It was a Year Marked by Numerous 'Firsts,'" *New York Times,* January 1, 1969, p. 25; "November 3, 1992: Year of the Woman," in "Senate Stories: 1964–Present," United States Senate History, available at http://www.senate.gov/artandhistory/history/min ute/year_of_the_woman.htm; Matthew Andrew Wasniewski, ed., *Women in Congress, 1917–2006* (Washington, D.C.: U.S. Government Printing Office, 2007); "Women Representatives and Senators by Congress, 1917–Present," available at http:// history.house.gov/Exhibitions-and-Publications/WIC/Histori cal-Data/Women-Representatives-and-Senators-by-Congress/.

68. "Shirley Chisholm Oral History," MSRC, pp. 10–11; Guild, "To Make That Someday Come," pp. 259–263; Gallagher, *Black Women and Politics,* pp. 171–180; Chisholm, *Unbought and Unbossed,* pp. 124–126, 162–163, 178–181.

69. Chisholm, *Unbought and Unbossed,* pp. 97–104; "House Negro Rids Self of Unwanted Job: Mrs. Chisholm Taken off Farm Committee," *Chicago Tribune,* January 30, 1969, p. 8.

70. Chisholm, *Unbought and Unbossed,* pp. 97–104; *New Journal and Guide,* February 1, 1969, B1.

71. Chisholm, *Unbought and Unbossed,* pp. 104–106, 96; Winslow, *Shirley Chisholm,* pp. 71–72; Gallagher, *Black Women and Politics in New York,* pp. 171–176.

72. Chisholm, *Unbought and Unbossed,* pp. 109–115; "Rep. Chisholm Takes Gun, Butter Stand," *Chicago Daily Defender,*

March 27, 1969, p. 1; "Rep. Chisholm Hits Arms Race, Calls End to Viet War," *Afro-American,* April 5, 1969, p. 11; "Chisholm Urges Women's Revolt," *Chicago Daily Defender,* February 18, 1969, p. 5.

73. "Women Face Most Bias: Rep. Chisholm," *Chicago Tribune,* January 25, 1970, p. 26; Gallagher, *Black Women and Politics in New York City,* pp. 173–174; Chisholm, *Unbought and Unbossed,* p. 177.

74. Chisholm, *Unbought and Unbossed,* p. 130; Gallagher, *Black Women and Politics in New York City,* pp. 172–176; Linda Greenhouse, "What Would Shirley Do?" *New York Times,* February 9, 2011, available at http://opinionator.blogs.nytimes .com/2011/02/09/what-would-shirley-do/.

75. "Cong. Chisholm's Charisma Is 'Catching,'" *Los Angeles Sentinel,* January 15, 1970, C1; Chisholm, *The Good Fight,* pp. 13–16.

76. Chisholm, *Unbought and Unbossed,* pp. 138–139, 171–174; Chisholm, *The Good Fight,* pp. 5–12; "'Paying Southern Debts' Says Shirley: Nixon's Policy Paper on Segregation Hit," *New York Amsterdam News,* April 4, 1970, p. 29.

77. Chisholm, *Unbought and Unbossed,* p. 173; Chisholm, *The Good Fight,* pp. 9–11; Theodore White, *The Making of a President, 1972* (New York: Harper Perennial, 2010), pp. 28–33.

78. Guild, "To Make That Someday Come," pp. 261–262; Manning Marable, *Race, Reform and Rebellion: The Second Reconstruction and Beyond in Black America, 1945–2006* (Jackson: University of Mississippi Press, 2007), pp. 118–120; Chisholm, *The Good Fight,* p. 29.

79. Chisholm, *The Good Fight,* pp. 28–31; "Shirley Chisholm Interview," SCC, p. 15.

80. "Women Organize for Political Power," *New York Times,* July 11, 1971, p. 1; "Women's Caucus Wants Half of Seats at '72 Conventions," *New York Times,* July 13, 1971, A1; "Lady Prez? Yez Yez!" *Women's Wear Daily,* July 15, 1971, p. 1; "Women's Po-

litical Caucus Draws Jokes—But Woman President? It's No Joke, Bub," *New York Amsterdam News,* July 17, 1971, A1, D10.

81. "Rep. Chisholm Considers Race for Presidency," *Boston Globe,* August 1, 1971, p. 1; "Rep. Chisholm Declares She May Run for President in 1972," *New York Times,* August 1, 1971, p. 40; "Woman President Gains as a Possibility," *Hartford Courant,* August 5, 1971, p. 24; "The Gallup Poll: Woman Could Win Presidency," *Baltimore Sun,* August 7, 1971, A5.

82. Chisholm, *The Good Fight,* pp. 27–30.

83. "Conyers Pushes Stokes for 1972," *Baltimore Sun,* September 14, 1971, A5; "Black Woman Plans to Run for President," *Los Angeles Times,* September 16, 1971, A4; "Chisholm Candidacy Gains: Meeting in Illinois," *Washington Post,* October 4, 1971, A9.

84. "Chisholm Candidacy Gains: Meeting in Illinois," *Washington Post,* October 4, 1971, A9; "Black Woman Plans to Run for President," *Los Angeles Times,* September 16, 1971, A4; "Chisholm for President," *Washington Post,* December 4, 1971, E7.

85. "Never Underestimate," *Afro-American,* December 18, 1971, p. 4; "Politics and Race: Negro Politicians Warn Democrats Not to Take Black Vote for Granted," *Wall Street Journal,* October 26, 1971, p. 1; Chisholm, *The Good Fight,* pp. 31–33; "Mrs. Chisholm President? Don't Take Her Too Lightly," *Los Angeles Times,* October 1, 1971, B7; Chisholm, *The Good Fight,* p. 34.

86. "Democratic Party Doesn't Need This Kind of Victory," *Boston Globe,* October 17, 1971, A7; "Patricia Harris Wins Fight for Key Dem. Convention Job," *Afro-American,* October 23, 1971, p. 1; "Most Women Possess Self-Destructive Urge?" *Atlanta Constitution,* December 13, 1971, 8B; "Mrs. Chisholm—She's Looking for a Coalition," *Los Angeles Times,* December 10, 1971, B1.

87. Chisholm, *The Good Fight,* p. 44.

88. Anthony Corrado, "An Overview of Campaign Finance

Law," in Paul S. Harrison, ed., *Guide to Political Campaigns in America* (Washington, D.C.: Congressional Quarterly Press, 2005); Gil Troy, *See How They Ran: The Changing Role of the Presidential Candidate* (Cambridge, Ma.: Harvard University Press, 1996), pp. 227–229; White, *Making of a President, 1972,* pp. 70–74; "New Hat in Ring: Mrs. Chisholm's," *New York Times,* January 26, 1972, p. 1.

89. Chisholm, *The Good Fight,* pp. 44–51; Winslow, *Shirley Chisholm,* p. 112.

90. Chisholm, *The Good Fight,* p. 71; "Shirley Chisholm Makes It Formal: She's a Candidate," *Washington Post,* January 26, 1972, A5.

91. Chisholm, *The Good Fight,* p. 71; "Shirley Chisholm: I'm Not Kidding," *Chicago Daily Defender,* January 24, 1972, p. 6; "New Hat in Ring: Mrs. Chisholm's," *New York Times,* January 26, 1972, p. 1.

92. Chisholm, *The Good Fight,* pp. 74–76; "Dream for Women: President Chisholm," *New York Times,* February 14, 1972, p. 19. On Abzug and Chisholm's candidacy see Alan H. Levy, *The Political Life of Bella Abzug, 1920–1976* (Lanham, Md.: Lexington Books, 2013), pp. 167–173.

93. "Shirley and Gloria, Feminism: Yes . . .," *Chicago Tribune,* January 22, 1972, p. 13; Chisholm, *The Good Fight,* pp. 76–77; Gloria Steinem, *My Life on the Road* (New York: Random House, 2015), p. 132.

94. "Shirley Chisholm Oral History," MSRC, pp. 4–6; Chisholm, *The Good Fight,* p. 66.

95. "Politics in Black," *New York Amsterdam News,* July 1, 1972, A7; Nora Ephron, "Miami," in *Crazy Salad and Scribble Scribble: Some Things about Women and Notes on Media* (New York: Vintage Books, 2012), p. 54; Judith A. Hennessee, *Betty Friedan: A Life* (New York: Random House, 1999), p. 170.

96. Chisholm, *The Good Fight,* pp. 64–66, 78–79; author's in-

terview with Lizabeth Cohen, September 23, 2015, Cambridge, Massachusetts.

97. Chisholm, *The Good Fight,* 94–99; "Black Panther Party for Shirley Chisholm," *Washington Post,* April 28, 1972, A4.

98. "Chisholm Wins TV Bid Time," *Chicago Tribune,* July 3, 1972, C1; Chisholm, *The Good Fight,* pp. 78–93, 100.

99. "Chisholm Recalls Crying over 'Dirty Tricks' Letter," *Afro-American,* April 13, 1974, p. 1; "Sent Phony Letters Segretti Says at Trial," *Atlanta Constitution,* April 3, 1974, 9A; "Excerpts from Segretti's Testimony before Senator Ervin's Select Committee," *New York Times,* October 4, 1973, p. 32; "Dwight Chapin Interview Transcription with Timothy Naftali," April 2, 2008, Richard Nixon Presidential Library, Yorba Linda, California, available at http://www.nixonlibrary.gov/virtuallibrary /documents/histories/chapin-2007–04–02.pdf.

100. Chisholm, *The Good Fight,* pp. 110, 118–124; Ronald W. Walter, *Black Presidential Politics in America: A Strategic Approach* (Albany: State University of New York Press, 1988), pp. 116–117; "Hillary Clinton versus Shirley Chisholm," *The Nation,* June 5, 2008, available at http://www.thenation.com/ article/hillary-clinton-versus-shirley-chisholm/.

101. "Hillary Clinton versus Shirley Chisholm," *The Nation;* National Visionary Leadership Project, "Interview with Shirley Chisholm," Part 11; Chisholm, *The Good Fight,* pp. 1, 163.

Epilogue: 2016

1. Hillary Rodham Clinton, *Hard Choices* (New York: Simon and Schuster, 2014), pp. 3–9; "Who Got the Most Presidential Primary Votes since 1992? The Answer Will Surprise You," *Washington Post,* January 8, 2015, available at https://www .washingtonpost.com/news/the-fix/wp/2015/01/08/where-will -2016-candidates-fall-on-the-brownback-to-clinton-vote-gett

ing-scale/; Brooks Johnson, "Clinton and the Popular Vote," FactCheck.Org, June 5, 2008, available at http://www.factcheck .org/2008/06/clinton-and-the-popular-vote/; "2008 Democratic Popular Vote," *Real Clear Politics,* available at http://www .realclearpolitics.com/epolls/2008/president/democratic_vote_ count.html; "2008 Presidential Democratic Primary Election Date–National–Primaries–by State," in *Atlas of U.S. Presidential Election,* available at http://uselectionatlas.org/RE SULTS/; Thomas E. Patterson, "Voter Participation in Presidential Primaries and Caucuses," pp. 12–13, available at http://jour nalistsresource.org/wp-content/uploads/2011/12/Voter-Turn out-in-Presidential-Primaries-and-Caucuses_Patterson.pdf.

Hillary Clinton's name was on the ballot in the Michigan primary but Barack Obama's was not. Clinton won 328,309 votes and 54 percent of the total in the Michigan primary. If that contest is counted, Clinton received more popular votes than Obama in the 2008 race for the Democratic presidential nomination. Michigan, however, had been sanctioned by the Democratic National Committee for violating party rules in setting a date for its primary. The DNC warned that it would not seat the delegation nor count its votes at the convention. Obama chose to withdraw from the primary, as did several other Democratic presidential candidates. In the end, the DNC seated the Michigan delegation and gave each delegate half a vote.

2. Clinton, *Hard Choices,* pp. 3–9.

3. "The Campaign That Never Was: A Pat Schroeder Strategist Tells the Inside Story of the Colorado Congresswoman's Try for the Presidency," *Los Angeles Times,* November 15, 1987, M11; "Schroeder, Patricia Scott," *History, Art, and Archives, U.S. House of Representatives,* available at http://history.house.gov /People/Detail/21313; "The Prime of Pat Schroeder," *New York Times,* July 1, 1990, SM12; "Schroeder, Assailing 'the System,' Decides Not to Run for President," *New York Times,* September 29, 1987, A1.

4. "Dole Bows Out of Presidential Race," *Washington Post,* October 20, 1999, available at http://www.washingtonpost.com /wp-srv/politics/campaigns/wh2000/stories/pmdole102099. htm; "Elizabeth Dole Drops Presidential Candidacy," *Baltimore Sun,* October 21, 1999, available at http://articles.baltimoresun .com/1999-10-21/news/9910210047_1_elizabeth-dole-can didacy-republican; "Says She Can't Compete against Fortunes of Forbes and Bush," *New York Times,* October 21, 1999, A22; "Braun Ends Candidacy, Supports Dean," National Public Radio, January 14, 2004, available at http://www.npr.org/templates /story/story.php?storyId=1600149; "In Crowded G.O.P. Field, Dole Was Hobbled by Her Stand on the Issues, Not Her Sex," *New York Times,* October 21, 1999, A22; Paula D. McClain, Niambi M. Carter, and Michael C. Brady, "Gender and Black Presidential Politics: From Chisholm to Moseley Braun," *Journal of Women, Politics and Policy,* vol. 27, no. 1/2 (2005).

5. Congressional Research Service, "Women in Congress, 1917–2015: Biographical and Committee Assignment Information, and Listings by State and Congress," April 27, 2015, available at https://www.senate.gov/CRSReports/crs-publish .cfm?pid=%270E%2C*PLS%3D%22%40%20%20%0A; Jennifer L. Lawless and Richard L. Fox, *Men Rule: The Continued Under-Representation of Women in U.S. Politics* (Washington, D.C.: Women and Politics Institute, 2012); Jennifer L. Lawless and Richard L. Fox, *It Still Takes a Candidate: Why Women Don't Run for Office* (New York: Cambridge University Press, 2010); Jo Freeman, *A Room at a Time: How Women Entered Party Politics* (Lanham, Md.: Rowman and Littlefield, 2002).

6. Barbara Burrell, "Political Parties and Women's Organizations: Bringing Women into the Electoral Arena," in Susan J. Carroll and Richard L. Fox, *Gender and Elections: Shaping the Future of American Politics* (New York: Cambridge University Press, 2010), pp. 210–220; Susan J. Carroll, "Voting Choices: The Politics of the Gender Gap," in Carroll and Fox, *Gender and*

Elections, pp. 117–118; Kelly Dittmar, "The Gender Gap: Gender Differences in Vote Choice and Political Orientations," *Center for Women and American Politics,* July 15, 2014, available at http://www.cawp.rutgers.edu/sites/default/files/resources /closerlook_gender-gap-07-15-14.pdf; "Long Term Gallup Poll Trends: A Portrait of American Public Opinion throughout the Century," *Gallup News Service,* December 20, 1999, available at http://www.gallup.com/poll/3400/longterm-gallup-poll -trends-portrait-american-public-opinion.aspx; "Little Prejudice against a Woman, Jewish, Black or Catholic Presidential Candidate," *Gallup News Service,* June 10, 2003, available at http://www.gallup.com/poll/8611/little-prejudice-against- woman-jewish-black-catholic-presidenti.aspx; "Some Americans Reluctant to Vote for Mormon, 72-Year-Old Presidential Candidates," *Gallup News Service,* February 20, 2007, available at http://www.gallup.com/poll/26611/some-ameri cans-reluctant-vote-mormon-72yearold-presidential-candi dates.aspx; "Are Americans Ready to Elect a Female President," *Pew Research Center,* May 9, 2007, available at http://www .pewresearch.org/2007/05/09/are-americans-ready-to-elect-a -female-president/.

7. "Hillary D. Rodham's 1969 Commencement Speech," Wellesley College, available at http://www.wellesley.edu/events /commencement/archives/1969commencement/studentspeech.

8. Hillary Rodham Clinton, *Living History* (New York: Scribner, 2003), pp. 64–75; "The National Law Journal Recognizes 100 Most Influential Lawyers in America," March 25, 2013, available at http://www.alm.com/about/pr/releases /national-law-journal-recognizes-100-most-influential-law yers-america; "Bill and Hillary's Double Trouble: Clinton's 'Two for the Price of One' Pledge Is Returning to Haunt Him," *Independent,* March 9, 1994, available at http://www.independent .co.uk/voices/bill-and-hillarys-double-trouble-clintons-two-for -the-price-of-one-pledge-is-returning-to-haunt-him-1427937

.html; "Hillary Clinton's Favorable Ratings One of Her Worst," *Gallup News Service*, September 4, 2015, available at http://www.gallup.com/poll/185324/hillary-clinton-favorable-rating-one-worst.aspx.

9. Bill Clinton, *My Life* (New York: Knopf, 2004), p. 201; "Clinton's Wife Hits Back at Sex Claims," *The Guardian*, January 20, 1992, p. 8; "Two for the Road," *Chicago Tribune*, March 16, 1992, E1.

10. Maureen Dowd, "Hillary Clinton as Aspiring First Lady: Role Model, or a 'Hall Monitor' Type?" May 18, 1992, A15; MaryAnne Borrelli, *The Politics of the President's Wife* (College Station: Texas A & M University Press, 2011), pp. 124–127; Bill Clinton, *My Life*, pp. 396–397.

11. Dowd, "Hillary Clinton as Aspiring First Lady," A15.

12. Clinton, *Living History*, pp. 105, 110.

13. Clinton, *My Life*, p. 482; "Hillary Clinton to Head Panel on Health Care," *New York Times*, January 26, 1993, A1; "Hillary Rodham Clinton's Job," *New York Times*, January 27, 1993, A22; "And Hillary Clinton's Job," *Washington Post*, January 27, 1993, A18; "New First Lady Shows Washington She, Too, Is Now at the Helm," *Wall Street Journal*, January 28, 1993, p. A1.

14. Clinton, *Living History*, p. 246; Theda Skocpol, *Boomerang: Health Care Reform and the Turn against Government* (New York: W. W. Norton & Co., 1997); "First Lady's Popularity Rebounds," *Gallup News Service*, January 16, 1997, available at http://www.gallup.com/poll/4417/first-ladys-popularity-rebounds.aspx.

15. Clinton, *Living History*, pp. 466, 476–481; "Admiration for Hillary Clinton Surges in 1998," *Gallup News Service*, December 31, 1998, available at http://www.gallup.com/poll/4108/admiration-hillary-clinton-surges-1998.aspx; "As Senate Hearings Begin, Hillary Clinton's Image Soars," *Gallup News Service*, January 13, 2009, available at http://www.gallup.com/poll/113740/senate-hearings-begin-hillary-clintons-im

age-soars.aspx; "Eight Dramatic Years Ending on a Positive Note for Hillary Clinton," *Gallup News Service,* January 3, 2001, available at http://www.gallup.com/poll/2149/Eight-Drama tic-Years-Ending-Positive-Note-Hillary-Clinton.aspx.

16. Clinton, *Living History,* pp. 107–108, 292–294, 380–386, 500; Rebecca Traister, *Big Girls Don't Cry: The Election That Changed Everything for American Women* (New York: Free Press, 2010), pp. 23–24.

17. Clinton, *Living History,* pp. 496–507; "Hillary Clinton Begins Pre-Campaign in a New Role for Her," *New York Times,* July 8, 1999, A1; "National Party Pumps Money to First Lady: Extra Funds Come Early into New York Senate Campaign," *New York Times,* August 10, 2000, B1.

18. "Hillary Clinton's Campaign Spurs a Wave of G.O.P. Fund-Raising: G.O.P. Fund-Raisers Focus on Hillary Clinton," *New York Times,* July 10, 1999, A1.

19. Clinton, *Living History,* p. 519; "The Victor: First Lady Emerges from Shadow and Is Beginning to Cast Her Own," *New York Times,* November 9, 2000, B1; "Huge Black Turnout Kept Gore in the Race: Hillary Clinton, Other Democrats also Buoyed," *Philadelphia Tribune,* November 10, 2000, 1A; "In Senate Race, Clinton Drew on Party Faithful," *New York Times,* November 12, 2000, p. 43; "In Poll, Mrs. Clinton Makes Gain among Women from the Suburbs," *New York Times,* September 21, 2000, A1; "Eight Dramatic Years Ending," *Gallup News Service;* "Hillary Clinton Retains Strong Appeal to American Women," *Gallup News Service,* March 20, 2015, available at http://www.gallup.com/poll/182081/hillary-clinton-ret ains-strong-appeal-american-women.aspx; "Metro Matters: By the Way Does He Bake Cookies," *New York Times,* November 9, 2000, D1; "It Took a Woman: How Gender Helped Elect Hillary Clinton," *New York Times,* November 12, 2000, WK5.

20. "The Victor," *New York Times,* November 9, 2000, B1; Clinton, *Living History,* p. 524.

21. "For Hillary Clinton, a Dual Role as Star and as Subordinate," *New York Times*, October 22, 2002, A1.

22. Traister, *Big Girls Don't Cry*, pp. 24–27; "Hillary Clinton's Gender Gap Advantage," *Gallup News Service*, February 24, 2005, available at http://www.gallup.com/poll/15025 /hillary-clintons-gender-advantage.aspx.

23. Maureen Dowd, "Can Hillary Upgrade?" *New York Times*, October 2, 2002, A27.

24. Ferraro quoted in Susan J. Carroll, "Ferraro Faced Hurdles with Strength and Grace," March 28, 2011, CNN Commentary, available at http://www.cnn.com/2011/OPINION/03/28 /carroll.ferraro/index.html.

25. Barbara Burrell, "Likeable? Effective Commander in Chief? Polling on Candidate Traits in the 'Year of the Presidential Woman,'" *PS: Political Science and Politics*, vol. 41, no. 4 (October 2008), p. 750.

26. "Obama Starts Bid, Reshaping Democratic Field," *New York Times*, January 17, 2007, A1; "Clinton Enters '08 Race, Fueling Race for Money," *New York Times*, January 21, 2007, p. 1; Victoria Woodhull "Letter of Acceptance," in "The Correspondence Between the Victoria League and Victoria C. Woodhull," in Madeleine B. Stern, *The Victoria Woodhull Reader* (Weston, Mass.: M & S Press, 1974), no page numbers.

27. "Marathon Benghazi Hearing Leaves Hillary Clinton Largely Unscathed," *CNN*, October 23, 2015, available at http:// www.cnn.com/2015/10/22/politics/hillary-clinton-benghazi-hearing-updates/; Douglas Kmiec, "Benghazi Backfire! Presidential Hillary Clinton Showcased by GOP," *Huffington Post*, October 23, 2015, available at http://www.huffingtonpost.com /douglas-kmiec/benghazi-backfire-preside_b_8363340.html; "Hillary Clinton and the Benghazi Gang," *New York Times*, October 23, 2015, A30; "Clinton's Curse and Her Salvation: Her Enemies," *Washington Post*, October 23, 2015, available at https://www.washingtonpost.com/politics/clintons-curse-and

-her-salvation-her-enemies/2015/10/23/7c6bbba4–7998–11e5
-a958-d889faf561dc_story.html; "The GOP's Unfortunate Benghazi Hearing," *Washington Post,* October 22, 2015, available at
https://www.washingtonpost.com/opinions/benghazi-business-
as-usual/2015/10/22/5a09b31e-7901–11e5-a958-d889faf561dc_
story.html.

ACKNOWLEDGMENTS

It is a great pleasure to acknowledge the many wonderful friends, colleagues, and institutions who made it possible for me to write this book. None, of course, bear any responsibility for any errors.

At the starting line, Jacqueline Ko at the Wylie Agency expressed such enthusiasm for this project that it made me feel it was possible to turn a vague thought into an engrossing research adventure and then a book. She "got it" at the jump and stayed with me throughout—I'm grateful for her support.

Theda Skocpol offered very helpful suggestions and never failed to answer, brilliantly, my unceasing questions. I benefited a great deal from our discussions, her wide knowledge of American politics, and her reading of the entire manuscript.

Elizabeth Hess, talented writer that she is, urged me on at a critical juncture. Her expert advice and her friendship were invaluable. The incomparable Florence Ladd also straightened me out more than once when doubt set in. Christopher Reed's enthusiasm was sustaining, as was that of Judith Vichniac, Margot Honig, and Gail Mazur.

Aida Donald played a central role in bringing this book to fruition. She encouraged me to go forward, read each chapter critically, made incisive suggestions, and last but far from least, led me back to Harvard University Press. Catherine Clinton very kindly introduced me to her friend Thomas LeBien, editor extraordinaire, and thus very much shaped this study.

Thomas LeBien's good judgment, keen historical understanding, brilliant instincts, and passion for his work made the often lonely task of writing feel like a collaborative undertaking. It has truly been my great privilege to work with him. The ultra-professionalism of everyone at Harvard University Press has been a wonder to behold. Many thanks to Christine Thorsteinsson, my talented manuscript editor, and to Michael Giarratano, publicist, Amanda Peery, editorial assistant, Graciela Galup, designer, Susan Donnelly, sales director, and William Sisler, director of the Press.

Elizabeth Pleck's deep historical knowledge and steadfastness rescued me at several points along the way. I thank her for investing so much of her valuable time and energy in reading critically and improving the entire manuscript. Likewise to my dear friend Ellen Rothman, whose literary flair and talent as a historian elevated my efforts. Winnie Rothenberg offered her expertise and served, as always, as an inspiration. My niece Brigid Wright wields a mean red pen and, much to my benefit, corrected her aunt on more than one occasion. Lyn Gaudiana supplied editorial acumen and avid interest while generously serving as one of the book's very first readers, as did Sue Carlson. My thanks to both and to Bette White for her steady support.

I am extremely grateful to fellow scholars and historians who took time from their own research and busy schedules to read chapters. Jama Lazerow offered superb comments that were discerning and helpful in equal measure. It was great fun to discuss the project with him and to learn from his astute historical perspective.

Mary Kelley read every word of the manuscript, offered detailed comments, and took such a generous interest in this project that I looked forward even to her most challenging corrections. She's been a great friend, as well, over decades, as has Jacqueline Jones, who made valuable suggestions and conveyed often her belief in the enterprise.

Morton Keller was generous in reading the manuscript and pushing me to consider and reconsider various aspects of the argument. The book is better for his instruction, as am I—an ever-appreciative student more than four decades after I first showed up at his office.

For their penetrating comments on the Woodhull chapter, I'm especially grateful to Ellen DuBois, Amanda

Frisken, Nicoletta Gullace, J. William Harris, Helen Horowitz, Jacqueline Jones, Winifred Rothenberg, and Lisa Tetrault—experts and outstanding historians all. Greg Gallant and Janann Sherman, each of whom has written a superb book on Margaret Chase Smith, were very kind to read my take on the senator and were magnanimous in their comments and in answering my questions. Frances Gouda also provided a thoughtful reading of my chapter on Smith, as did Rebecca Mitchell; both offered warm encouragement throughout, as did Ben Harris. Catherine Clinton, Anastasia Curwood, Linda Earle, Vanessa Northington Gamble, and Jason Sokol deepened my understanding of Shirley Chisholm. Their comments did much to enlarge my perspective. Anastasia was especially generous in sharing findings from her forthcoming biography of Chisholm. Vanessa offered wonderfully astute observations and corrections along with her unswerving friendship. Lizabeth Cohen took time from her packed schedule to convey thoughtfully her memories of the Chisholm campaign with me.

For their persistence, energy, patience, and skill in tracking down important data and leads, I want to thank the talented research assistants who worked with me: Jordan Coloumbe at the University of New Hampshire, Nadia Farjood now at Harvard Law School, Karen Mylan in Illinois, James Pyle at Rutgers, and Elena Sokoloski at Harvard University. As always, librarians and archivists make it all possible. Angie Stockwell at the Margaret Chase Smith Library was crucial. She offered a gracious welcome, her vast knowledge of Senator Smith, and superb guidance in using the collection in Skowhegan. Librarians and staff at the Schlesinger Library at the Radcliffe Institute for Advanced Study, the Baker Library at Harvard Business School, the Lyndon Baines Johnson Presidential Library, the Moorland-Spingarn Research Center at Howard University, Rutgers University Library Special Collections, Brooklyn College Library and Special Collections, and Southern Illinois University Special Collections Research Center were likewise tremendously helpful.

Kenneth Fuld, Dean of the College of Liberal Arts, and Eliga Gould, Chairman of the Department of History at the University of New Hampshire, made possible the research leave that allowed me to write this book. I couldn't have done it without them.

To my family, especially my wordsmith sister Maureen, and the many friends who sustained me throughout my work on this book, including Brita Carhart, Peter Badini, Susan O'Hara, Sara Rimer, and Alice Kelikian, my deepest thanks. To Steven Come and Ann Lambert, who took me sailing every summer day we could get away, made me laugh, and provided such great company, a special thanks. I look forward to more good times on land and sea.

ACKNOWLEDGMENTS

Revan Miles's warm encouragement, wisdom, humor, and amazing equanimity kept me moving forward
in this endeavor as in life. I wish there were words to
convey the depth of my appreciation.

My mother was born two years after women gained
the right to vote. She took a keen interest in this book.
One of my great pleasures in writing it was our frequent exchanges about its composition and contents.
For reading every word, for always being there, and
for being who she is, I will be forever grateful. She has
lived a life that has inspired me, her other children, her
grandchildren, and now another generation.

INDEX

INDEX

INDEX

INDEX

Primary elections, 129–130, 211, 226

Prostitution, 40, 91

Providence, R.I., 204–205

Puerto Ricans, 176, 180–181, 184–185, 194, 198, 216

Purvis, Robert, 21

Race riots, 186

Racism, 158, 160, 198

Rankin, Jeannette, 83

Reagan, Ronald, 232

Reconstruction, 8–10, 19, 32, 43, 146, 162, 191, 251–252, 267n33

Redistricting, 184

Refugees, 83

Reproductive rights, 197–198, 228

Republican Party, 83, 99, 229, 231–232, 248; during Reconstruction, 7, 32, 44, 46, 61; and election of 1964, 65–67, 119–120, 122, 124–126, 135, 138, 141–142; in Maine, 74, 76–77, 80–82, 85–88, 90, 94, 97–98; in Senate during Smith's tenure, 100–102, 104, 107–111, 113, 120, 125, 132, 247; and McCarthy, 104, 106–111, 113; and election of 1972, 152, 200, 203, 210; in New York, 188, 225, 243–244; and Clinton's run for Senate, 225, 243–244, 248; and election of 2008, 227; during 1990s, 236, 243; and election of 2016, 253–254

Revels, Hiram Rhodes, 35, 251, 267n33

Revolution, The, 19–20, 25, 48

Rockefeller, Nelson, 66, 120, 122–124, 129, 141, 188

Roosevelt, Franklin D., 67, 78, 85, 87–88, 200

Ross, Nellie Taylor, 125

Rotary Club, 137

Saddam Hussein, 241, 249

St. Hill, Charles Christopher, 152–154, 156–160, 167, 169–170

St. Hill, Muriel, 153

St. Hill, Odessa, 153

St. Hill, Ruby Seale, 152–160, 169–170

St. Hill, Selma, 156

St. Louis, Mo., 16

Salem, N.H., 1

Sand, George, 39

Sanders, Bernie, 253

San Francisco, Calif., 16, 25, 36, 142

Schroeder, Patricia, 228–229

Seale, Emmeline, 154–155

Secession, 8–9, 31

Second Great Awakening, 12–13

Secretary of state, 251, 253–254

Secret Service, 239

Securities and Exchange Commission, 93

Segregation, 10, 148, 151, 186, 219

Segretti, Donald, 221

Self-nomination, 27–28, 60

Senate, U.S., 9, 230, 251, 254; Smith in, 65–67, 100–143, 192–194, 218, 231; campaigns for, 94–100, 225, 242–246; Clinton in, 231, 244, 246–249. *See also* Congress, U.S.

Senate Aeronautical and Space Sciences Committee, 115

Senate Appropriations Committee, 115

Senate Armed Services Committee, 115, 249

Senate Government Operations Committee, 113

Senate Judiciary Committee, 45

Senate Permanent Investigations Subcommittee, 111–112

Seneca Falls women's rights convention, 15

316

INDEX

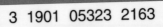